A ROMANTIC CENTURY
IN POLISH MUSIC

ALSO BY MAJA TROCHIMCZYK

POETRY

Miriam's Iris, or Angels in the Garden
Rose Always – A Court Love Story
Glorias and Assorted Praises

MUSIC HISTORY

After Chopin: Essays in Polish Music
The Music of Louis Andriessen
Polish Dance in Southern California

FORTHCOMING

Chopin with Cherries: A Tribute in Verse
The Nightingale in Space: Essays on Music
Conversations with Henry Brant

A ROMANTIC CENTURY
IN POLISH MUSIC

Studies edited by
Maja Trochimczyk

Los Angeles 2009

This book is a publication of

Moonrise Press
P.O. Box 4288, Los Angeles – Sunland, CA 91041-4288
www.moonrisepress.com

© Copyright 2009 by Maja Trochimczyk

All Rights Reserved
No part of this book may be reproduced or utilized in any form or by any means, electronic or mechanical, including photocopying and recording, or by any information storage and retrieval system, without permission in writing from the publisher.

Prior publication of articles by Maria Zduniak, Krzysztof Rottermund, Magdalena Dziadek, and Krzysztof Szatrawski in original Polish versions is hereby gratefully acknowledged.

Book design and layout by Maja Trochimczyk using fonts: Garamond, Arial and Tahoma. Illustrations from Maja Trochimczyk Collection, Los Angeles, unless otherwise indicated. Used by Permission.

Cover design by Maja Trochimczyk, based on a postcard issued by Towarzystwo Szkoły Ludowej, Kraków, Poland, ca. 1870-1880, no date.

MANUFACTURED IN THE UNITED STATES OF AMERICA

The Library of Congress Publication Data:

Trochimczyk, Maja, b. 1957–
A Romantic Century in Polish Music / Maja Trochimczyk, editor
       pp. 248+xvi. 15.2 x 22.9 cm.
Includes 50 illustrations, 4 music examples, and index.

ISBN 978-0-9819693-3-6 (paperback)

1. Music—Poland—19th Century—History and criticism.
2. Music—Poland—20th Century—History and criticism.
2. Music History   I. Trochimczyk, Maja, b. 1957.   II. Title.

10   9   8   7   6   5   4   3   2   1

A ROMANTIC CENTURY IN POLISH MUSIC

TABLE OF CONTENTS

Introduction by Maja Trochimczyk..vii

Chapter 1..1
Maja Trochimczyk – From Mrs. Szymanowska to Mr. Poldowski:
Careers of Polish Women Composers

A Romantic Interlude I..47
Two postcards with a peasant couple and krakowiak couplets

Chapter 2..49
Maria Zduniak – Karol Lipiński's Concerts in Wrocław
Translated by Maja Trochimczyk

Chapter 3..77
Krzysztof Rottermund – Stradivari, Guarneri, and Amati:
A History of Karol Lipiński's Violins
Translated by Maja Trochimczyk

A Romantic Interlude II...98
A postcard with Cracovian newlyweds and a patriotic couplet

Chapter 4..99
Martina Homma – True Virtuosity and Ungraceful Music:
Henryk Wieniawski's Activities in Germany and His Attitude
towards Joseph Joachim
Translated by Maja Trochimczyk and Martina Homma

A Romantic Interlude III..120
Three postcards with a peasant couple and krakowiak couplets

Chapter 5..**123**
Magdalena Dziadek – Polish Reception of Wagner's Music and Ideas
Translated by Maja Trochimczyk

A Romantic Interlude IV...**150**
Three Preludes of Chopin interpreted by Sigismund Ivanovski

Chapter 6..**153**
Magdalena Dziadek – Portraits of Composers and Musicians in 19th Century Polish Music Criticism
Translated by Maja Trochimczyk

A Romantic Interlude V..**175**
Four postcards with a peasant couple and krakowiak couplets

Chapter 7..**179**
Maja Trochimczyk – Searching for Poland's Soul: Paderewski and Szymanowski in the Tatras

A Romantic Interlude VI...**220**
Three postcards with a Polish nobility couple

Chapter 8..**223**
Krzysztof D. Szatrawski – Feliks Nowowiejski: A Late Romantic from Warmia
Translated by Maja Trochimczyk

Index..**243**

INTRODUCTION

Maja Trochimczyk

In his 1833 collection of Polish and Russian folk songs from Galicia, *Pieśni polskie i ruskie ludu galicyjskiego*, Wacław Zaleski (Wacław z Oleska) devoted a considerable attention to the topic of "nationality" in folk music and poetry.[i] Citing poet Kazimierz Brodziński who introduced Romanticism to Polish literature in 1818 and collected folklore as his eminent predecessor,[ii] Zaleski articulated a typical Romantic belief that folksong expresses the particular spirit of each nation:

> A nation that loves battles sings of the deeds of its heroes; a tranquil and tender nation sings of love; a witty nation loves puzzles; the songs of a nation with a vivid imagination are filled with allegories, similes and lively images; a passionate nation also sings passionately; likewise, a nation surrounded by terrifying objects, imagines terrifying gods. . . [Folk song] is a treasure trove of everything that is the closest to the nation; it is a national archive of sorts, an outpouring from the people's hearts, an image of domestic life with its joys and sufferings, and an expression of feelings in the bedroom and at the tombstone.[iii]

When referring to "song" in his collection of nearly 1,500 folk texts in two languages and many dialects, Zaleski meant "poetry" not "music." The latter was provided in the form of transcriptions and arrangements by violinist and composer Karol Lipiński (1790-1861). Simultaneously, Zaleski's concept of "lud" (people) was geographic, not based in ethnic/linguistic distinctions: Polish and Russian songs are mixed up in his volume, juxtaposing various languages and cultures of one "people of Galicia."[iv] His description of various nations as if they had distinct personalities, expressed in their folklore, seems completely anachronistic today. Yet, it was one of the tenets assumed without questioning throughout the romantic century, filled with the greatest musical achievements (Chopin) and periods of apparent stagnation (before Szymanowski).

The present volume seeks to cast light on some of the less known aspects of music making in Poland in the 19th century. Eight studies of diverse aspects of Polish musical culture are presented chronologically, from about 1818 (the date of Brodziński's essay defining Polish romanticism), to 1918, the year when Poland regained its independence, and, in some cases, to 1939, the outbreak of World War II. The subjects range from a sociological-feminist account of the presence of women composers throughout this period (Chapter 1), through detailed studies of narrowly defined topics in the lives of violin virtuosi, Karol Lipiński (Chapters 2 and 3) and Henryk Wieniawski (1835-1880; Chapter 4), to critical reviews of the scope of interests of Polish music critics (Chopin, Paderewski, and Wagner; Chapters 5 and 6), to a re-evaluation of the roles of Ignacy Jan Paderewski (1860-1941) and Karol Szymanowski (1882-1937) as Poland's "national composers" (Chapter 7), and to a re-introduction of Feliks Nowowiejski (1877-1946) as an unjustly forgotten late romantic (Chapter 8).

Who are the protagonists in this story? Karol Lipiński (1790-1861) was one of the most celebrated Polish composers, an older colleague of Fryderyk Chopin. As a brilliant virtuoso violinist, he toured Europe and made a mark on the musical life of many countries. In **Chapter 2, Prof. Maria Zduniak** focuses on his links to the city of Wrocław (Breslau) in Silesia. On the basis of archival research, old newspaper publications and concert programs, a detailed account of the virtuoso's concerts emerges, with additional information about his reputation, tributes he received during his tours, and forms of cultural life of Polish minority in the predominantly German-speaking city. The author is Professor Emeritus at Karol Lipiński Academy of Music in Wrocław, Poland, and the former Dean of the Faculty of Humanities. Zduniak is a specialist in 19th and 20th century music and has published books on: *Wrocław Musical Life* (Wrocław, 1999); Olivier Messiaen (Wrocław, 2001), and *Brahms in Wrocław* (Wrocław, 2004). She contributed numerous articles and book chapters to collected works, conference proceedings and scholarly journals. Also active as a organizer of musical life in Wrocław, Prof. Zduniak initiated the construction of a Chopin memorial and is a crucial figure in the current revival of scholarly interest in Karol Lipiński.

The article by **Dr. Krzysztof Rottermund (Chapter 3)** traces the history of Lipiński's violins—one made by Andrea Amati, one by Antonio Stradivari in 1715, and one by Giuseppe Guarneri del Gesù in 1736. Using 19th and early 20th century sources, the author corrected erroneous information found in two monographs on the Polish violinist (written by Józef Powroźniak and Vladimir Grigoriev) and supplemented these corrections with his own findings. The article also deals with aspects of Lipiński's performances in the context of the features of his instruments. Dr. Rottermund is a music theorist and historian of music instruments, professor at Szczecin University, Poland. A graduate of Polytechnical High

School in Kalisz, specializing in piano construction, as well as of the Academy of Music in Wrocław, Rottermund received his doctorate in 1992 from the Institute of the Arts, Polish Academy of Sciences in Warsaw, for *The Building of Musical Instruments in Wielkopolska in 19th century and the first half of the 20th century*. His second book is on *Piano building in Silesia before 1945* (Szczecin, 2004) An author of numerous scholarly and popular publications, Dr. Rottermund is a specialist in antique pianos, frequently collaborating with the National Center of Research and Documentation of Monuments in Warsaw and the Museum of the History of Industry in Opatówek near Kalisz. His scholarly interests focus on Polish musical culture, especially of the 19th century, and the history of music instruments.

Another famous violinist-composer, Henryk Wieniawski, has been equally neglected by music historians, though, at least, still recognized by violinists. In **Chapter 4, Dr. Martina Homma** fills in a gap in research concerning Wieniawski's links to Germany, including his tours and reception in German-speaking countries as well as his relationship to violinist Josef Joachim. Homma's study goes beyond narrating historical facts, as she focuses on the issue of musical "virtuosity" itself, its manifestations in performances by various musicians, and its significance for German music critics. Dr. Homma received her doctorate from the University of Cologne, for an award-winning dissertation on Witold Lutosławski (1995). Fluent in Polish, French, and English, she authored three books, and about 40 articles on $20^{th}/21^{st}$ and 19th century music. Her topics range from music history to the present situation in Eastern Europe, Polish music, sketch studies, problems of reception and analysis, and women composers. She made many contributions to reference works such as *Lexikon Komponisten der Gegenwart*, and *The New Grove's Dictionary of Music and Musicians*. She taught at the University of Cologne and University of Chicago, and gave numerous papers at international conferences and guest lectures in Germany, Poland, Italy, Lithuania, Denmark, Slovakia, and the U.S. Dr. Homma organized many international conferences dedicated to Lutosławski, women composers, and Polish music. She received honorary medals from the Polish Composers Union (2004) and the International Witold Lutosławski Society (2005).

Interactions between Polish and German music cultures attracted also **Prof. Magdalena Dziadek**, who dedicated her study (**Chapter 5**) to the topic of Polish reception of music and ideas of Richard Wagner. According to Dziadek, it "reflects a deep change in cultural consciousness of those participating in the musical and literary life in the main centers of the three partitioned areas: Warsaw, Lwów, Kraków and Poznań, in the years 1890-1914." Ranging from open hostility to total admiration, Polish critical responses to Wagner's world of *Kunstwerk der Futur* and *Leitmotifs* were grounded in the critics' own ideologies and objectives. One paradoxical element in the process of introducing Wagner into Polish culture was the transmission of these ideas through the writings of French philosophers and critics. Writers from the Young Poland movement who were associated with the neo-romantic ideology (Górski, Jabłonowski, Gostomski, and Miller) drew inspiration from the writings of Catulle Mendès, Eduard Schuré, Friedrich Nietzsche and others to create an elevated, "Promethean" image of Wagner. This image incorporated some features from the cult of "three prophetic poets," Mickiewicz, Słowacki, and Krasiński. This study was first published in Poland in 2001. The second chapter penned by **Prof. Dziadek (Chapter 6),** deals with ways of presenting composers in the context of various ideologies and aesthetic beliefs, starting from "positivistic" approaches, which emphasized modesty, humility and hard work of composers seen as social workers, and reaching the extravagant decadence of the *fin-de-siècle* Young Poland movement, with its cult of the artist and fascinations with spirituality. Contemporaneous critics presented composers in the context of *Weltschmerz*, sorrow and morbidity on the one hand, and the heroic mythology of national prophets-bards ("wieszcz") on the other. Dziadek traces these conceptual extremes in the critical reception of Chopin and Paderewski.

A specialist in Polish musical life of the 19th century, she teaches at the Silesian University, and at the F. Chopin University of Music in Warsaw. The author of several seminal books on the history of Polish music culture at the outset of the 20th century, Dziadek published research on source studies, music criticism, aesthetics, and women composers. Her monumental, two-volume study of *Polish Music Criticism 1890-1914* (Cieszyn, 2002), is based on her post-doctoral dissertation. She edited *Musica Polonia Nova na Śląsku* (New Polish Music in Silesia), with Bogumiła Mika and Anna Kochańska (Katowice, 2003) and a volume on women composers.[v] She also serves as editor for *Opcje*, a cultural periodical published in Katowice, and *De Musica*.

The final **Chapter 8** by **Prof. Krzysztof Szatrawski** presents the career of Feliks Nowowiejski, born in a patriotic Polish family in the Warmia region of Eastern Prussia. Nowowiejski, first trained as a church musician, studied in Berlin and Regensburg; he worked in Olsztyn, Kraków, Berlin, and Poznań. An organist and a serious, pious, romantic man, Nowowiejski remains best known for his music to the patriotic anthem, *Rota*, celebrating the tenacity of Polish peasants in the face of German/Prussian oppression. His major works include Symphonies and Concerti for organ solo, several operas and large-scale oratorios. *Quo Vadis*, based on themes from Henryk Sienkiewicz's Nobel-Prize-winning novel of the same title, was Nowowiejski's best known and most widely played composition during his lifetime. The author discusses Nowowiejski's quest to be recognized as a Polish composer and various political and social obstacles on this path. In conclusion, he cites a number of recent efforts to recover the composer's nearly forgotten music and restore him to the proper position in Polish music history. Dr. Szatrawski, born in Kętrzyn, Mazury, studied at the Faculty of Humanities, Higher School of Pedagogy in Olsztyn and at Christian Culture Institute in Olsztyn. He received his M.A. degree in 1984, for a thesis, *Experimental Music as a Subject of a Cycle of Classes for Young People*. In 1994, Szatrawski received his Ph.D. from the Nicholas Copernicus University in Toruń, for a dissertation *Sacral Space in the Mazurian Hymn-book*. A prolific writer, poet and music historian, Szatrawski penned six volumes of poetry, two novels, a cycle of short stories, and music history studies dedicated to creative individuals from the area of Warmia and Mazury. The article published here in an enlarged form first appeared in the journal *Borussia*, vol. 18/19 (1999).

I left the introduction to my own work for the end. Born and raised in Poland, I came to study Polish music quite late in my academic career. After completing a doctoral dissertation on *Space and Spatialization in Music: History and Analysis, Ideas and Implementations* (Montreal: McGill University, 1994), I received a Postdoctoral Fellowship from the Social Sciences and Humanities Research Council of Canada for two projects on Polish music, one of them dedicated to women composers (1996). The study of women's participation in music culture as professional composers **(Chapter 1)** is a result of this research project, that also gave rise to publications on Grażyna Bacewicz, Maria Szymanowska, Marta Ptaszyńska, and reception of Chopin's music by women composers.[vi]

I became interested in Ignacy Jan Paderewski after joining the faculty of the University of Southern California in Los Angeles in 1996. My inspiration came from the unwavering commitment to Polish music of the late Wanda Wilk, founder of the USC Polish Music Center that I directed from 1996 to 2004. There is a fallacy in the traditional picture of this composer as a romantic pianist without much compositional talent. My study of Paderewski's contribution to Polish "national style" and of his influence on Karol Szymanowski stems from a decade of research presented at national and international conferences since 2001. In **Chapter 7**, I attempt to rectify the historical record pertaining to the relationship of Paderewski to the younger Szymanowski, who assumed the mantle of the national composer in the 1920s. In reviewing this controversial topic, I touch upon issues of constructing national identity in music, patriotic and racist dimensions of national ideologies, the changing images and lasting fame of Paderewski, and the historical importance of his forays into Tatra Mountains in the early 1880s, when Szymanowski was just a toddler.

Since the majority of studies included in this volume interpret the theme of "a romantic century" from the perspective of national ideologies and preoccupations, including encounters with neighboring German cultures, I decided to enliven this scholarly content by adding some "romanticism" of a different kind. A series of visual vignettes, called Romantic Interludes, provides humorous or poignant commentaries on the themes discussed by the authors. Period postcards are also used as illustrations in Chapters 1, 3, 4, 6, 7, and 8. Interludes I, III, V, and VI bring the elated subject matter down to the level of popular art, or kitsch, as it were. These late 19th century postcards present peasant or noble couples expressing their love and attraction to each other. This popular history of "romance" was illustrated with simple folk poetry of the kind that Wacław Zaleski collected and published in 1833, including two krakowiak couplets found in his volume and reproduced here. According to Zaleski, "krakowiak" was the most important form of the national folksong, disseminated not only in the region of Galicia, but also in the entire country. Paderewski's use of this dance and of the Cracovian folklore provides an interesting link, highlighted by the romantic content of his only opera, *Manru*. Another connection is via the person of Karol Lipiński who arranged the music for Zaleski's massive undertaking.

Romantic Interludes I and III are from the same set of postcards featuring a married couple in Cracovian costumes from the area of Kraków in Małopolska. The Interlude V is the most ribald—as can be seen in the attire and gestures of the characters. Note the short skirt of the woman and her boldness in sitting on the lap of the man. In contrast, in Interlude VI, the gentleman and gentlewoman wearing idealized Polish nobility costumes of the 17th century engage in modest displays of affection, articulating the three stages of courtship. The traditional "romantic" pathway proscribed for Poles of a higher class leads from a man falling in love, through engagement, to marriage. In the Romantic Interlude II, we encounter an actual newlywed peasant pair from the Kraków region, who are somberly staring at the camera. The accompanying poem brings the subject matter back to the national sphere, as it proclaims: "In the home country, we will be happy / It is sweet to live and die for the homeland."[vii]

Unlike these cheap, kitschy, postcards, the Romantic Interlude IV contains material of actual artistic value. Three engravings are based on drawings by a Polish-American artist, Sigismond Ivanovski (Ivanowski), who is, by now, almost entirely forgotten. These visual interpretations of Chopin's Preludes op. 28 bring to light the late romantic emphasis on spirituality, morbidity, the occult, and the idea of the correspondence of the arts.

* * *

In conclusion, I would like to acknowledge the patience and dedication of scholars whose work appears here: the book was planned for 2005, but was delayed by life events of various kinds. Five papers, by Zduniak, Rottermund, Szatrawski, Homma and Dziadek, were originally scheduled for publication in the online, peer-reviewed *Polish Music Journal*, as its vol. 7 (2004). Since the Journal is now on indefinite hiatus (I should like to say, "defunct," but it may be revived in the future), the idea of transforming the material into a book emerged and is finally coming to its fruition. I thank, especially, Dr. Martina Homma of Cologne and Prof. Halina Goldberg of Indiana University for their thoughtful reminders about the importance of my work as a musicologist that motivated the completion of this volume. An expression of gratitude is also due, posthumously, to Dr. Stefan and Mrs. Wanda Wilk, who founded the Polish Music Center, brought me to California, and inspired me with a passion for Polish music history.

Research and publications of my Polish and American colleagues provided valuable insights. In Poland, I worked with: Dr. Teresa Chylińska (PWM Edition), Prof. Magdalena Dziadek (Silesian University), Prof. Maciej Gołąb (University of Wrocław), Prof. Zofia Helman (University of Warsaw), Dr. Wojciech Nowik (University of Warsaw), Dr. Małgorzata Perkowska (Jagiellonian University), Prof. Irena Poniatowska (University of Warsaw), Prof. Mieczysław Tomaszewski (Jagiellonian University), and the editorial team at Polish Musicological Quarterly, *Muzyka*, among others.

In the U.S., I should mention Polish American scholars: Prof. Mieczysław Biskupski, Prof. Anna Cienciała, Prof. Patrice M. Dabrowski, Sławomir Dobrzański, Prof. Mary Patrice Erdmans, Prof. Halina Filipowicz, Dr. Thaddeus V. Gromada, Prof. Ann Hetzel Gunkel, Prof. Anna Jaroszyńska-Kirchmann, Prof. Barbara Milewski, Prof. James S. Pula, Prof. Bożena Shallcross, Prof. Anne Swartz, and Dr. Barbara Zakrzewska. Credits for various insights and inspirations should also be given to: Prof. Michael Beckerman (New York University), Prof. Timothy J. Cooley (UCSB), Prof. Steven Huebner (McGill University), Prof. Beth Holmgren (Duke University), Prof. Jeffrey Kallberg (University of Pennsylvania), Prof. Jolanta T. Pekacz (Calgary University), Prof. James Parakilas (Bates College), and Prof. Antony Polonsky (Brandeis University), and Prof. Richard Taruskin (University of California, Berkeley). I should not ignore my doctoral dissertation advisors, the late Prof. Bo Alphonse and Prof. Susan McClary (now at UCLA), even though my dissertation was not on Polish music.

I would like to express gratitude to librarians and staff at the following institutions: Archiwum Akt Nowych in Warsaw, the Polish Institute of Arts and Sciences of America in New York, New York Public Library, Los Angeles Public Library, Polish Music Center at University of Southern California in Los Angeles, and the Paderewski Studies Center at Jagiellonian University. At the end, I should also thank all the sellers on E-Bay who, over the years, supplied me with many items for my personal collection of music ephemera and memorabilia that, in my mind, enriched *A Romantic Century in Polish Music* and brought it to life.

ENDNOTES

[i] Wacław z Oleska (Wacław Zaleski), *Pieśni polskie i ruskie ludu galicyjskiego z muzyką instrumentalną Karola Lipińskiego* (Polish and Russian Songs of Galician People with Instrumental Music by Karol Lipiński), Lwów: Nakładem Franciszka Pillera, 1833.

[ii] Kazimierz Brodziński (1791-1835) published two important essays, *O klasyczności i romantyczności tudzież o duchu poezji polskiej* (On classicism and romanticism and on the spirit of Polish poetry; 1818) and *O idylli pod względem moralnym* (On idyll and its moral aspects; 1823), introducing Romanticism to Polish literature. Zaleski refers to his 1826 publication of Polish folksongs in a Warsaw daily, Zaleski, op. cit., p. vii.

[iii] Zaleski, *op. cit.*, p. xxix: "Naród kochający się w bojach śpiewa czyny bohatyrów; naród spokojny i czuły śpiewa o miłości, naród dowcipny kocha się w zagadkach; pieśni narodu z żywą wyobrażnością pełne są alegoryj, porównań, i żywych obrazów; naród namiętny I namiętnie śpiewa; tak jak naród strasznemi otoczony przedmiotami, strasznych sobie wyobraża bogów... Zawsze jest to skarb wszystkiego tego, co się narodu najbliżej dotyczé; jest to jak gdyby archivum narodowe, wyraz serca ludu, obraz jego domowego życia w radości i w ucisku, wyraz czucia przy łożnicy i przy grobie."

[iv] Jolanta T. Pekacz. *Music in the Culture of Polish Galicia, 1772–1914.* (Rochester Studies in Central Europe.) Rochester, N.Y.: University of Rochester Press. 2002.

[v] Magdalena Dziadek, *Oto artyści pełnowartościowi, którzy są kobietami... Polskie kompozytorki 1816-1939* [Here are fully-valuable artists who also are women. . . Polish women composers 1816-1939], catalog of an exhibition held in Katowice, 2003; co-edited with Lilianna M. Moll.

[vi] In reverse chronological order: "Maria Szymanowska's Vocal Music," in Sławomir Dobrzański, *Maria Szymanowska: Pianist and Composer.* Los Angeles: USC and Figueroa Press, 2006; "From Art to Kitsch and Back Again? Chopin's Reception by Women Composers," in Irena Poniatowska, ed., *Chopin and His Work in the Context of Culture [Proceedings of the Second International Chopin Congress, October 1999].* (Kraków: Musica Iagellonica, 2003), vol. 2, 336-353. Papers published as Maria Anna Harley: "Composing in Color: Marta Ptaszyńska"s *Liquid Light*" in Martina Homma, ed., *Frau Musica (nova). Komponieren heute/ Composing today,* (Sinzig: Studio Verlag, 2000), 307-330; "Chopin and Women Composers: Collaborations, Imitations, Inspirations," *The Polish Review* 45, no. 1 (2000): 29-52; "Bacewicz, Picasso and the Making of *Desire*," *Journal of Musicological Research* 16, no. 4 (1997): 243-282.

[vii] The postcard was published in Kraków: Wydawnictwo Salonu Malarzy Polskich, 1901. With handwritten inscriptions in French, dated 11 March 1902, it was sent from Kovno (Lithuania, then Russia), to Barcelona, Spain.

A ROMANTIC CENTURY
IN POLISH MUSIC

Studies edited by
Maja Trochimczyk

Chapter 1

From Mrs. Szymanowska to Mr. Poldowski: Careers of Polish Women Composers

Maja Trochimczyk

I. A Matter of Choice

It was not that ladies were inferior to me; it was that they were different. Their mission was to inspire others to achievement, rather than to achieve themselves. Indirectly, by means of tact and a spotless name, a lady could accomplish much. But if she rushed into the fray herself she would first be censured, then despised, and finally ignored. Poems have been written to illustrate this point. There is much that is immortal in this mediaeval lady. The dragons have gone, and so have the kings, but still she lingers in our midst.

(Forster, *A Room with a View*)[1]

The struggle for recognition that women composers[2] engaged in throughout the nineteenth century mirrored the fate of Forster's mediaeval (or rather, Victorian) lady who was first "censured, then despised, and finally ignored."[3] The obstacles to women's entry into the composing profession were many, from the idealized image of the "eternally feminine" that proscribed for women a limiting role of beautification of the male-oriented world, through lack of access to formal musical training or professional positions, to a class-based prejudice against women's participation in the musical profession and, in particular, their engagement in popular music, and to the gender characteristics of the key concept of musical "genius"— a Great Composer, the creator of masterpieces.

During the first half of the nineteenth century there were no female conductors, music directors, leaders of orchestras or choirs, nor female university teachers of music, and very few organists and instrumental soloists active in the European music world. According to James Parakilas, women were unable to find positions within well-established public institutions, so many of them opted to create their own, small music schools, or give private lessons in the shelter of their homes.[4] Married women were expected to devote their time to their families and children, not to the pursuit of artistic careers. Few women found success as traveling virtuosi and even fewer such as the "exceptional" Clara Wieck Schumann managed to balance marriage, motherhood and the burden of frequent pianistic concert tours.[5]

When studying works by male composers, historians and critics almost never ponder the question of "masculinity" of these compositions. In contrast, the issue of "feminine" (soft, delicate, charming), or "non-feminine" (i.e. exceptionally strong, dynamic or virile) character of music by women was raised in the majority of its critical discussions.[6] Marcia Citron's research into issues of gender and the musical canon highlighted ways in which women were excluded from contributing to the repertoire of masterpieces.[7] Women were not supposed to possess the mental capacity to create large-scale compositions that alone deserved the title of the masterpiece. Since they were also deprived of the educational, institutional, and social support that would have provided them with skills for composing such works, the vicious circle of gender-based exclusion continued in perpetuity. Citron and other feminist scholars claimed that as a result male composers established a canon of masterpieces solely through gender-based forms of creativity.[8]

Therein was the source of the fundamental problem with women's career choices: the deep-seated prejudice against female ability to think and engage in rational activities, such as planning large-scale complex compositions, or envisioning their orchestral embodiments. Arguments against women ever being able to become Great Composers were reiterated for the past 100 years, often recurring as if nothing was ever refuted and no dispute closed. In a book of 1880, reissued in 1895, George Upton summarized his convictions about women's inherent inability to compose by stating:

> Man controls his emotions, and can give an outward expression of them. In woman they are the dominating element, and so long as they are dominant she absorbs music. . . When the emotions lose their force with age, her musical power weakens. . . She will always be the recipient and interpreter, but there is little hope she will be the creator.[9]

Since to be musical women had to be emotional, not rational, and since emotion and reason were the opposites that could not coexist in one person, there was no solution to this circuitous argument that denied women the power of creativity. If they became "rational" and composed complex, large-scale pieces, they lost their female identity. Upton blamed women's apparent lack of compositional achievements on their passivity and inherent inability to think without emoting. From today's perspective, the argument should be not whether women could not compose, but why they were prevented from doing so and why, if they did compose, their music was not welcome, discussed, or recognized, but simply dismissed into a "woman's sphere."

II. Gender and Genres

The idealized Woman, "the priestess of the home" may have been revered, yet she was also disallowed access to positions in the "temples of music," i.e., public concert halls. Here, a digression is due to touch upon philosophical aesthetic and the role of the notion of "absolute music" in excluding large swaths of music making, primarily occupied by women, from the realm of the "sublime" and truly "artistic."[10] If, as the philosopher Arthur Schopenhauer put it, the elusive Will of the World, the life-force itself, was fully and directly expressed only in one art, "absolute" instrumental music (and imperfectly mirrored in the remaining arts), only such content-less symphonic, instrumental music was worthy of serious study and attention.[11] There could be no "Will of the World" lurking amidst the notes of a mere mazurka or a love song played at home. The lower status of salon music in comparison with concert music, based on the condemnation of "Trivialmusik" as an unworthy distortion of the lofty "Absolute Musik," kept the women within their circumscribed domestic sphere.[12]

In Poland during the partitions, this sphere extended to include educating children and the nation in Polish language and culture. Women, aristocratic or bourgeois, participated in this task and thus selflessly served the patriotic cause. After the fall of Napoleonic Empire and the incorporation of the Duchy of Warsaw into Russia in 1815, female members of the Warsaw Music Society, sponsored the creation of Julian Ursyn Niemcewicz's *Śpiewy Historyczne* (Historical Chants; 1816), a collection of songs praising Poland's kings and nobles. By setting poems for this patriotic collection, women composers—Cecilia Beydale, Franciszka Kochanowska, Salomea Paris, Maria Szymanowska, Countess Zofia Zamoyska-Czartoryska and others—contributed to the educational efforts designed at reviving the national spirit after the loss of Poland's independence in 1791. While doing so, these women were cast in their subsidiary roles as men's assistants and facilitators. It was Niemcewicz's text that truly mattered and the musical settings were just vehicles for its transmission. Nonetheless, the composers, including a professional (Szymanowska) and a group of amateurs, an aristocrat (Czartoryska) and her *protégé* (Beydale), were united in this praiseworthy and ambitious undertaking: using songs to enlighten Poles about their country's historical past, the legends of kings and heroes. Here, musical composition served a national purpose and female composers assisted the poet to hold up the flame of national remembrance. In a way, these women presaged by over seventy years and fulfilled an ideal upheld by the creator of an anonymous postcard expressing "positivistic" philosophy of the role of the arts in Polish society after the failed January Uprising of 1863.

Fig. 4: Postcard issued by Towarzystwo Szkoły Ludowej, Kraków, ca. 1870-1880, no date. Inscription: "Niechaj żywi nie tracą nadziei, i przed narodem niosą oświaty kaganiec" (Let the living not give up hope and carry the light of education before the nation). Maja Trochimczyk Collection.

The postcard bore a quotation from a poem by Juliusz Słowacki, "My Last Will" ("Testament Mój"), which became the motto of the positivistic movement of the 1870s: "Let the living not give up hope and let them carry the light of education before the nation." This light was placed in the hands of a woman, with two children reading books at her side. This model of womanhood embracing the interrelated roles of a mother (guaranteeing the biological survival of the nation) and an educator (ensuring the continuing cultural vitality and existence of the nation) was firmly connected to the principles of "positivism"—a cultural philosophy predominant in Polish lands after the failure of yet another national uprising which had sought to regain Poland's independence through military action.

The patriotic engagement in preserving national traditions may also be seen in the women composers' prolific output of dance music based on Polish national rhythms. The majority of women composers surveyed here wrote mazurkas, obereks, cracoviennes, or polonaises. Most of this music was purely utilitarian, though: it was music that one danced to, nothing more.[13] This was music for private enjoyment at the salon, at the piano in the drawing room. According to the distinction between "artistic" and "trivial" music advocated for by German musicologists cited above, this type of music, composed to be played at home, at private performances with friends and family, predestined its creators, women composers, for obscurity. Neither national dances, nor romances, nor salon piano pieces found much lasting recognition in the annals of music history.[14] From the point of view of "innovation" and "sublimity" they had no aesthetic value. Let me rephrase this statement: only songs and piano pieces by the Great Composers (who established their reputations mostly in symphonic music) were regarded as deserving of note and study.

Furthermore, if a piano piece became popular despite not being penned by a Great One, the danger was that its author would face ridicule and rejection. Popularity by itself did not guarantee affirmative recognition. Consider the example of Tekla Bądarzewska-Baranowska (1839-1862). She was not forgotten by historians; quite the contrary: she became infamous. At the age of 18, the young Tekla committed an unforgivable sin: she wrote a piece of popular music, gave it a title of *La prière d'une vierge* and sent it on its way to corrupt the musical tastes of the masses. Music historians' hostility towards this sentimental and charming miniature, designed to show off the beauty, musical talents, and piety of the "piano girls"[15] laboring to entertain their families and potential suitors extends to entries in major reference works. Bądarzewska's miniature, with its long-lasting and universal popularity (with over 80 editions around the world, even in Australia), is immediately dismissed as a prime example of "musical kitsch"—for instance in *The New Grove Dictionary of Music and Musicians*.[16]

The Maiden's Prayer is seen as a cheap substitute of true musical values; yet, compared with some of the miniatures by Felix Mendelssohn, Edward Grieg, or Piotr Tchaikovsky, it does not stand out as being significantly worse, or belonging to a different universe of musical thrash. If all French, German, English, Italian, American, and even Australian brides-to-be continued to impress their domestic circles with this particular composition, the music itself cannot be dismissed as completely irrelevant. However, its relevance is not based on the notions of innovation and complexity—instead, it stems from a realization in sound of the ethical, social and aesthetic values of the middle-class families that embraced domesticity, devotion, education, hard work and personal development.

Fig. 2: Cover of Bądarzewska's *The Maiden's Prayer*.
Melbourne Edition, National Library of Australia, used by permission.

An eminent Polish-Canadian historian, Jolanta T. Pekacz, has thoroughly examined this issue in her extensive study of *Music in the Culture of Polish Galicia, 1772-1914*, criticizing the theoretical and aesthetic biases of traditional European musicology, which has contemptuously rejected popular music, placing it beyond the boundaries of serious art, in the domain of kitsch.[17] Pekacz writes:

> Nineteenth-Century European musical culture has been particularly susceptible to the interpretations in terms of the elite-versus-popular polarity. The modernist master narrative of music as the artistic production of individual geniuses, rather than of music in relation to social and cultural forms, the modernist preoccupation with masterpieces and distrust of music other than 'elite," and an ideology of modernism obsessed with defending 'culture" against the forms of wide consumption, reinforced the bipolar perception of a musical universe...

While Pekacz does not separate women's music into a sub-category of her study, her remarks about the intensity of irreconcilable differences between elite and popular music worlds have relevance here, highlighting the general aesthetic and methodological bias that hitherto excluded women composers from historical narratives of classical music. Towards the end of the 19th century, eighty years after the beginning of Szymanowska's distinguished and exceptional career, women still could not find the recognition they deserved as composers or performers.

In 1893, Ludmiła Jeske-Choińska (Mikorska) won a prize for her composition called *Rusałka (Water Nymph)*, performed at the World's Columbian Exposition in Chicago. Recent studies revealed to what extent the music programs at the Exposition were structured to marginalize non-European and female musicians. Women had their own Women's Pavilion and they engaged in organizing separate concerts and competitions.[18] Their works were not included in general music programs and, thus, their activities were assured of marginality. Still, why Polish music historians did not take note of Jeske-Choińska's American success, however limited? Why was she so completely forgotten? Is it because Jeske-Choińska's, by virtue of being a member of the fledging "women in music" movement, found herself among the amateurs and second-class citizens in the world of classical music?[19]

III. The Case of Szymanowska

While reviewing secondary literature on Polish music, it is not difficult to notice that almost no female composers achieved a stature comparable to that of Fryderyk Chopin and Stanisław Moniuszko in the 19th century, and Karol Szymanowski, Witold Lutosławski, or Krzysztof Penderecki in the 20th century. Only the names of Maria Szymanowska, née Wołowska (1789-1831) and Grażyna Bacewicz (1909-1969) have regularly appeared in history surveys, and in the programs of concerts and conferences.[20]

In 1828, Adam Mickiewicz wrote an ode to Szymanowska, a virtuosa pianist and composer whose musical salon in Petersburg had been the site of many joint poetic-musical improvisations by the two artists.[21] Mickiewicz called Szymanowska "the Queen of Tones" while praising her musical skills and artistic originality. Goethe called her "the charming Almighty of Sound" (in *Aussohnung*), and Malewski considered her "exceptional among women." Romantic writers, such as Maurycy Mochnacki, praised Szymanowska for the brilliance and expressive quality of her tone: she made the piano speak and sing.[22] As a gifted composer and extraordinary performer, she was able to create her own world in sound, a world admired throughout Europe.[23] Szymanowska has been seen primarily as a brilliant virtuosa pianist, an older colleague of the German child prodigy, and member of the musical establishment, Clara Wieck Schumann.[24] Her music earned her the title of "Chopin's predecessor," but not one of a Great Composer.[25]

Szymanowska's life illustrates the tension between family obligations and artistic interests faced by nineteenth-century women composers.[26] Born to Jewish parents, she was baptized as Marianna Agata Wołowska. Her marriage to a much older nobleman, Józef Szymanowski, lasted from 1810 to 1820; after the separation, their three children remained with the mother. During the marriage, she performed mainly for friends and visitors at the Szymanowski rural estate in Walewice, and focused on composition. From this period come her best piano works (*Vingt Exercices et Preludes*) and the majority of her songs. Her publications usually concealed her pre-married identity. It was her choice, though: after leaving her husband she retained the protection of the "married woman image." Being a "Mrs." and traveling with a female companion (her sister, Kazimiera Wołowska), she was free to avoid inappropriate male attention, maintain her public image of a respectable person, and focus on her music. The familiar double standard emerges: Franz Liszt could enchant all his female listeners during the concerts, and then seduce some of them afterward, privately; Maria Szymanowska could charm everyone on the stage, but had to resolutely guard her virtues and the appearance of propriety everywhere else.[27]

Among circa 100 compositions penned by Szymanowska during her lifetime, the most numerous and interesting are piano miniatures. A gifted virtuosa, praised for spectacular displays of pianistic technique, she composed miniatures: songs, etudes, preludes, and mazurkas for salon entertainment. She also wrote over 20 songs with piano accompaniment and three chamber pieces. Her compositions are characterized by brilliant virtuosity, innovative textures and harmonies (piano works), pensive expressiveness (romances), and simplicity of form (i.e. the absence of polyphony and motivic development). She was awarded a place in compositional history as an important forerunner of Chopin, especially in the use of *stile brillant*, Polish national dances, and the development of the genres of concert etude, mazurka, and the nocturne.[28] Her oeuvre does not include large-scale sonatas or piano concertos. For this type of repertoire for her concert performances she looked elsewhere, preferring music by the now-nearly-forgotten Hummel and Kalkbrenner to that by the great Beethoven or Mozart.

While engaged in composing during her marriage, Szymanowska was somewhat resentful of the seclusion inherent in the lifestyle of the landed gentry. In 1815, she wrote to her parents about the limited scope of her travels, arranged by her husband. She reported that a recent trip was constrained to her neighborhood: Łowicz, Nieborów, and Arkadia, with the return home for the night to Walewice.[29] These neighboring estates were all that the nobleman's young wife was allowed to visit. However, her horizons widened considerably after the separation: since 1820 Szymanowska's career acquired an international dimension, as she immediately embarked on a series of European concert tours. During the years 1823-1827, she toured Germany, England, France, Switzerland, Italy and Russia. Everywhere, she was welcomed with praise and acclaim. In Berlin and London, she performed for the royal courts, in Weimar—for Goethe.

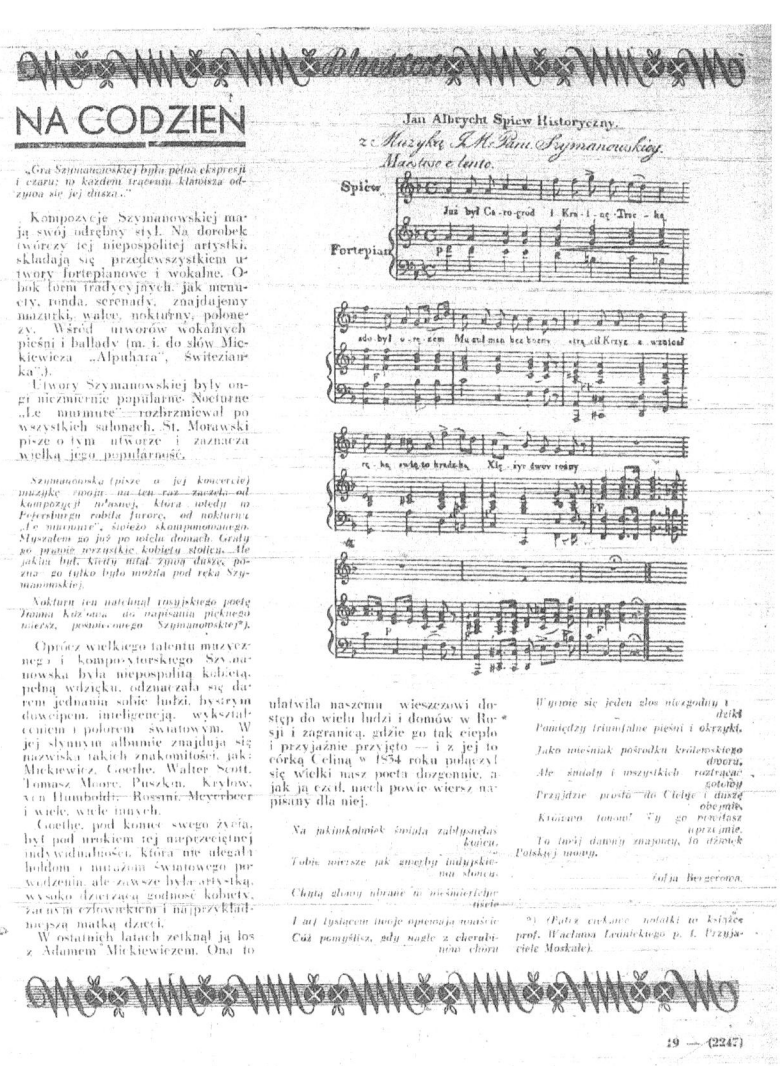

Fig 3: Szymanowska's song *Jan Albrycht* from *Śpiewy Historyczne* to texts by Julian Ursyn Niemcewicz, reproduced with an article by Zofia Bergerowa in a periodical for women, *Bluszcz, (the Ivy)* no. 19 (1889).

The separation from her husband resulted from Maria's need to pursue her artistic ambitions. She had no interest in agriculture and rural life, while her husband preferred staying at home and working on his estate. Therefore, one has to assume that they were both relieved, when Maria returned to the life of a professional musician. Like Clara Schumann, Szymanowska was able to support herself, her siblings and her three children with earnings from concert appearances and music publications. Moreover, similarly to the German virtuosa, she relied on the help of family members, especially her unmarried sister, Kazimiera, who accompanied her on travels, or cared for her children while the eminent pianist was away concertizing.

Szymanowska clearly preferred a lifestyle of international travels to a sedentary existence on a family estate. However, when it was time to present her daughters to future suitors, she settled down in one, glamorous city where she was assured of a high social status and could assemble a rich circle of educated and sophisticated friends. Thus, Maria chose St. Petersburg as her permanent home; she lived there since 1828 to her untimely death of cholera just three years later. Since she was honored to serve as the court pianist of the Tsarina, she could support her family by giving music lessons to affluent aristocrats associated with the imperial court. Szymanowska's social standing in St. Petersburg's society was partly measured by the success of her musical salon which was frequented by the most distinguished members of the local elite, including Polish and Russian artists and aristocracy, including such notables as Mikhail Glinka, Alexander Pushkin and Adam Mickiewicz who later married her daughter, Celina.

There is no doubt that the pianist's performing career flourished after the marital separation. Yet, as a composer she thrived in the seclusion of her husband's estate—and was able to create her most important compositions while simultaneously fulfilling the function as unglamorous as that of a "stay-at-home" mother and wife. During her more active performing career, the combined pressures of performing, teaching, and social networking to expand her circle of students and peers, have not been beneficial to the scope and quality of her compositional achievement. Paradoxically, she is remembered for the works created under the most severe personal constraints. Greater personal liberty allowed her to flourish as a interpreter, but not as a composer.

IV. Women? What Women?

In Polish music history, Szymanowska has played the role of an "Exceptional Woman"—who confirms the inferiority of her kin by her unique ability to transcend the assumed general lack of compositional capabilities of the fair sex. Szymanowska, and other musical exceptions (like Grażyna Bacewicz, 1909-1969), have been treated as living proofs of the unspoken rule that women have no creative and intellectual powers that would enable them to engage in serious compositional work.

Yet, there were many other female composers active in Poland in the 19th and the early 20th century. I compiled a list of names from entries in *Słownik Muzyków Polskich* of 1962-1967 (*Dictionary of Polish Musicians*, henceforth abbreviated to DPM), still the most detailed source of information about Polish composers and musicians.[30] I compared this list with entries in the *New Grove Dictionary of Music and Musicians II*, online version (2003; abbreviated to NGDM), and with entries added to the *Norton/Grove Dictionary of Women Composers* (1994, abbreviated to NGDWC). One reference comes from Magdalena Dziadek's monumental history of Polish music criticism between 1890 and 1914, published in 2002.[31] Another name was found in Leon Błaszczyk's as yet unpublished dictionary of Jewish musicians active in Poland in the 19th and 20th centuries.[32] Eight composers were identified through copies of their songs published in the period in Warsaw, Kraków, Kiev, Lwów, and Leipzig by women about whom I have not yet been able to find any additional information. The songs are included in the Walter Martin Polish Song Collection, held at the Polish Music Center, University of Southern California, Los Angeles.

No.	Name	Dates and biographical details
1	Tekla, née **Bądarzewska, Baranowska**	born 1834, died 29 September 1861, Warsaw (amateur composer, wrote the famous exemplar of "kitsch" - *The Maiden's Prayer*, 1856 and 80 international editions; other solo piano works of the same salon type)
2	Cecylia **Beydale**	b. ?, d. 1854, Paris (pianist, composer; raised by countess Maria Czartoryska Wirtemberska, student of F. Lessel; wrote songs for *Śpiewy Historyczne*), (not in NGDM)
3	Irena née **Białkiewicz**, married **Andrault de Langeron**	b. 6 February 1891, Nieżyn, Ukraine, d. 14 April 1957, Warsaw (singer and composer, studied composition with Rytel, Noskowski, Statkowski in Warsaw, piano with Michałowski, singing with Battistini in Italy; also played piano and violin; 1924-31 lived in the U.S.; after returning to Poland taught and composed; works include two symphonies, violin concerto, two piano concertos, a piano sonata, small pieces for piano, 100 songs for voice and piano with her own texts, *W Godzinach smutku i tęsknoty*, six songs, with Italian trans. , 1914) (not in

		NGDM, in DPM as "Bialkiewiczówna-Andrault de Langeron")
4	Maria **Borkowicz**	b. 1886, Warsaw, d.? (composer, studied with Urstein in Warsaw, wrote for piano, *Ghiribizzo, Plaintes des fleurs, Daphnis et Chloe*, and for violin and piano, e.g. (not in NGDM)
5	Filipina **Brzezińska**, née **Szymanowska**	b. 1 January 1800, d. 11 November 1886, Warsaw (sister of Szymanowska's husband, studied piano with a student of Field, wrote songs, music for organ, piano, mostly simple and sentimental, e.g. *Nie opuszczaj nas! Prośba do Matki Boźkiej*, pub. Kaufman in Warsaw) (not in NGDM, in NGDWC)
6	Jadwiga née **Brzowska, Mejean,** Pseudonym **Jadwiga Jagiełło**	b. 1830,Warsaw; d. after 1886, Paris (daughter of Józef Brzowski composer and cellist; studied with father, performed as a pianist around the world, directed Music Institute in New Orleans for 3 years, 1860 married French ambassador, Count Mejean, soon divorced, returned to Brussels, lived in Paris, taught piano, gave benefit concerts, all music lost) (not in NGDM)
7	Julia née **Brzozowska, Niewiarowska**	b. 1827, Warsaw, d. December 1891, Warsaw (pianist and composer, studied with Freyer; led an artistic salon, with writer Aleksander Niewiarowski, composed piano music and songs, some published in 1850s) (not NGDM, in NGDWC)
8	Jadwiga **Burzyńska**, née **Eminowicz**	? (late nineteenth c. published four songs, with no. 3-4. to texts by Tetmajer, *Słodka dziewczyno*, no. 1, *Żal mi myśli*, trans. into Esperanto) (not in NGDM, DPM)
9	Janina, Countess **Czertwertyńska-Jełowicka**	? (composed a simple *Mazurka "Spójrz na mnie"* for voice and piano, dedicated to Countess Franciszka Potocka, publ. Warsaw, Gebetner i Wolff, n.d.)
10	Łucja **Drège-Schielowa**	b. 13 February 1883, Warsaw, d. 26 January 1962, Łódź (composer and teacher, studied in Warsaw, composition with Szopski and piano with Badowska; composed chamber music, Violin Sonata, Partita for flute, cello and piano, songs to texts by Polish poets, Staff, Wolska, Rydel, Gałczyński, Tuwim, piano music: Sonata, Toccata, Ballada, etudes, dance stylizations; later also mass songs; published songs include *Cyprys* text by Staff, op. 3 no. 1, 1917)
11	Julia Helena	b. 22 May 1895, Sosnowiec, d. 20 July 1944,

	Dorabialska	Wołomin near Warsaw (composer, pianist, musicologist, studied in Warsaw, Moscow, Krakow, doctorate from Jagiellonian University in 1924, composition with Statkowski, teacher of harmony, form, piano, history at the Warsaw Conservatory to 1939; wrote reviews for *Robotnik*; composed three operas (*Dewaki, Hanusia*, a comic opera *Koncert*), a mass, numerous songs, *Workers' Songs* for chorus, chamber music for violin and piano: *Arietta, Lullaby, Melody*, String Quartet, piano music incl. *Lilije* illustrations for Mickiewicz, preludes, etudes, capriccio, triptych, etc.) (not in NGDM)
12	Ida **Erwest**	b. 1895, Warsaw?, d. ca. 1942, Warsaw? (popular singer and composer, active in popular music theatre and cabaret, e.g. Qui pro Quo around 1928, died in the Warsaw ghetto; wrote popular and cabaret songs) (not in NGDM, DPM, Błaszczyk only)
13	Klementyna **Grabowska**	b. 1771 in the Duchy of Poznan, d. 1831 in Paris (studied clavichord performance in Warsaw, since 1813 in Paris; composed for solo piano, two sonatas, variations, polonaises) (not in NGDM)
14	? **Grewe Sobolewska**	? (published a song *Muchy* to texts in Russian by Aleksej Apuchtin and Polish transl., Warsaw: Leon Idzikowski, n.d., ca. 1900) (not in NGDM, DPM)
15	Krystyna **Grottger**	? (composer of patriotic songs in first half of 18th c. popular during the Spring of the Nations) (not in NGDM, in DPM as "Grottgerowa")
16	Julia **Grodzicka-Rzewuska**	? (early 1800s, singer and composer, lived in Kraków; composed comic operas: *Dinner with Magdusia, Malwina and Ernest, Husband of all Women*, and songs) (not in NGDM, DPM does not say which one is her birth name)
17	Maria **Gruszecka**	? (composed songs, wrote poetry; published ten stylized urban folk *Pieśni sielskie*, Warsaw: M. Arct, 1896, her texts, e.g. *Prasowaczka, Goniec, Oberek*) (not in NGDM, DPM)
18	Gabriela **Gwozdecka**	? (pianist, improviser, arr. Beeethoven's Adagio from Pathetique Sonata for string quintet, wrote theater music) (not in NGDM)
19	Ludmiła **Jeske – Choińska**, née	b. 1849, Małachów near Poznań, d. 2 November 1898, Warsaw (studied singing,

	Mikorska	theory, composition with Noskowski and Munchheimer, taught in Poznan and Warsaw; gifted composers of songs and comic operas, piano works, ballad *Rusalka* for orchestra won a special diploma at Chicago's World Fair, 1893, and at Antwerp, 1894; also wrote a novel *Muzykanci*, songs, e. g. *Naiwna*, or *Kowal*, published as "Ludmiła Mikorska" in Vienna)
20	Natalia Maria Cecylia **Janotha**	8 June 1856, Warsaw, d. 9 June 1932, The Hague (virtuosa pianist, child prodigy, studied with Brahms and Clara Schumann; a Chopin specialist, wrote about 400 piano works and songs, edited/translated books on Chopin)
21	Anna Maria née **Klechniowska**, married **Klechniowska-Sas**	b. 15 April 1888, Borówka, Ukraine, d. 26 August 1973, Warsaw (member of the Young Poland generation, studied piano and composition, in Warsaw, Leipzig, Vienna, Paris, with Nadia Boulanger; she composed symphonic music, ballet, songs, later mostly teaching, she wrote pieces for children, schools for piano, as well as orchestral works: *Wawel*, 1917, *The Seasons*, 1953, cantatas, ballets, e.g. *Bilitis*, 1930, performed in Chicago in 1935; songs, etc.)
22	Franciszka **Kochanowska**	b. 1787, d. 13 December 1821 (singer, wrote *Kazimierz I* for *Śpiewy Historyczne*) (not in NGDM)
23	Wiktoria **Kowalewska**	? (early 1800s, wrote a waltz for orchestra) (not in NGDM)
24	Apolonia **Krokiewicz**	? (composed ca. 40 songs, e.g. dedicated to count Lubomirski, *Wysłuchaj mnie*, op. 25, and count Piniński, *Morze*, op. 40, self-published as "Krokiewiczowa" around 1900, Lwów) (Not in NGDM, DPM)
25	Halina **Krzyżanowska**	b. 4 August 1867, Paris, d. 18 January 1937, Rennes (pianist, composer, worked as piano teacher; studied at the Paris conservatoire, officer of the Academie de France and piano professor at Rennes; wrote a symphony, fantasy for piano and orchestra, opera *Magdusia*, oratorio, songs to French and Polish poetry, 2 piano sonatas, various other piano, chamber works) (not in NGDM, in NGDWC)
26	Stefania **Lachowska**	b. 20 August 1898, Lwów, d. 24 May 1966, Kraków (pianist, composer, studied with Frieman and Sikorski, privately with

		Szymanowski; composed folkloristic pieces for orchestra, piano, arrangements of Polish folksongs from various regions and from Kolberg's collection) (not in NGDM)
27	Wanda **Landowska**	b. 5 July 1879, Warsaw, d. 16 August 1959, Lakeville, USA (keyboard player and composer, leading the revival of the harpsichord; piano studies with Kleczyński and Michałowski; composition studies in Berlin with Urban; composed songs, *Rhapsodie orientale* for orch., *Pologne* - variations for two pianos, *Paysage triste* for strings, arrangements of Polish folksongs.
28	Iza **Leśniewicz**	? (songs to poetry by Tetmajer, *Gdzie jest twój sen?*, *A kiedy będziesz moją żoną*, self-published as "Leśniewiczowa;" distributor Gebethner, Warsaw, ca. 1920) (not in NGDM, DPM)
29	Helena **Lessel**	? (active around 1850; related to Franciszek? Wrote a *Serenade* for piano 1858) (not NGDM)
30	Natalia née **Lipińska, Parczewska**	? (daughter of Karol Lipinski, ;pianist and composer, wrote mazurkas dedicated to Chopin, 1838, other dances) (not in NGDM)
31	Helena née **Łopuska, Wyleżyńska**	b. 1878, Vilna, d. 24 May 1920, Moscow (pianist, composer, influential music critic; studied piano with Kleczyński and Michałowski, composition with Noskowski in Warsaw, then in Leipzig; wrote a *Ballade* for orchestra – won a prize at the composition competition of the Warsaw Philharmonic; a cantata to poetry by Słowacki, piano and violin sonatas, piano miniatures) (not in NDGM, DPM)
32	Eliza **Markowska-Garłowska**	? (mid 1800s; pianist and composer from Poznań, wrote a piano concerto, chamber music) (not in NGDM, DPM does not say which one is her birth name)
33	Władysława **Markiewicz**	b. 5 February 1900, Bochnia; studied with Jachimecki in Kraków, Leichtentritt in Berlin, in 1929-39 and after the war, piano professor at Katowice Conservatory, composed chamber music in neoclassical forms, sonatas and sonatinas for trumpet, oboe, bassoon, clarinet, various wind instruments; piano music in neoclassical and folkloric styles, songs to texts by Tetmajer, Iłłakowicz, Iwaszkiewicz, later mass songs) (In DPM as "Markiewiczówna")
34	Zofia **Obtułowicz**	? (composed songs, *Piosenka* to Mickiewicz's poem won first prize at a competition of Lwów

		Music Society, published as "Obtułowiczówna" by Krzyżanowski, Kraków, ca. 1910; songs with texts by Tetmajer, published Breitkopf & Härtel) (not in NGDM)
35	Amelia **Ogińska**	? (daughter of Prince Michał Kleofas, composed a polonaise and two romances, published in 1820s), (not in NGDM, not in DMP)
36	Zofia **Ossendowska** née **Iwanowska-Płoszko**	b. 18 February 1887, Sieradz, d. 1943, Warsaw (violinist, composer, studied with Barcewicz in Warsaw, Berthelioz in Paris, and Thompson in Brussels; in 1908 founded a music school in Warsaw, composed orientalist pieces for violin *Hidalgo e gitana, Capriccio di Sevilla, Onango-Fetish Dance, Melancolie;* a five-mvt. cycle *Afrique occidentale* for piano, songs, e.g. *Śnieg prószy*, ded. to her husband, *Triste berceuse* ded. to the memory of her young son, self-published as "Ossendowska" reprinted by Gebethner i Wolff, Warsaw; *Noc* as "Iwanowska-Ossendowska") (not in NGDM)
37	Helena **Ottawowa (Ottawa?** née Rogalska?**)**	b. 6 February 1874, Lwów, d. 15 August 1948 (pianist composer, teacher, managed her own music school 1902-1914, professor of Lwów Conservatory) (not in NGDM)
38	Teodozja **Papara**	b. 1797 Lwów (composer, wrote 40 works for piano, including salon dances, a fantasy, funeral march; wrote commentaries for her music in prose and poetry, constructed a keyboard for silent practice) (not NGDM)
39	Salomea **Paris (Parys?)**	b. 1800, d?, Warsaw (pianist, singer, harpist, composer, teacher responsible for all the female students at the Warsaw Conservatory, 1822 gave concert of her own music including *Cherubini Variations;* wrote 3 songs for *Śpiewy Historyczne*) (not in NGDM)
40	Teofila **Polanowska**	? (pianist, composer, taught piano in Paris 1840-1850; published about 20 salon piano pieces, e.g. *Polonaise brillante, L'Aurore valse brillante*, op. 18) (not in NGDM)
41	Jadwiga **Sarnecka**	b. 1877, Sławuta, Ukraine, d. 29 December 1913, Kraków (pianist, composer, teacher, poet, studied with Michałowski in Warsaw, Leschetitzky in Vienna; supported herself with teaching piano, suffered a nervous breakdown; composed 4 ballades for piano, one awarded

		prize at Chopin Competition 1910, other piano music, solo songs; gave a lecture on creativity and virtuosity at the Chopin Congress in Lwów, 1910) (not in NGDM)
42	Jadwiga **Stalewska**	? (composed waltzes published in 1860 in Warsaw) (not in NGDM)
43	Ilza née **Niekrasz** – **Sternicka**	b. 1898, St.Petersburg, d. 27 June 1932, Warsaw (composer, pianist, studied with Glazunov in St. Petersburg, with Melcer, Statkowski and Szymanowski in Warsaw; composed *Baśń* (Fairy tale) a fantasy for piano and orchestra, *Chess*, a symphonic grotesque, piano suite *Colors* (*Liliowy* arr. for orchestra), an oratorio, songs, works for piano (not in NGDM)
44	Paulina **Szalit**	b. 1887 Brody, Ukraine, d. after 1920, in a mental hospital abroad (composer and teacher; Polish Jew, studied with uncle Henryk Szalit, D'Albert, J. Hofmann, and Leschetitzky in Vienna, child prodigy touring Europe; last concert in 1913 with Paul Kochański; composed piano music: capriccio, mazurkas, preludes, stylized dances) (not in NGDM, in DPM as "Szalitówna")
45	Maria **Szymanowska**, née Marianna Agata **Wołowska**	b. 14 December 1789, Warsaw, d. 25 July 1831, St. Petersburg (from a Jewish family converted to Catholicism, studied with Lisowski and Gremm, 1810 debut as pianist in Warsaw; married with 3 children, left husband to perform, 1822 settled in St. Petersburg, Court pianist to the Tsarina; composed over 20 songs, including some for *Śpiewy Historyczne*, and about 50 solo piano pieces, two chamber works)
46	Leokadia **Wojciechowska,** née **Myszyńska**	b. 9 May 1858, d. 12 September 1930 (composer, studied with Roguski, Żeleński and Noskowski in Warsaw; composed chamber music: Trio, Violin Sonata, Romance for cello; works for piano, and numerous solo, choral and church songs; e.g. *Na Fujarce* to text by Konopnicka) (not in NGDM)
47	Irena Régine née **Wieniawska,** pseudonym **Mr. Poldowski,** married **Lady Dean Paul**	b. 16 May 1880, Brussels, d. 28 January 1932, London (daughter of famous composer-violinist Henryk Wieniawski, studied with Gevaert in Brussels, in London; at Schola Cantorum in Paris with D'Indy, 1901 married Sir. Aubrey Dean Paul, lived in London; composed operetta *Laughter*, opera *Blind* and symphonic drama

		Silence, based on plays by M. Maeterlinck, now both lost; symphonic works, *Nocturne, Pat Malone's Wake*, for piano and orch., over 30 songs, mostly to French poetry, esp. Verlaine, also a Violin Sonata, works for wind ensemble, violin and piano, and solo piano) (in NGDWC as "Poldowski" in Polish as "Wieniawska")
48	Zofia **Wróblewska**	? (composed songs, to text by Tetmajer *Pod gorzkim smutkiem*, Lwów: Piller & Neumann, n.d., ca. 1920) (not in NGDM, DPM)
49	Zofia née **Zamoyska, Czartoryska**	b. 1779, d. 1837 Florence (aristocrat-amateur; singer and composer, president of Warsaw Music Society in 1815, organized a Charitable Society, composed songs for *Śpiewy Historyczne*) (not in NGDM)
50	Maria née **Zyberk – Broel,** married **Plater**	? (perhaps married to either composer Karol or Gustav Plater; composer; publications dated 1884 and 1885; religious music *Ecce Panis, Tantum ergo* for voices with organ, songs to Polish and Italian poetry) (not in NGDM; in DPM as "Platerowa- Broel- Zyberk")

Women composers, who were not performers as beautiful and charismatic as Szymanowska, have not fared well in the annals of music history. Without public recognition as virtuosa performers, without a will and resources to travel extensively, being tied down to their domestic lives, these women disappeared from the historical record. Despite this fact, I was able to compile an extensive list of women who managed to compose and publish: maybe just some piano works, maybe just a set of songs, or one polonaise or a mazurka. The majority of them remain unknown today—their music is neither played, nor studied.[33]

The difficulty of researching the music and careers of women composers listed above becomes immediately apparent when realizing that their names, with few exceptions, such as Wanda Landowska (famous as a virtuosa harpsichord player) and Maria Szymanowska, do not appear in most reference works, historical surveys of music in Poland, and other sources. Even the dates of their lives are frequently not known. Exact dates of birth and death are available only for 14 of the 50 composers listed in the table. Much of the music has been lost; for instance, all of the works by Brzowska-Mejean, or orchestral music by Wieniawska.

The location of many manuscripts is not known, including the whereabouts of Natalia Janotha's 400 songs which may have been destroyed. Some women's names are remembered only due to a performance or publication of one work (Wiktoria Kowalewska, Gabriela

Gwozdecka, and Helena Lessel). There are almost no modern editions of these women's music in Poland; though, thanks to a revival of interest in women composers in the U.S., selected works by Landowska, Szymanowska and Wieniawska have been reissued by Hildegard Press.

V. Career Options

What were the career options of these musical women? Why weren't they better known and appreciated? Let me start from the choices of careers and the array of "stations in life" at a disposal of a 19th-century woman. First, let us consider the standard ranking of composers, seen in the context of their status and other activities:

(1) *Great Composer*: recognized as an innovator in musical language of classical music (writes symphonies, operas, chamber and solo music, works studied in history textbooks); Example: Chopin.

(2) *composer–performer–conductor–music director*: a pillar of musical life, a member of the professional and opinion-making elite (mentioned in history studies, but the music not studied in detail); "Kleinemeister" belong here—people who contributed to change, but did not transform musical style or language by themselves; Examples: Paderewski, Moniuszko.

(3) *composer–teacher–writer–editor*: with an advanced degree, member of an institution of higher learning, shaping future generations and their view of music; their own works are somewhat neglected; Examples: Żeleński, Noskowski. Woman: Klechniowska.

(4) *virtuoso performer–composer*, writing music for personal use in concerts, mostly virtuosic displays of little lasting historical value. Examples: Lipiński, Szymanowska?

(5) *composer of popular music, often also conductor and performer*: a member of music industry and the middle class; music noted only in social histories of music culture, not in typical "music" histories; Examples: Sonnenfeld, Bądarzewska.

(6) *composer–amateur, writing for personal use*; historically negligible, without impact. Examples: the majority of women composers.

During the early 19th-century, composing could be an acceptable occupation for women in Poland, as long as it served as an expensive hobby, a status symbol associated with the piano and its role in the middle-class home. In 1817, Anna Krechowiecka advocated performing music and composition as proper occupations for women, much more appropriate than reading "boring and useless novels" and studying mathematics or astronomy "disciplines useless for women."[34] For Krechowiecka, "it would be good if women learned composition and ... tried to set a fantasia or a capriccio." Moreover, she believed, they would derive pleasure from setting their own poetic texts. She did not consider an option of the music's public performances or publication. Nonetheless, the large number of female composers of miniatures for solo piano found in various sources attests to the practicality of this admonition: while spending long hours at the keyboard, women created and played music of their own.

Women's career choices were not determined by consciously deciding to become a Great Composer or one of the "Kleinemeister." Rather, they stem from the availability of careers and access to professions. In the 19th century, due to societal constrains, women's life and career options were limited to the following range:[35]

(1) *wife and mother* from a middle/upper class household; not working, engaged in music for social purposes or as a private hobby, dedicated to educating the children; the stereotype of the heroic "Matka-Polka," or Polish Mother (see the image from a 19th-century postcard of a woman holding a flame enlightening her children reproduced above);

(2) *single working woman, usually a teacher*, especially pianist; numerous women gave private lessons at home or established private schools, but few had positions at public conservatories (e.g., Krzyżanowska, Landowska, Ottawowa, or Klechniowska);

(3) *single woman, traveling virtuosa*, giving public and private concerts, known internationally during her lifetime, but mostly forgotten afterwards (e.g. Szymanowska, Janotha, Brzowska-Mejean, Szalit);

(4) *theatre/opera performer, a singer–actor*, who may be married to a member of the same troupe; these actors-singers rarely composed;

(5) *church organist,* an exceedingly rare occupation for women, even in convents.

The majority of creative women listed in the table above were "composer-pianists" who wrote music for their instrument. They displayed a marked preference for two genres associated with the salon: the character piece for solo piano (brief works, either stylized dances or programmatic pieces with sentimental titles) and the solo song with piano accompaniment. These two genres predominate among pieces published by women composers until the time of Grażyna Bacewicz. Even though many of women composers mentioned above wrote large scale symphonic and stage works, music publishers were only interested in releasing their songs and piano miniatures for home use.

Numerous women penned operas, comic operas and operettas, symphonies, overtures, fantasies, and concertos for piano or violin with orchestra. Their ranks include: Irena Białkiewicz-Andrault de Langeron (two symphonies and three concerti), Julia Dorabialska (three operas, one Mass), Ludmiła Jeske-Choińska (comic operas and the orchestral ballad *Rusałka* performed at the Chicago World Fair in 1893), Anna Maria Klechniowska-Sas (associated with the Young Poland movement, a colleague of Szymanowski and a student of Nadia Boulanger; composer of neo-romantic orchestral poems, suites, and ballets), Halina Krzyżanowska (composed a symphony, opera, oratorio, and a fantasy for piano and orchestra), Wanda Landowska (world famous as a harpsichordist and pioneer of early music revival, she also composed *Rhapsodie orientale* for orchestra), Eliza Markowska-Garłowska (wrote a piano concerto), Julia Grodzicka-Rzewuska (author of a series of comic operas), Helena Łopuska-Wyleżyńska (penned a prize-winning *Ballade* for orchestra and a cantata to poetry by Juliusz Słowacki), Ilza Niekrasz-Sternicka (wrote a *Fairy Tale* and *Chess* for orchestra, among other large-scale pieces), and Irena Wieniawska, known as Mr. Poldowski—the author of a series of modernist symphonic works and music settings of symbolic dramas by Maurice Maeterlinck.

VI. Name, Class and Status

The hyphenated names of many women point to another problem with the public recognition of the talent and achievements of female musicians and composers. It is hard to establish a solid, lasting position in the annals of music history, if a person continuously shifts her public identity, expressed in the name. Zofia Iwanowska-Płoszko-Ossendowska and Ludmiła Jeske-Choińska-Mikorska are the most difficult cases here, for it is hard to ascertain whether the birth name or the name most often used during their lifetimes (Iwanowska or Ossendowska, Jeske or Mikorska?) should appear in biographical publications and scholarly writings.

The trouble with names does not end here. The Polish language indicates a woman's marital status by adding suffixes to last names and some women composers followed this practice themselves. The *Dictionary of Polish Musicians* lists wives (with the suffix "-owa") and unmarried maidens (with the suffix "-ówna"). Among the former are: Łucja Drège-Schielowa, Krystyna Grottgerowa, Iza Leśniewiczowa, Helena Ottawowa, and Maria Platerowa. The maidens include: Irena Białkiewiczówna, Władysława Markiewiczówna, Zofia Obtułowiczówna, Natalia Janothówna, and Paulina (Paula) Szalitówna. These women were unmarried and their names revealed their relationship status in a unique way. In accordance with this lasting tradition, Grażyna Bacewicz was for many years called "Bacewiczówna" in Polish music publications; her married name was Biernacka, but she never used it. Curiously, the form "Bacewiczówna" appears even in recent Polish reference sources, as late as mid-1980s.[36] This name form is not neutral, though; it designates its bearer as either as an immature young woman, or a spinster who failed to marry and have children. As such, it is inappropriate for an older, accomplished career woman, such as Bacewicz or Markiewicz.

Fig 4: Wanda Landowska in 1917 (1879-1959).

This linguistic flexibility spells potential trouble for disseminating information about women composers in non-Polish biographical sources, where Grottgerowa or Bacewiczówna would be considered a different person than Grottger or Bacewicz. Male composers, regardless of their marital status, or the number of wives, had no trouble with this issue at all: once Paderewski, always Paderewski. Similarly, Wanda Landowska, who was a child prodigy and a famous pianist before her marriage kept her birth name throughout her life. She was married to a folklorist Henry Lew from 1900 to 1919 when he died.

The role of a name as an indicator of a woman's marital status is just one aspect of the problem with names as signs of personal identity. Irena Wieniawska, also known as Lady Dean Paul (her British title, acquired through marriage), or Mr. Poldowski (her pen name), is a paradigmatic example of the name-and-identity issues. In some biographical sources she is identified as Irene Poldowski, in others as Regina (her middle name) Wieniawska, or Iréne Régine Wieniawski. In still other studies and dictionaries she is called Lady Dean Paul. In Polish, she is usually referred to as Irena Wieniawska; "Regina" is listed in biographic sources as her second name. However, her birth certificate spelled her name as Régine Wieniawski.[37] None of these names, Irena(e) nor Regina(e), had an obvious male counterpart.

What was her personal choice, though? According to her biographer, Myra Brand, Wieniawska created a pen name for herself to use in her published music in order to avoid being overshadowed by either the international fame of her virtuoso-violinist and composer father, Henryk Wieniawski, or the respectability of the British aristocracy of her husband, Sir Aubrey Dean Paul. Yet, while assuming a public identity with a pen name based on a combination of the two private ones—"Pol" (for Paul) and "-dowski" (an allusion to Wieniawski)—she also concealed her gender. As a result, in her publications, Wieniawska became a "Monsieur" without a first name.[38] I will return to Mr. Poldowski and her music in the final part of this chapter.

In general, the marital status of women (single, married, separated, divorced, or changing names and identities in a series of multiple marriages) played a great role in enhancing or limiting opportunities for their professional development in music. Marriage typically had a detrimental impact on their careers as performers and composers. The woman's vocation as a home-maker was usually perceived as encompassing her whole identity and taking up all of her time. The requirements of a musical career run contrary to requirements of family life.

Zofia Ossendowska (nee Iwanowska-Płoszko) accompanied her husband, scientist, writer, journalist and professor, Antoni Ferdynand Ossendowski (1876-1945) on his frequent travels around the world. Therefore, she could not really pursue an extensive musical career, though her experience in Africa provided an inspiration for music, e.g., *Onango-*

Fetish Dance for violin and piano, or a five-movement suite for piano, *Afrique Occidentale*. These works remain virtually unknown today.

Women were encouraged to learn and practice music (especially singing and piano) primarily in order to provide cultural entertainment for family gatherings and courtship. However, their decisions to wholeheartedly follow their musical vocations and use their talents to the most of their ability typically spelled the end to the marriages.

Fot. J. Majewski.
Ferdynand Ossendowski z małżonką w namiocie w Afryce środkowej.

Fig. 5: Zofia Iwanowska-Płoszko, married name Ossendowska (1887-1943) with her husband Ferdynand in Africa. The original caption reads: "Ferdynand Ossendowski with his wife in a tent in central Africa." Photograph found by Magdalena Dziadek. Used by permission.

Maria Szymanowska left her husband in order to be able to perform and tour Europe: she felt too educated and talented to bury herself in quotidian matters of life on their rural estate. Since she took her children with her and supported her entire "single-mother" household, including her sister, Kazimiera. It seems that she did not perceive motherhood as an obstacle on the way to fame.

A one-time Countess Mejean (Jadwiga Brzowska), left her French aristocratic husband to teach music and enjoy the rich cultural life in the metropolitan center of Paris. She was considered quite successful in both teaching and performing; she was known for organizing benefit concerts for charitable causes (presumably, she was free from financial need). In contrast, Helena Łopuska who married a fellow musician, Adam Wyleżyński, ended her days in such abysmal poverty that, according to the musicologist Stefania Jagodzińska-Niekraszowa, she died of hunger in 1920 in the Pavlov hospital in Moscow.[39] How did she end up there? Apparently, she was driven from her native Wilno (Vilnius) by a scandal, a highly publicized love affair of her husband. In 1914, she moved away to avoid being exposed to gossip and social discomfort in her private life and to teach at the Moscow Conservatory. While she was spared the ravages of World War I in Wilno, she unwittingly placed herself at the epicenter of the Soviet revolution. Her marital tragedy started a chain reaction of events that resulted in her death.

In pursuing her artistic interests as a composer, Irena Wieniawska appeared to have had a full support of her husband, British baronet, Sir Dean Paul, who not only gave her freedom to study and write, but also supposedly paid for some of her publications and performances. He even participated in her concerts, singing some of her songs himself, under the pseudonym Edward Ramsey.[40] The seemingly perfect married life had a hidden, darker side and, ultimately, harmed Wieniawska's career as a musician. These issues will be discussed below.

At this point we encounter another significant issue that influences women's success in musical careers: the question of their origins, status and belonging to a particular social class. Since aristocratic ladies—such as Countesses Zofia Zamoyska-Czartoryska, Janina Czertwertyńska-Jełowicka, or Amelia Ogińska—were initially allowed to pursue musical interest only as a hobby, the accident of noble birth or marriage permanently damaged the women's chances of embarking upon a professional music career. Neither Zamoyska nor Ogińska composed or published much music. Even a protégé of an aristocrat (Cecylia Beydale) sharing the high-society lifestyle did not accomplish much as a composer.

In contrast, family background consisting of many professional musicians, provided an inspirational context and engendered musical ambitions in these women who were daughters of composers and teachers (Jadwiga Brzowska, Natalia Lipińska, Irena Wieniawska, and Helena Lessel). Yet, their position in society was ambiguous, due to the contrast between their ambitions and potential for accomplishment—resembling that of their male relatives—and their actual career opportunities. Men could be employed as conductors and directors of musical institutions, but equally talented women had limited social horizons and were directed towards family duties.

This situation was by no means exclusive to Poland: Felix Mendelssohn and Fanny Mendelssohn-Hensel provide the most famous case of musical siblings advised to enter the public sphere of the concert hall (Felix) and the private salon (Fanny), with the obvious consequence of the male achieving fame and recognition, and the female languishing in obscurity.[41] According to her biographers, Fanny was older, more musically talented and accomplished than her brother, Felix, yet she was directed by her family towards the ideal feminine role of a mother and a domestic musician. She organized concerts at home, conducted an orchestra during the Sunday musicales, but could not seek employment outside, or even publish her own music under her name. Since pursuing publication and a professional career was not seen as appropriate for a woman of her high stature, her authorship had to be erased, if her music were to be known. Consequently, some of her early songs appeared as Felix's. Her affluent bourgeois family denied her the support that was so richly awarded to her younger brother. Only after marrying, thanks to the kindness of her husband, was Fanny Hensel able to publish her first opus numbers; unfortunately she died without realizing her full potential. This strict separation of gender roles, of the male "public composer" and the female "musical guardian of the home," was not intended as discrimination, but as an expression of societal principles of propriety and status. Musical professions of a conductor or a music director were included in this general prohibition of employment that predestined generations of 19th-century educated women to a life of enforced leisure that limited their creativity.

There are many similar stories among Polish women composers, women even whose dates of birth and death are not known. Ogińska, Lessel, Lipińska, Krzyżanowska… these female members of musical families could not hope to become equal to their fathers or brothers. They just could not be employed outside of the home: it was not done. Since recognition of one's being a composer actually required working as one, they were *de facto* prohibited from joining the profession. Is it, therefore, surprising, that there was not much to say about their musical activities? It suffices to compare the amount of space awarded in the *Dictionary of Polish Composers* to Wincenty Lessel (1750-1825), Franciszek Lessel (1780-1838) or their female relative, Helena Lessel, who received a mere one-paragraph mention. According to Danuta Gwizdalanka, in Poland, as elsewhere, musical pursuits in the salons, while of high artistic merit, were not recorded for posterity in the same way as public concerts.[42]

To a greater extent than their male colleagues, female pianists and composers were taught at home: private lessons and self-education (reading and studying alone) played an important role in their way of life. Over time, however, an increasing number of women was admitted to conservatories. Some female students received gold medals upon graduation and went on to teach and concertize. By the end of the 19th century, the vocation of a music teacher was chosen predominantly by single women, who decided to forgo marriage for the sake of personal accomplishment as a professional.

One obvious path to success in the field of music was through becoming an "Exceptional Woman"—like Maria Szymanowska—who bewildered listeners with her talents as a child prodigy, and subsequently made a successful transition from a youthful miracle to a mature musician. During her lifetime, Natalia Janotha, now almost entirely forgotten, was known both as a child prodigy and as a talented and prolific composer-pianist. Hundreds of her songs and solo piano pieces were lost, so unfortunately we cannot fully gauge the scope of her compositional talent.

Fig 6: Photo of Paula (Paulina) Szalit from the collection of Universitaetsbibliothek Frankfurt am Mein, used by permission.

VII. Illness and Depression

An equally precocious pianist and composer, Paulina (Paula) Szalit, emotionally fragile to start with, was destroyed by an exploitation of her talents that manifested themselves early in her childhood. Born in Lemberg (Lwów, now Lviv) and educated in Vienna, as a student of d'Alembert and others, she did not have the emotional endurance to survive the pressures of an artistic career and ended her life in a mental hospital.

Serious mental problems are also mentioned in the biography of Jadwiga Sarnecka. Her musical talent merited a compositional prize and her oratory talents brought her as a speaker to the 1910 Congress of Polish Musicians celebrating the 100th anniversary of Chopin's birth in Lwów.[43] Her speech about the relationship between the virtuosity of performance and composition addressed one of the crucial issues studied by music psychologists until today: the mapping and "dissecting" of a creative mind.[44] A gifted, romantic poet, she composed songs to contemporaneous poetry (e.g. *Szumny wichrze głuchych pól / Vent qui cours la plaine* to text by Rydel, dedicated to Count Henryk Tyszkiewicz, published in Kraków by Piwarski, no date).

She also wrote her own verse and set it to music, for instance *Lux in Tenebris* dedicated to Helene de Gałęzowska and also issued by Piwarski. Let us consider the emotional tone of one of Sarnecka's poems that she set to music:[45]

Przed nocą wieczną
Niech Twój głos usłyszę
Jak pieśń nadziei w godzinę skonania.

/ *Before the eternal night*
/ *Let me hear your voice*
/ *Like the song of hope at the hour of agony*

A może wtedy ponad grobu ciszę
Wzejdzie mi blady księżyc
zmartwychwstania?

/ *And then, perhaps*
/ *A pale moon of resurrection*
/ *Will rise above the silence of the tomb.*

A jeśli płacząc na zgasłych źrenicach
Złożysz, złożysz jak kwiaty
Twoje ciche ręce, Grób spłonie ogniem

/ *But if you, crying, on your dead irises*
/ *Will place, like flowers,*
/ *Your quiet hands, the tomb will burn with fire*

I w stu błyskawicach
Słońc nieśmiertelnych,
Słońc nieśmiertelnych obleją mnie wieńce.

/ *And in a hundred lightnings*
/ *Of immortal suns, I will be covered*
/ *By wreaths of immortal suns.*

Sarnecka's poem ostensibly celebrates the *fin-de-siècle* theme of death and resurrection-plus-transfiguration, known from symphonic poems of

Richard Strauss (*Death and Transfiguration*, op. 24) or Mieczysław Karłowicz (*Odwieczne pieśni*, Eternal Songs, Op. 10, 1904-1906). Her musical setting is original and experimental, suffused with strongly dissonant, late-romantic harmony. The rhetorical content of the text, featuring a dramatic pause after the mention of "fire" is magnified by musical means of a discontinuous narrative—an interruption in mid-phrase and a shift to a new tonal area and rhythmic patterns. The overall key signature of a triumphant D major is used ambiguously, since the work begins in D minor and after the impassioned exclamation descends to a highly chromaticized, lugubrious key of C minor.

The dark subject matter and dramatic musical setting of *Lux in Tenebris* has many counterparts in other chromatic and sorrowful works by women composers, from *In the Hours of Sorrow and Longing* by Irena Białkiewicz(ówna) to *In Bitter Sorrow* by Zofia Wróblewska.[46] This preference for themes of sorrow, longing, vague emptiness and meaninglessness of life, interspersed with exclamations of darkest despair, is interpreted as a *signum temporis* of the generally "depressed" mood of the "Young Poland" poets in the music by male composers.

Nonetheless, the same traits have been regarded as a symptom of mental instability in the music by women. The Young-Poland poetry of Leopold Staff and Jan Kasprowicz was the main inspiration for poetic efforts of Irena Białkiewicz, who, with about 100 published songs was a popular and prolific song writer. The text of her *Preludium 3* from *Cztery Preludia* for one voice with piano, (published by Gebethner i Wolff, n.d.), entitled *Na duszę moją padł cień* (A Shadow Covered my Soul) features the following confession about a profound depression of the lyrical subject:[47]

Na duszę moją padł cień, / A shadow was cast upon my soul
Brzemienny łez rozpaczą, / Pregnant with the tears of despair
Zamroczył mi jasny dzień / It darkened the bright daylight
Nad drogą mą tułaczą... / On my pilgrim's way

Odchodzę w ciemną dal, / I walk away into darkness
Samotnych tęsknot drogę / Along the path of lonely longing
Unoszę w sercu żal, / I carry a sorrow in my heart
Zadławić go nie mogę / That cannot be vanquished.

Białkiewicz's songs are filled with expressions of darkness, sorrow, and longing. Was it a mannerist gesture of depression characteristic in the Young-Poland culture, or an expression of a more personal emotional affliction? She arranged six songs to her own words with Italian translations into a set *W godzinach smutku i tęsknoty (In the Hours of Sorrow and Longing)*: *Serenada, Smutno, Wspomniena, W zapamietaniu, Noc majowa,* and *O Zmroku*

(*Serenade, Sadly, Memories, In Forgetfulness, A May Night,* and *At Dusk*). Another set of three songs includes Italian versions by the poet/composer herself: *Śnieg/La Neve, Kołysanka/Berceuse,* and *Lilja/Il Giglio*. Vagueness and moodiness and indefinite longings of the *fin-de-siecle* era are clear in the following reflection on the "snow:"[48]

Lecą płatki śniegu	/ Snowflakes fly
Jedne drugie gonią	/ Chasing each other
Dzwonki sanek w biegu	/ The bells of the moving sled
Dzwonią...	/ Jingle
Marzę w dziwnem upojeniu,	/ I dream in an enchanted swoon
Myślą w złudzeń dążę szlak...	/ My thoughts fly on illusion's path
Pragnę w sennem zachwyceniu	/ In sleepy enchantment, I long
Wiecznie marzyć tak	/ To dream like that for eternity

While skillfully employing romantic conventions in portraying the literal meanings and moods of her poetry (thus providing the programmatic imagery and general emotional quality of the music), Białkiewicz's songs are not particularly original. These songs present their period's standard musical practice—unlike Sarnecka's or Wróblewska more experimental and harmonically adventurous attempts to underscore verbal articulations of depressed feelings with radically dissonant, chromatic, and disjointed musical means.

A good example is a setting of Tetmajer's poem *In Bitter Sorrow* by Wróblewska. The music is suffused with chromatic alterations (flats and sharps juxtaposed in one motive or chord) and dissonances (minor seconds, thick, altered chords). It does not even have a key signature, though it ends with a G minor triad. The composer consistently uses chromaticism for expressive purposes—in complete accordance with the well-established rhetorical tradition of *pathopoeia*, according to which melodic use of very small or very large intervals, sudden leaps, or unresolved dissonance, were appropriate for musical imagery of suffering. Perhaps by channeling their negative and troubled emotional states some of these women were able, for a time, to overcome the demons of depression?

VIII. Mr. Poldowski or Ms. Wieniawska?

Almost a century passed since the artistic triumphs of Maria Szymanowska, but women still could not find success and recognition of their compositional talents if they tried to achieve them as women. The most famous case of "passing" as a man is that of Irena Regina Wieniawska (1879-1932), the daughter of Henryk Wieniawski, who published her music as a Mr. Poldowski, a gentleman without the first name. She studied in Brussels, England, and in Paris with Vincent d'Indy. Unlike many others, who had to sacrifice their professional aspirations for the sake of their families, Wieniawska continued to study and compose after marrying a British baronet, Sir. Dean Paul, and becoming an English lady.[49] Her aristocratic and affluent husband provided financial support for her intense preoccupation with the musical art. Wieniawska's *oeuvre* includes over thirty songs, an operetta, works for orchestra, a woodwind suite, eleven pieces for piano, and two violin and piano pieces.

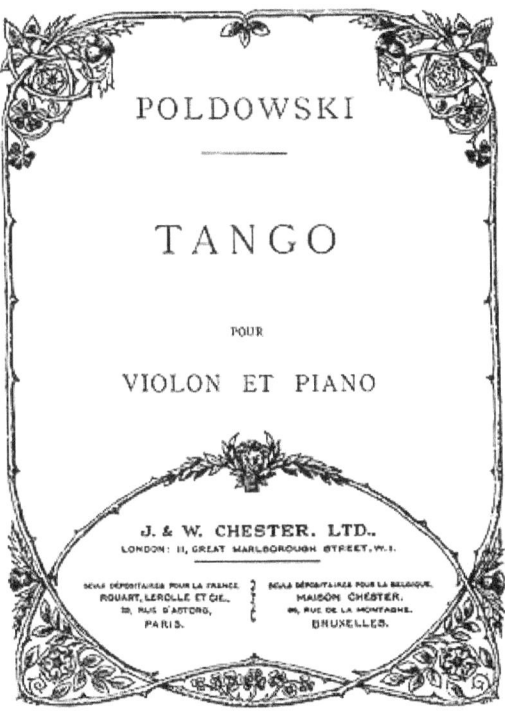

Fig. 7: Cover of Irena Wieniawska (Poldowski), Tango for Violin and Piano.

Letters of a fellow composer, Karol Szymanowski, contain references to long, sincere and emotional conversations with Irena and to her profound unhappiness about the state of her marriage in the early 1920s. In 1921 and 1922 both composers spent time in New York, giving concerts of their music, networking and trying to establish themselves professionally in the New World. When Szymanowski met Wieniawska on 29 January 1921, he noted in his diary: "very nice Lady!"[50] During another encounter on 13 February 1921, she played some of her songs which Szymanowski dismissed with a blunt comment: "nice, without a special talent."[51] Nonetheless, he admired her *Suite Minature des chansons a danse* for eight wind instruments, which he heard at the Aeolian Hall in New York on 15 February 1921. A long, all-night conversation on 20 March 1921 implied an exchange of confidentialities and secrets, which apparently continued on 24 March, with the evening summarized in a judgment: "poor Irena! Still she is wise, *et telle a de la noblesse.*" Despite his reservations about Wieniawska's compositional talents, Karol Szymanowski relied on her as a promoter of his own music: she organized his concerts in New York and, later, also in London. In gratitude for her assistance, Szymanowski planned to dedicate to her *Dryads* from *Myths* for violin and piano; instead, he chose to offer the whole set to its true inspiration, violinist Paweł Kochański.[52] Wieniawska also composed pieces for violin and piano for this extraordinary musician, for instance *Berceuse de l'enfant mourant,* or *Tango.*

Szymanowski's social and musical interactions with Wieniawska continued through mid 1920s. Yet, this friendship seemed to have cooled off after the influential American music critic Henry E. Krehbiel erroneously named both Poldowski and Szymanowski as representatives of Russian and Polish Jewry invading the concert stages of New York, to the apparent detriment of American musical life.[53] Szymanowski was deeply hurt by this case of mistaken identity, and—one may assume—also by being placed on a par with Wieniawska's male *alter ego.* Despite that fact Irena Wienawska continued to promote Szymanowski's music in New York and London.

Between 1915-1935, the British publisher J. W. Chester LTD (now Chester Music) issued some of her songs and they are still available in print. However, a significant number of her compositions remained in manuscript format, and the majority of her larger works, especially her symphonic music, was destroyed during World War II. Before that tragic event, Wieniawska's music was well-known in European concert halls. The eminent conductor, Sir Henry Wood championed her orchestral music and featured her works, like the *Miniature Suite* in the programs of the London Proms. Furthermore, he commissioned her *Nocturne* for performance at the same popular concert series. We have to note, however, that Wieniawska's name is not to be found on the cover of her published songs or the Proms' concert programs: instead, they feature the name of Mr. Poldowski.

By hiding behind a male pseudonym and obliterating both her female identity and the fact of belonging to a famous musical family, Wieniawska sought to be judged solely for the quality of her music. Paradoxically, while doing so, she created obstacles for a full recognition of her place in Polish music history. After all, Johann Christian Bach was not compelled to hide his relationship to his father, the great Johann Sebastian. Why did she? One possible explanation was given earlier: she was forging an identity separated from, though related to, her father and/or her husband. As a composer of serious ambitions, she may also have felt it necessary to distance herself from ill-regarded *Trivialmusik*—insignificant women's work. She avoided being grouped with such purported makers of musical trifles as Tekla Bądarzewska in Poland and Loisa Puget, or Cecile Chaminade in France. These prolific composers of popular, widely disseminated musical miniatures for voice and piano, were denied an entry to the musical Parnassus; they were discounted as mere producers of musical confection, if not outright trash.[54]

The danger of publishing music as a woman was not limited to being relegated to the inconsequential category of entertainers. It is impossible that Irena Wieniawska was not aware of the fate of Augusta Holmes (1847-1903) a highly talented composer of symphonic and dramatic music that was widely performed and well-liked by her audiences, yet intensely vilified by the French music critics. While, as the research of Jann Pasler conclusively demonstrates, Holmes was the most often performed composer during her lifetime, with operas, concertos, symphonies, chamber and solo music to her credit, her status as a female composer was marred by a critical resistance and ongoing campaigns aimed to ruin her social status by portraying her as a woman without moral principles.[55] Pasler showed that the anti-Holmes efforts were directed by Camille Saint-Saens and his influential colleagues. Being a female and daring to compose music were the sole reasons for these attacks. Thus, the sophisticated Wieniawska, or Lady Dean Paul, felt it necessary to distance herself from public discussion of her music which would also involve speculations about her character and her private life. She wanted to protect her social status and to see her music studied and considered solely on musical terms.

The majority of Wieniawska's extant works are songs for voice and piano or other solo instruments.[56] The 32 songs to poetry by Paul Verlaine, published between 1910 and 1920, are a rare gem. Even when considered the entire *oevure* of the composer (due to the loss of her orchestral music), these songs have the power to transform her image into one of Poland's most important song-writers. Inspired by Debussy, Ravel, and Faure, Wieniawska was among the country's the most prominent representatives of mature impressionism and post-impressionism in music. Her poetry settings are being recognized as an immensely valuable contribution to the genre of French art song, the *melodie*. Performers and historians note, with delight, the harmonic and motivic richness of her songs, the complexity of links between the music and the text, and the sonorous beauty of melodic lines and shimmering pianistic textures.

In *Mandoline,* the piano imitates the strumming arpeggios of the instrument from the title, accompanying a pliable, expressive melody of the voice. Verlaine's poetic reimagining of Greek antiquity comes to life here in a different form than in the far more famous setting of the same poem by Gabriel Faure. The fleeting trills in Wieniawska's *Le Faune* take the listeners into the languid realm of Debussy's orchestral *The Afternoon of a Faun.* The capricious *Sur l'herbe,* shimmers with chromatic color, while dispensing entirely with key signatures, like the other songs from this set. When key signatures appear, as in *Cythère,* setting one of the most famous Verlaine poems, Wieniawska enriches the music with irregularity of phrasing and pianistic textures vividly depicting the luxurious world of roses, perfume, and the joy of sensuous love evoked by the poem.

Fig. 8: Wieniawska (Poldowski), *Mandoline,* the piano part.

This rarefied world of symbolist poetry and richly harmonized, ethereal and expressive music has attracted numerous performers to Wieniawska's songs. There are now several recordings available and researchers have started to survey her music. At present, this research is limited to two performers-scholars who sang her songs and wrote D.M.A. dissertations to accompany their vocal recitals, Myra Brand and Sarah Gillian Hopkins.[57] Wieniawska's inclusion in the standard accounts of Polish music history has not yet taken place and books and article continue to be written alleging that there was no interesting or outstanding songs by Polish composers before Karol Szymanowski was able to "fill in this gaping void" with the fruit of his talent.[58] But there was no void: Wieniawska's adventure with Verlaine's poetry was preceded by another "impressionistic" set of songs by Ignacy Jan Paderewski, *Douze melodies sur de poesies de Catulle Mendès,* Op. 22 (1903). This music remains practically unknown.

The majority of Wieniawska's songs were published between 1910 and 1920; Szymanowski composed his song sets on oriental and fantastic themes (*The Songs of the Fairy Princess* 1915, *The Songs of the Infatuated Muezzin* 1918) in the same period.[59] While at this time, Szymanowski did not know Wieniawska personally and probably had not studied her songs either, her works in the song genre are representative of the same generation. In terms of their musical sophistication and inventiveness, these exemplars of the French art song are on a par with the songs of Szymanowski.

A solo piano piece published in 1928 and entitled *Hall of Machinery – Wembley* highlights Wieniawska's unwillingness to accept the limiting musical conventions established for women's music. This is a "futuristic" portrayal of industrial soundscape, an exuberant musical image of an explosion of urban noises. The machine sounds are imitated via dissonant chords (parallel tetrachords with major sevenths, semitonal clusters), sharp accents and shifts of register, repetitive ostinati in motoric eight-note patterns and chromatic meandering melodies, and, finally, layers of sustained trills juxtaposed with percussive or repetitive motives. This work reveals Wieniawska's mastery of harmony, as well as her wit and keen talents of aural "observation" and imitation of urban sound world that was unparalleled in contemporaneous Polish music. Yet, I have never seen this work cited as an early instance of Polish "futurism" or modernist avant-garde and it remains overlooked by historians and performers alike.

The futuristic innovations in the *Hall of Machinery – Wembley* would merit Wieniawska a label of Poland's first futurist of a "bruitist" orientation. She was hardly a pioneer on the European stage, though; such machine noises appeared in western music since the 1910s. Wieniawska's interest in urban soundscapes of modern city has prominent predecessors in the Italian Futurists (e.g., Russolo's russolophones), Eric Satie (especially his ballet *Parade*), Georges Antheil (*Ballet mécanique*, 1926),[60] and Arthur Honegger (the overture *Pacific 231*, a portrayal of a steam locomotive, published in 1923). While Wieniawska's piece was published and copyrighted in 1928, four years before the composer's death, it may have been composed much earlier. Towards the end of her life, Wieniawska was quite destitute and her royalties were assigned to her creditors: it is quite likely that she brought out earlier, unpublished compositions to be released and somewhat reduce her debts by providing her creditors with royalties.

This hypothesis is partly confirmed by the existence of another "noisy" song by Wieniawska, published in 1914. This dramatic setting of a symbolist text by Jean Moréas is entitled *Nocturne (des Cantilènes)*. The title itself seems somewhat ironic, since the song's refrain features a musical portrayal of strikes of a hammer on a coffin in which the poet's rejected love was to be buried. The loud banging noises are imitated in the piano part by an alternation of low, pounding octaves and high, widely-spaced chords, played *fortissimo* with strong accents. In addition, the composer asks the singer to onomatopoetically imitate the sound of the hammer by shouting "toc!" *fortissimo*, when the pianist hammers on the resounding low octave. The pitch of these exclamations remains the same, to further the impression of a realistic sound image, rather than singing. This auditory "realism" extends the declamatory verses of the song, which recounts the tragic story of a rejected lover.

These two examples of avant-garde experiments in Wieniawska's oeuvre give us a glimpse into her compositional universe. Portrayals of repeated sequences of urban, machine, or labor sounds may have also occurred in her symphonic pieces, for instance in a dramatic composition depicting the *Tenements* (lost work) or the pictorial eight-part cycle for piano, capturing the lively colors and environment of the *Caledonian Market* (published by Chester in 1923). The latter, engaging set of pieces captures the liveliness of a crowded market scene in colorful aural imagery, such as: the repeated cries of the *Street Hawkers*, trying to outdo each other, popular tunes heard from *Mouth Organs, Musical Box, Bloomsbury Waltz*, and childhood joys, pets and toys (*Child Talking to the Cat, Running Tops,* and *The Bouncing Ball*). The witty, light-hearted character of this set is underscored by its conclusion with a *Picture of Clowns*. Artistic portrayals of everyday subjects and imagery, in the manner of *Neue Sachlichkeit*, seemed to have an increasing appeal for Wienawska in the final stages of her compositional career. In 1927 she wrote *Deux Poèmes Arisophanesques* to French poetry by Laurent Tailhade which she described with enthusiasm as "the most inspiring poems one could wish to find. They deal with everyday events and everyday types…"[61]

Whether she was Poland's first and most gifted musical "futurist" we will never know, since neither her work list, documenting the origins of each composition, nor her larger symphonic and dramatic pieces have survived. A similar case, of a limited output, but extremely high quality works, is the oeuvre of Ruth Crawford Seeger (1901-1953), considered an important American modernist composer despite the small number of her extant compositions.[62] One of the most interesting parallels to Wieniawska's "machinistic" compositional style is Seeger's *Piano Study in Mixed Accents*. The motoric quality, oscillating direction, and persistent chromaticism of the melodic line endows Crawford Seeger's Piano Study with a characteristic "ultra-modern" sound, associated with a fascination with the modern, urban life, noisy and powerful technology and the freedom that it entailed, including unlimited potential for artistic experiment. Seeger's Piano Study features a continuous line of even eightnotes which move up and down the keyboard in a oscillating motion. The melodic line is all the more prominent that it is played by two hands in unison rhythm (octaves), and interrupted by sudden, irregular accents.

Placed within this context, Wieniawska's music may, too, be called "ultra-modern" and revered for its unique position in Polish music history. There is a peculiar echo of Wienawska's machine imitations in Grażyna Bacewicz's "Dance with the Machine"—a section in her last work, the ballet, *Desire* (1967-69) inspired by a comic play by Pablo Picasso.[63] Both sets of musical machinery emit unusual noises, in the extreme high and low range. Both engage in rhythmic repetitions of extremely fast, or interrupted motions, both include staccato, *sforzando*, triple *forte*, and other means of "mechanistic" articulation and dynamic that onomatopoeically represent the banging and clashing of metal on metal destroying the hearing of workers in modern factories.

Wieniawska spent the years 1921 and 1922 in New York and may have met Ruth Crawford Seeger there, though the American composer was much younger and lived in Chicago at that time (she moved to New York in 1929). The later dates of Crawford Seeger's compositions suggest that the influence may have been from Wieniawska to her American colleague. Wieniawska's *Miniature Suite for Winds* was well known since its 1912 performance in London by Sir. Henry Woods, a great advocate for her music, as mentioned above. According to the correspondence of Karol Szymanowski, this work was included in concerts in New York in 1921. It could have been heard by Crawford Seeger who composed her *Suite for Five Wind Instruments and Piano* in 1927 and her *Piano Study in Mixed Accents* in 1930. Wieniawska's (or, actually, Mr. Poldowski's) futuristic explorations preceded Crawford Seeger's modernist masterpieces.

A curious aesthetic similarity of ironic, vivid imagery in works by Wieniawska and Crawford Seeger may be deciphered also in the American composer's *Five Songs, poetry from Carl Sandburg* (1929). In 1948, Crawford Seeger wrote to composer Edgard Varèse about the main traits of her compositional technique, listing the "clarity of melodic line, avoidance of rhythmic stickiness, rhythmic independence between parts, feeling of tonal and rhythmic center, and experiment with various means of obtaining, at the same time, organic unity and various sorts of dissonance."[64] While Wieniawska's similarly explicit statements about her compositional priorities and main characteristics of her personal style have not survived, her three articles about music, published in an obscure British journal entitled *The Chesterian* (i.e. promotional publication of Chester, her London publisher),[65] reveal a strong and independent mind and a broad range of interests. Like Crawford Seeger, Wieniawski was fascinated with jazz; this shared interest was by no means typical of all classical musicians, as demonstrated by the whole-scale rejection and condemnation of jazz by American classical musicians grouped around the piano journal *The Etude* in mid-1930s.

An interesting aspect of Wieniawska's aesthetic views is her feminist interpretation of musical creativity. In her essay on "Man and Modernism" (1923), the composer made a distinction between what in art is "professorial" and what is truly "creative." She equates the "rational" "constructed" and "unimaginative" with a masculine approach to musical creativity through complexity and calculation. According to Wieniawska, the woman's way is the "intuitive" and "inventive"—the only truly creative approach to composing music. Women are wary of the mechanical and contrived way of composing that Wieniawska associated with extreme experimentation in modern music: "All the harmonic revolutions will not give us a new music! It is merely old music in convulsions, the convulsions of second childhood. Man is too theoretical to create, too much of a Professor to learn."[66]

Not a radical modernist, Wieniawska also kept away from the traditional neo-romantic world of the salon tradition of sweet and sentimental miniatures, created and cultivated primarily by women and for women. Her *Berceuse de l'enfant mourant* (*A Lullaby of a Dying Child*) is a good example of the composer's way of subverting this tradition.[67] The piece begins gently enough, with a rocking accompaniment carrying forward a delicate, tranquil melody. Yet, this musical portrayal of the child's death is far from serenity: soon, dissonances and unusual textural changes will depict the suffering of the young one—the belabored breathing, the fear, the agony. There is no well-articulated conclusion as the music simply dies away. This miniature reveals the expressive range of Wieniawska's talent and the ambivalence that a truly gifted and ambitious composer must have felt towards a genre that, through its association with the salon, maintained a secondary status in the hierarchy of serious compositions.

Fig. 9: Fragment from Wieniawska's *Berceuse* for violin and piano.

The interpretation of the music changes, though, when details from her personal biography are known: Wieniawska's first-born son, Aubrey Donald Fitzwarren Dean Paul (b. 22 October 1902) died on 12 January 1904. She has left him in the care of a nanny while studying in Paris with André Gédalge.[68] This tragic event, the death of a future baronet who inherited his father's first name, profoundly influenced the course of Wieniawska's life: she interrupted her studies, returned to England, and never completed her formal music education. Her absence from the deathbed of her first son, may have also contributed to the marital difficulties she later experienced. While Wieniawska's attempt to study abroad and leave her son when he was only a year old may be shocking in contemporary world, throughout the 19th century, children of aristocracy were raised by nannies, not their biological mothers, who enjoyed pursuing their personal interests instead of spending their time in the nursery. Regardless of this context, Wieniawska's personal trauma must have been quite intense, since she immortalized the memory of a dying child in her Lullaby composed twenty years later.

In the final years of her life, Wieniawska was estranged from her husband and found herself in financial troubles, so much so that her royalties were assigned to her creditors. According to her biographer, Myra Brand, due to her poverty and staggering debt, Lady Dean Paul was forced to engage in commercial enterprises in which she was not very successful. She died in poverty and left no estate. Her son, Brian (1904-1972), not her husband, was at her deathbed. According to her niece (daughter of an older sister), Francis Patterson-Knight, all the family documents given to Irena by her mother, Isabel Hampton Wieniawska, and inherited by her surviving children, Brenda and Brian (both single and childless), were subsequently lost. Wieniawska's children sold off the most precious documents and did not preserve their mother's legacy and family history.[69]

IX. The End of the Circle?

From the public recognition of the great Szymanowska, who gave up her marriage for fame and self-fulfillment as a creative person, to the obscurity and loss of the (great?) Wieniawska, who gave up her name to publish as a man, women's choices seem not to have expanded through the course of the nineteenth century. There is a persistent sense that the whole project of "woman composer" has, for a hundred years, followed the trajectory of a "vicious circle." Only in recent years, this circle has gradually started to open up into an ascending spiral.

While Maria Szymanowska's achievements were welcomed by the press and her musical colleagues; Wieniawska's works, even when published under a male name, did not attract much critical attention. The career choices of both composers resulted in personal hardships and constraints. Women's music remained in manuscript format or in scattered publications, and was often lost after the composers died. In this way, female composers continued to be erased from the history of music, an art which continued to attract new generations of women, struggling under an illusion that, with very few exceptions, they were, and are, the first. The outright dismissal of women's talent based on their gender may be highlighted by the juxtaposition of two critical statements written about Wieniawska's music, one when she posed as a man, Mr. Poldowski (1921), and another one written after her death when her identity was fully known (1932):

> The music of Poldowski's shows, undoubtedly the influence of the modern French School. . . yet there is a strong individuality that runs through it and there is no sense of imitation. There is an unusual power of expression, of the interpretation of the spirit of the verses, of the establishment of a mood. (Richard Aldrich)[70]

> Irena Dean Paul was a very intelligent woman; but there was nothing that grated, nothing angular or aggressive in her mind. Hers was the true woman's intelligence, devoid of mental prejudice, with a wise and rare sympathy, unfailing intuition, and a sense of humor and of the ridiculous which shone through everything she said and did... (Patrick Balfour)[71]

By the middle of the 20th century, Grażyna Bacewicz reached the level of international recognition: she became the first Polish female composer of a stature equal to men, the first ever considered to be capable of composing music equal to, or better than, written by men, the first ever about whom books were published during her lifetime.[72] This state of affairs, despite Bacewicz's obvious and unusual talent, did not stem solely from her musicality, or the quality of her oeuvre: it was the most unequivocally positive result of the imposition of socialist rule on Poland after World War II. In the new "socialist" state where equality of women was a fundamental tenet of official ideology and the subject of state propaganda (regardless of ridiculous forms that this propaganda often assumed, such as widely-satirized posters of female tractor-drivers or masons), a female composer could be—and often was— construed as an "equal" to her male colleagues. In the 1960s, Bacewicz's works had a greater number of publications and performances in Poland than any other composer, except Chopin. She wrote symphonies, concerti, operas, ballets, chamber music, and pieces for solo instruments: her oeuvre spanned the full range of genres available to a "serious" composer of contemporary music.

In contrast, women composers of the 19th century did not have the luxury of such generous state support, publishing opportunities, or commissions. They wrote for themselves, for performances at the salon, at home. Those who attempted to enter the male field of composing for the concert stage, were exceptions confirming the rule that was finally broken in the second half of the 20th century.

ENDNOTES

[1] E. M. Forster, *A Room with a View* (New York: The Modern Library, 1993), 44.
[2] My research on Polish women composers was initiated with a postdoctoral research project "Women Composers In the Polish People's Republic (1945-1989)" conducted at McGill University (Montreal) in association with the University of Warsaw (Poland) and funded by a Postdoctoral Fellowship from the Social Sciences and Humanities Research Council of Canada (1994-1996). I thank Ms. Wanda Bacewicz for assistance with my research about her sister, Grażyna Bacewicz, the staff at the Jagiellonian Library in Krakow and the library of Muzeum Literatury in Warsaw, for providing me with materials about Maria Szymanowska; Prof. Irena Poniatowska and Dr. Zofia Chechlińska of Warsaw, Poland, for sharing with me the results of their research into the music of nineteenth century; Dr. Myra Brand for providing me with copies of her articles published in 1980s; and Jolanta Pękacz for her book on music in Galicia. An earlier version of this paper was first read at the special session organized by Prof. Beth Holmgren for the annual meeting of the Association for the Advancement of Slavic Studies held in November 2002.
[3] The ideal of the "Eternal Woman" (ewige Weiblichkeit) originated in the early 19th century and was not medieval; feminist historians have mapped vast areas of autonomy and accomplishments inhabited by truly 'medieval' ladies. See "The Women Troubadours," by Meg Bogin, New York: W.E. Norton, 1980; Audrey Davidson, Audrey, Ekdahl,*Wisdom Which Encircles Circles: Papers on Hildegard of Bingen*. (Kalamazoo, Michigan: Medieval Institute Publications, Western Michigan University, 1996). For a general overview of the history of women in music see Karin Pendle, ed. *Women & Music: A History* (Bloomington: Indiana University Press, 1991).
[4] See the chapter "The Piano Lesson" in James Parakilas, ed., *Piano Rolls: Three Hundred Years of Life with the Piano*, (Yale University Press, 1999).
[5] Nancy B. Reich, *Clara Schumann: The Artist and the Woman* (New York: Cornell University Press, 1985).
[6] Feminist approaches to the "feminine/masculine" stereotypes in music, may be found in Sophie Drinker, *Music and Women: The Story of Women in their Relation to Music* (New York: Feminist Press, 1995; 1st ed. 1948); Kimberly Marshall, ed. *Rediscovering the Muses: Women's Musical Traditions* (Boston: Northeastern University Press, 1993); and Susan McClary, *Feminine Endings: Music, Gender, and Sexuality* (Minneapolis: University of Minnesota Press, 1991).
[7] Marcia J. Citron, *Gender and the Musical Canon* (Cambridge University Press, 1993).
[8] Jane Bowers and Judith Tick, eds. *Women Making Music: The Western Art Tradition, 1150-1950*. (Chicago: University of Chicago Press, 1986).
[9] George Putnam Upton, *Woman in Music* (Chicago: A.C. McClurg and Co., 1880, reprinted in 1895). Excerpt reprinted in Neuls-Bates, op. cit., p. 206-210.
[10] Carl Dahlhaus, *The Idea of Absolute Music* (Chicago: University of Chicago Press, 1989). Originally published as *Die Idee der absoluten Musik*.
[11] Arthur Schopenhauer, *The World as Will and Representation*, (alternately translated in English as *The World as Will and Idea*. Original German is *Die Welt als Wille und Vorstellung*), 1818/1819, vol 2, 1844, Dover edition 1966. The philosopher's misogynist essay, "On Women (Über die Weiber), from 1851, influenced the dissemination of views denying women higher talents, based on biological determinism. See also Gerard Mannion, *Schopenhauer, Religion and Morality - The Humble Path to Ethics*, Ashgate Press, New Critical Thinking in Philosophy Series, 2003.
[12] The notion of "trivial music" plays an important role as the antinomy of "art music" in German musicology, especially in the work of Carl Dahlhaus and his students. See Carl Dahlhaus, *Studien zur Trivialmusik im 19. Jahrhunder.t* Series: Studien zur Musikgeschichte des 19. Jahrhunderts, No. 8 (Regensburg: Bosse, 1967); Helga de la Motte-Haber, ed., *Das*

Triviale in Literatur, Musik und bildender Kunst, Series: Studien zur Philosophie und Literatur des 19. Jahrhunderts (Frankfurt am Main: Klostermann, 1972). About 70 % of entries about "trivial music" listed in the RILM database were published in German (data of June 2003). Unlike their American colleagues, German scholars tended to apply this term to various types of popular, or urban vernacular music, including rock.

[13] For a spirited and articulate apology of such "lived" practical music, contrasted with "serious" music in the Galician society, see Jolanta Pekacz, *Music in the Culture of Polish Galicia, 1772-1914* (University of Rochester Press, 2002), esp. Chapters 1 and 7.

[14] With recent exceptions, such as studies by Magdalena Dziadek, "Utwory fortepianowe polskich kompozytorek do 1939 roku. Kontekst kulturowy, strategie wyboru gatunków i środków." in Muzyka fortepianowa XIII, ed. Janusz Krassowski (Gdańsk 2004), 543-560.

[15] This term is borrowed from Judith Tick's essay in Jane Bowers and Judith Tick, eds. *Women Making Music: The Western Art Tradition, 1150- 1950*. Chicago: University of Chicago Press, 1986.

[16] See the entries on Tekla Bądarzewska-Baranowska in the *New Grove Dictionary of Music and Musicians*, ed. Stanley Sadie (London: McMillan, 1980), and the *New Grove Dictionary of Music and Musicians II*, London: McMillan, 2000; online edition 2003).

[17] Pekacz, *op. cit.*.

[18] Kiri Miller, "Americanism Musically: Educating the Public at the Columbian Exposition, 1893," paper read at the 2002 meeting of the American Musicological Society.

[19] Since the 1980s, American feminist scholars are busily recovering such "lost traditions" of forgotten or marginalized women composers. See Dianne Peacock Jezic, *Women Composers: The Lost Tradition Found*. Ed. Elisabeth Wood (New York: The Feminist Press, 1994).

[20] Biographical studies in Polish based on primary sources include: Maria Iwanejko, *Maria Szymanowska*. (Kraków: Polskie Wydawnictwo Muzyczne, 1959); Józef Mirski and Maria Mirska, *Maria Szymanowska, 1789-1831. Album: Materiały biograficzne, sztambuchy, wybór kompozycji*. Kraków: Polskie Wydawnictwo Muzyczne, 1953). The most extensive biography of Szymanowska to-date is by Teofil Syga and Stanisław Szenic, *Maria Szymanowska i jej czasy* (Maria Szymanowska and her times) (Warszawa: Państwowy Instytut Wydawniczy, 1960). Pioneering research in English was conducted by Anne Swartz who published research studies and edited a selection from Szymanowska's piano works for *Women Composers: Music Through the Ages*, vol. 3, *Composers Born 1700-1799*. Sylvia Glickman and Martha Furman Schleifer, eds. Boston: G. K. Hall, 1998, 396-600; the music was reprinted (Bryn Mawr: Hilgard Press, 1998).

[21] Adam Mickiewicz's poem, written in 1827 in Moscow, is reproduced in Józef Mirski and Maria Mirska, *Maria Szymanowska, 1789-1831. Album: Materiały biograficzne, sztambuchy, wybór kompozycji (*Kraków: PWM, 1951), 47.

[22] By F. Malewski, cited in Belza (1987): 15. See Syga and Szenic (1960), Swartz (1984).

[23] A recent overview of Szymanowska's life and career may be found in Sławomir Dobrzański's *Maria Szymanowska: Pianist and Composer* (Polish Music Center, 2005). See also Maria Iwanejko: *Maria Szymanowska* (Kraków: Polskie Wydawnictwo Muzyczne, 1959); Maja Trochimczyk (previously: Maria Anna Harley), "Chopin and Women Composers: Collaborations, Imitations, Inspirations." *The Polish Review* 45 no. 1 (2000): 29-52.

[24] Nancy B. Reich, *Clara Schumann, op. cit.*

[25] See Jerzy Gołos, "Some Slavic predecessors of Chopin," *The Musical Quarterly* 46 (October 1960): 437-447; Anne Swartz, "Goethe and Szymanowska: The years 1823-1824 in Marienbad and Weimar" *Germano-Slavica* 4 no. 6 (fall 1984): 321-330; Anne Swartz, "Maria Szymanowska and the salon music of the early nineteenth century," *The Polish Review* 30 no. 1 (1985): 43-58; and Sławomir Dobrzański, "Maria Szymanowska and Fryderyk Chopin: Parallelism and Influence," *Polish Music Journal* 5 no. 1 (2002), online.

[26] The most extensive study of Szymanowska published in English is by Sławomir Dobrzański, *Maria Szymanowska: Pianist and Composer* (Los Angeles: Polish Music Center, 2005). It is a revised DMA dissertation, with a review of existing research and new insights into her music. The book also includes a chapter on vocal music by Maja Trochimczyk. See review by Anne Swartz, *The Polish Review* 54, no. 1 (2009): 105.

[27] Testimony to this concern with proper, respectable behavior may be found in her letters to her family (reprinted in Mirski and Mirska, 1953) and in many incidents described by Syga and Szenic. See also Halina Goldberg, "Album Musical de Maria Szymanowska," *Music and Letters*, 83, no. 4 (2002): 671-673.

[28] See the previously cited study by Dobrzanski, *Maria Szymanowska*.

[29] A letter of 31 August 1815, sent by Szymanowska to her parents, reproduced from Jozef Mirski and Maria Mirska, *Maria Szymanowska, 1789-1831. Album: Materiały biograficzne, sztambuchy, wybór kompozycji* (Kraków: PWM, 1951), 25.

[30] The work, published by PWM under strict censorship, has various shortcomings, the most important one being the distortion of the role of Jewish musicians in Polish culture. One of the contributors, Prof. Leon Błaszczyk had to remove a large number of entries and prepared a different Dictionary of Jewish Musicians in Poland, completed in 2002 after 40 years of research. I thank Bret Werb of the Holocaust Museum in Washington, D.C. for sharing with me Prof. Błaszczyk's as yet unpublished opus, the source of biographical information about composers Ida Erwest and Paulina Szalit.

[31] Magdalena Dziadek, *Polska krytyka muzyczna w latach 1890-1914* (Polish Music Criticism in the Years 1890-1914), vol. 2, *Czasopisma i autorzy* (Periodicals and Authors) (Cieszyn: Uniwersytet Śląski, filia w Cieszynie, 2002).

[32] Leon Błaszczyk, *Żydzi w kulturze muzycznej na ziemiach polskich w XIX I XX wiekuL Słownik*. Unpublished, pre-publication copy courtesy of Bret Werb, Holocaust Memorial Museum, Washington, D.C.

[33] The exceptions include a series of exhibitions on women composers organized in Katowice by Magdalena Dziadek and Lilianna M. Moll: *Oto artyści pełnowartościowi, którzy są kobietami... Polskie kompozytorki 1816-1939* [Here are fully-valuable artists who also are women... Polish women composers 1816-1939], catalog of an exhibition held in 2003; *Odrodźmy się w muzyce! Muzyka na łamach polskiej prasy kobiecej i „kobieca" krytyka muzyczna 1818-1939*. [Let us renew ourselves in music. Music in Polish women's press and women's music criticism, 1818-1939]. Catalog of an exhibition (Katowice, 2005).

[34] Anna Krechowiecka, "O edukacji kobiet," *Pamiętnik Lwowski* 1817, April, 315-321. Cited from Jolanta T. Pekacz, *Music Culture of Polish Galicia (1772-1914)* (University of Rochester Press, 2002), 153-14. On women's writings on music, see also Magdalena Dziadek, "'Female' Music Criticism in Poland 1890-1939," in *Interdisciplinary Studies in Musicology. 6. Music-Erotica-Culture* (Uniwersytet Adama Mickiewicza w Poznaniu, Poznań 2007), 155-168.

[35] Bianka Pietrov-Ennker, "Women in Polish society. A historical introduction," in R. Jaworski and B. Pietrow-Ennker, eds, *Women in Polish Society*. (Boulder, Colorado: East European Monographs, 1992), 1-30.

[36] *Almanach polskich kompozytorów współczesnych* (Dictionary of contemporary Polish composers), Mieczyslawa Hanuszewska and Boguslaw Schaeffer, eds. (Kraków: PWM, 1982, new edition).

[37] Brand, "Lady Dean Paul," 7.

[38] Myra Friesen Brand, *Poldowski (Lady Dean Paul): Her Life and Her Song Settings of French and English Poetry*. DMA dissertation, University of Oregon, 1979; "Lady Dean Paul (Poldowski): Composer, Performer, Wife and Mother in the Early 1900's" (*The Triangle of Mu Phi Epsilon*, vol. 74, no. 1 (Fall 1979): 7-11, 22.

[39] S. Jagodzińska-Niekraszowa, "Zarys twórczości polskich kompozytorek XIX i XX wieku," (*Muzyka Polska*, no. 8 (1935): 247. Cited from Dziadek, vol. 2, 392.
[40] Brand, "Lady Dean Paul," 8.
[41] See Marcia J. Citron, *The Letters of Fanny Hensel and Felix Mendelssohn* (New York: Pendragon Press, 1987); Carol Neuls-Bates, "Fanny Mendelssohn Hensel," in Neuls-Bates, ed., *Women in Music: An Anthology of Source Readings from the Middle Ages to the Present*. Boston: Northeastern University Press, 1996), 143-155.
[42] Danuta Gwizdalanka wrote about women's musical life at home in "Muzy(cz)ka dla dam. Kobieta a muzyka kameralna na przełomie XVIII i XIX wieku" (Music for ladies: Women and chamber music at the turn of the nineteenth century), *Monochord: De musica acta, studia et commentarii*, vol. 2 (1994): 13-19.
[43] " Twórczość a wirtuozja kompozycji muzycznej," in *Obchód setnej rocznicy urodzin Chopina i Pierwszy Zjazd Muzyków Polskich we Lwowie*, Lwów 1912.
[44] See Martina Homma's article on Wieniawski in the present volume.
[45] English translation of this and other poems by Maja Trochimczyk.
[46] Studies of music and depression focus on issues of music therapy and the usefulness of music as a cure in acute psychological afflictions, such as severe bi-polar disorder or clinical depression with suicidal preoccupations. See, Georgia Hudson Smith, "The song-writing process: A woman's struggle against depression and suicide," in *Case studies in music therapy* (Phoenixville: Barcelona, 1991), 479-496. See also David F. Hoeniger, "Musical cures of melancholy and mania in Shakespeare," in *Mirror up to Shakespeare: Essays in honour of G.R. Hibbard* (Toronto, Ontario: University of Toronto, 1984), 55-67.
[47] The cycle featured all Polish texts of these poems on separate pages, preceding the musical setting of each. Published by Leon Idzikowski (Kijów, Warsaw, 1914).
[48] *Śnieg/Snow* by Irena Białkiewicz, published by Gebethner and Wolff, Warsaw, n.d.
[49] The most extensive studies of Wieniawska's life and music are in two D.M.A. dissertations by American singers, Myra Jean Brand, *Poldowski (Lady Dean Paul): Her Life and her Song Settings of French and English Poetry*, D.M.A. dissertation, University of Oregon, 1979, 134 pages, including reprints of Poldowski's three articles, bibliography and music examples. Sara Gilliam Hopkins, *Verlaine in Song: How Six Composers of Melodie Responded to the Innovations of his Verse*, D.M.A. document, (University of Maryland, College Park, 1996), 77 pages.
[50] Teresa Chylińska, ed., *Szymanowski: Korespondencja, 1920-1926*, vol. 2 (Kraków: PWM, 1994), 192.
[51] Chylińska, *Korespondencja*, 206; the following two comments are on pp. 221, 225.
[52] Szymanowski's letter to Emil Hertzka in Vienna (director of Universal Edition), from Paris, 6 May 1921. In Chylińska, 240.
[53] Review in *The New York Herald Tribune*, 6 February 1922, in Chylińska, *Korespondencja*, 343.
[54] Marcia J. Citron, *Cécile Chaminade: A Bio-Bibliography* (New York: Greenwood Press, 1988).
[55] See Jann Pasler's entry on Augusta Holmes in the *New Grove Dictionary of Music II*, and her book on musical life in Paris, 1880-1900, *Composing the Citizen: Music as Public Utility in Third Republic France* (University of California Press, 2009).
[56] Wieniawska/Poldowski's publications include: *Seven songs ; Soir* : with oboe d'amore (New York, N.Y.: Bryn Mawr, Pa.: Classical Vocal Reprints; distributor, Hildegard Pub. Co., 1997, 1912); *Dans une musette,* text by Jean Dominique (London: J. & W. Chester, 1918); *L'heure exquise = O tempting hour* (Boston : C.W. Homeyer, 1917); *Colombine* to text by Paul Verlaine, (London: J. & W. Chester, 1913); *Cythère*, to text by Verlaine (London: J.&W. Chester, 1900-1964?); *Cortège*, text by Verlaine (London: J. & W. Chester, 1900-1928?); *Mandoline*, text by Verlaine (London: J. & W. Chester, 1900-1964); *Dansons la gigue* (Radio City, N.Y., E.B. Marks Music Corp. 1942); *Le faune*, to text by Verlaine (London, J. & W. Chester, 1919); *Pannyre aux talons d'or*, to text by A. Samain (London, J. & W. Chester, 1919); *Nocturne (des*

cantilènes) to text by Jean Moréas (London, J. & W. Chester, 1914); *Sérénade (Le forêt bruissante)* to text by Adolphe Retté (London, J. & W. Chester, 1914); *Fantoches* to text by Verlaine (London: J. & W. Chester, 1913); *L'attente* to text by Verlaine (London: J. & W. Chester, 1912); *Dimanche d'avril* to text by Verlaine (Paris : Durand, 1911), *To love* (London: J. & W. Chester Ltd. 1927); *Narcisse. Pour chant avec accompagnement de quatuor à cordes.* (London, J. & W. Chester, 1927); *Reeds of innocence* to text by William Blake (London, J. & W. Chester Ltd. 1924); *La passante* (London: J. & W. Chester, 1923); A poor young shepherd ; Verlaine, Paul, Publication: London: J. & W. Chester, 1923); *Soir: poesie de Albert Samain pour chant avec accompagnement de piano et d'hautbois d'amour* (London: J. & W. Chester, 1920); *Sur l'herbe* text by Verlaine (London, J. & W. Chester, 1918); *Spleen = Melancholy,* text by Verlaine (Boston, Mass. : Charles W. Homeyer, 1918); *Brume* to text by Verlaine (London: Charles W. Homeyer & Co., 1915); *Berceuse d'armorique, to* text by Anatole Le Braz (London, J. & W. Chester, 1914).

57 Brand, 1979, *op. cit.,* Gillian Hopkins, 1996, *op. cit.*
58 Statement paraphrased from an entry on Szymanowski in *The New Grove Dictionary of Music and Musicians II,* by Jim Samson (online version, 2003).
59 Zofia Helman, Teresa Chylińska, and Alistair Wightman, *The Songs of Karol Szymanowski and his Contemporaries* (Los Angeles: Polish Music Center at USC, 2002).
60 George Antheil (1900-1959), scored for 1 pianola with amplifier, 2 pianos, 3 xylophones, electric bells, small wood propeller, large wood propeller, metal propeller, tam-tam, 4 bass drums, and siren, an earlier version of this work was for sixteen pianolas run electrically from a common control. See Linda Whitesitt, *The Life and Music of George Antheil, 1900-1959* .Ph.D. dissertation, (Ann Arbor, Michigan: UMI Research Press, 1983).
61 Poldowski, "*Poèmes Arisophanesques,*" *The Chesterian* 8 (1927): 269. Cited after Brand, "Lady Dean Paul": 9.
62 Joseph Strauss, *Ruth Crawford Seeger* (Cambridge: Cambridge University Press), 1995; Judith Tick, *Ruth Crawford Seeger.* (Cambridge University Press, 1997).
63 See Maria Anna Harley (now: Maja Trochimczyk), "Bacewicz, Picasso and the Making of Desire,"*Journal of Musicological Research* 16 no. 4 (1997): 243-282.
64 Cited from Carol Neuls-Bates, ed., *Women in Music: An Anthology of Source Readings from the Middle Ages to the Present* (Boston: Northeastern University Press, 1996, revised edition), 310.
65 Wieniawska's articles were published under her *nom-de-plume,* Poldowski: "Man and Modernism," *The Chesterian* New Series 34 (1923): 6; "*Poèmes Aristophanesques,*" *The Chesterian* 8 (1927): 269; "The Influence of Jazz," *The Chesterian* 9 (1927): 10-12. This quarterly journal was edited by Georges Jean-Aubry and published between 1915-1961 (London: J. & W. Chester).
66 Poldowski, "Man and Modernism" (1923): 6.
67 Poldowski, *Berceuse de l'enfant mourant : pour violon et piano* (London: J. & W. Chester, 1923). A Recording of this work is available on a TROY 338 CD issued by Albany Records in 1999: *Polish Romantic Violin Music of late 19th & 20th Centuries* (Tyrone Greive, violin and Ellen Burmeister, piano). Greive also edited her chamber music for Hildegard Publishing Co.
68 Brand, "Lady Dean Paul": 7. Gédaldge (1856- 1926) was a French composer and teacher was renowned for his study of counterpoint and a textbook on the fugue. Conservative in his own music, he encouraged students to pursue excellence in their personal styles. His students included Milhaud, Ravel and Honegger.
69 Letter from Francis Patterson-Knight to Teresa Chylińska, 1 December 1984, in Chylińska, *Korespondencja,* 194.
70 Richard Aldrich, "Poldowski's Recital," *New York Times* (19 January 1921): p. 14 col. 2.
71 "Obituary, Lady Dean Paul, Composer and Pianist," *London Times* (29 January 1932): p. 17 col. 2.

[72] See Stefan Kisielewski's *Grażyna Bacewicz*, further references in Maja Trochimczyk and James Harley, "Grażyna Bacewicz - Bibliography." *Polish Music Journal* 5, no. 1 (2002), online. A comprehensive biography of Bacewicz is by Małgorzata Gąsiorowska, *Bacewicz*. Series: Kompozytorzy Polscy XX wieku (Kraków: Polskie Wydawnictwo Muzyczne, 1999).

A Romantic Interlude I

Fig. 1: A Polish postcard of a village couple in Cracovian costumes (from the Małopolska region), with a krakowiak couplet. The woman's head scarf in this and all the following postcards indicates her married status. Translation: "My Marysia / my black eyes, / It seems that for you / My heart will leap out." Published in Kraków, Poland, ca. 1890. Maja Trochimczyk Collection.

Fig. 2: A Polish postcard of a village couple in Cracovian costumes (from the Małopolska region), with a krakowiak couplet: "A nightingale cannot / part from another / And I have to leave you; / Oh, my mighty God!" Published in Kraków, Poland, ca. 1890. Maja Trochimczyk Collection.

This text is No. 99 in the section of krakowiaks in Wacław z Oleska, *Pieśni polskie i ruskie ludu galicyjskiego z muzyką instrumentalną Karola Lipińskiego* (Polish and Russian Songs of Galician People with Instrumental Music by Karol Lipiński), Lwów: Nakładem Franciszka Pillera, 1833, p. 117.

Chapter 2

Karol Lipiński's Concerts in Wrocław

Maria Zduniak

Relatively little is known about the life, concert activities and compositions of Karol Lipiński, the most famous Polish violin virtuoso active in the first half of the 19th century. Born on 30 October 1790 in the family of a court musician, Feliks Lipiński, Karol spent his childhood on the Potocki estate in Radzyń Podlaski, near Lublin.[1] There, from an early age, he studied violin performance under the direction of his father. According to Józef Powroźniak's biography of the composer, young Karol revealed his outstanding musical abilities already in this early period. The development of the child's talent greatly benefited from the change of residence of Lipiński family: in 1799 they moved to Lwów, a large city in Galicia, a province of Austro-Hungarian Empire created out of south-eastern Poland (now Lviv in Ukraine; also known as Lemberg). At that time, the young violinist was also interested in other string instruments than the violin, especially the cello. Luckily for the later admirers of his talent, practicing the cello did not distract him from mastering the violin, the main subject of his music studies. Actually, the result of this fascination with the cello was quite positive: it helped Lipiński to develop a beautiful, rich tone that characterized his violin performance style well into his old age.

Over the years, Lipiński became active in many areas of Lwów musical life. He performed chamber music, conducted, and served as a soloist for a variety of concerts given in the city. He worked as an orchestral musician and a composer.[2] During the Lwów period of his career, he wrote three symphonies in classical style as well as an overture, a series of violin pieces, and stage music for a Lwów theater which was directed by Jan Nepomucen Kamiński. Interestingly, in this period the composer also developed an avid interest in folklore. Fascination with folklore was quite widespread at the time; in Lipiński's case, it resulted in publishing a collection of Polish and Russian folk songs from Galicia, co-edited by Wacław Zaleski (Wacław of Olesko) and entitled *Polish and Russian Songs of the Peasants of Galicia*.³

The turning point in Karol Lipiński's artistic biography was his departure for Vienna at the end of 1814. There, he met Louis Spohr —an eminent violin virtuoso, composer and conductor, who was then at the peak of his fame. From that time onward, Lipiński found the idea of a virtuoso career to be increasingly attractive. The way to accomplishing this goal led through perfecting his violin technique and expanding his repertoire. He dedicated three years to these tasks. A subsequent turning point in Lipiński's career may be located in the year 1817, when the violinist embarked on his first artistic tour as a virtuoso soloist, a tour that he described a decade later in the following words:

> After working in this position for five years (i.e. the position of the concertmaster of the opera theater in Lwów—M.Z.) I left in 1817—I went alone to travel abroad. Subsequently, I gave public concerts in many notable cities, for instance, after arriving in Italy I appeared in recitals in Trieste and Venice.⁴

The first concert tour abroad was of great significance in Lipiński's life as a virtuoso, primarily because the young violinist had an opportunity to meet Nicolo Paganini (1782-1840). In 1818, they even gave concerts together in the Italian town of Piacenza. Lipiński's musical challenge of the famous Italian ended well for the Pole, for he gained Paganini's admiration and learnt the secrets of his new, virtuoso style of performance. The Polish virtuoso's first successful artistic tour was followed by an extended series of concert travels that the violinist embarked upon, incessantly criss-crossing the continent for over 20 years, with only short interruptions.

Karol Lipiński began his career as a virtuoso violinist in an extraordinary era, when great virtuosi traveled around the European continent on concert tours. He belonged among the most eminent musicians of the first half of the 19th century and was the most famous Polish musician before Chopin. He was also a zealous patriot, who emphasized his Polish background by his multifaceted activities and by his creativity. Without doubt, he was one of the greatest violinists of his time. This judgment was confirmed by Paganini's opinion, who, when asked about the best concert violinist, responded coyly: "Who is first, I do not know, but the second is undoubtedly Lipiński."⁵ The Polish violinist developed a personal performance style that was unique among his colleagues. Among elements of this individual style, the greatest attention is due to his extensive musical background and sensitivity, to his technical perfection, spotlessly pure intonation, and, last but not least, his wonderful, profound tone.

Lipiński's concert repertoire was quite extensive, but he mostly featured his own compositions in his concert programs. Obviously, he was their incomparable and most distinguished interpreter. His repertoire included: sonatas by Giuseppe Tartini; various solo and chamber works by Johann Sebastian Bach; Violin Concerti by Giovanni Battista Viotti; as well as Beethoven's Violin Concerto in D major, Op. 61. He was not a stranger to contemporary violin literature, which he added to his concert repertoire. The list of contemporary compositions consisted of works by Jean Pierre Rode, Charles Philippe Lafont, Charles-Auguste de Bériot, Pierre Baillot, and Louis Spohr. Only occasionally, though, did he play any music by Nicolo Paganini.

The Polish virtuoso's accomplishments as a composer are also notable. His catalog of works includes three symphonies, an overture, chamber music, as well as many other vocal, instrumental and stage compositions. The most prominent position in his oeuvre is assumed by pieces for solo violin, including eleven capriccios, as well as works for violin and piano or orchestra. These compositions include four violin concerti, among which the Second Violin Concerto, in D major, Op. 21, known as "The Military," takes the position of honor. An important place in his oeuvre should be assigned to various Rondos, Variations and Fantasies, based on themes usually borrowed from fashionable operas by other composers. These works reveal his sensitivity to music novelties and changes of fashion: current opera repertoire entered his own music immediately, in the form of variations or fantasies with variations, based on operatic arias and themes by such composers as Gioacchino Rossini, Vincenzo Bellini, Giacomo Meyerbeer, Giuseppe Verdi, or, in Poland, Jan Stefani.

Many of Lipiński's works are saturated with national characteristics, expressed, for instance, through the genre of the polonaise, his favorite form of artistic expression. He wrote over 30 polonaises; these compositions were both very popular and highly regarded. Franz Liszt wrote: "in Lipiński's polonaises the heart beats joyously, as it did before the disaster" (i.e. the disaster of the partitions and the fall of the November Uprising—MZ).[6]

In this study based on archival documents from the libraries of Wrocław, Dresden, and Lwów, I will focus on a little-known aspect of

Lipinski's musical career: his links to, and performances in the Silesian city of Wrocław (Breslau). Of Lipinski's his early concerts in Poland, the 1819 appearances in Krzemieniec and Kraków are worth noting, followed by a return to these cities two years later. In June 1821, he performed in Poznań during the so-called St. John Contracts ("kontrakty świętojańskie"). As the local press reported, the violinist played in Poznań twice that year—on 26 June in the Rezusa Hall on Grobla St. and on 30 June in the Exhibition Hall.[7] Immediately after these two concerts, Lipiński departed for Wrocław; local press noted his arrival there on 18 July 1821.[8] In addition to a print advertisement about his concert, an anonymous author published an article filled with praise of the virtuoso's astounding capabilities. Apparently, the reviewer had met the musician during one of the so-called "musical soirées," held in the salons of affluent bourgeoisie.

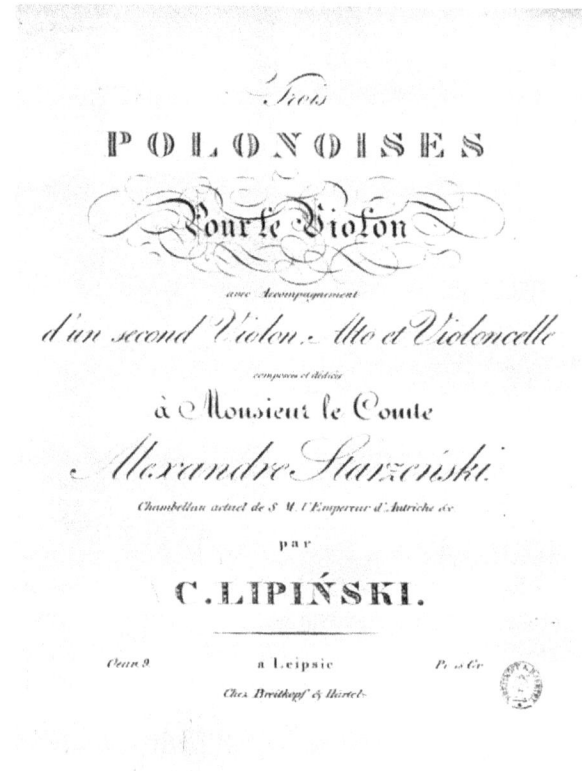

Figure 1: Cover of Lipiński's Polonaises.

At that time, out-of-town virtuosi frequently participated in such exclusive forms of private entertainment. The unknown author of this anonymous article compared the type of virtuosity represented by Lipiński to the performance style of Louis Spohr, whom local music lovers knew in person, since he had given concerts in Wrocław in 1809. In addition, the article brought to the public's attention the fact that the Polish violinist was well appreciated in Moscow and St. Petersburg.[9]

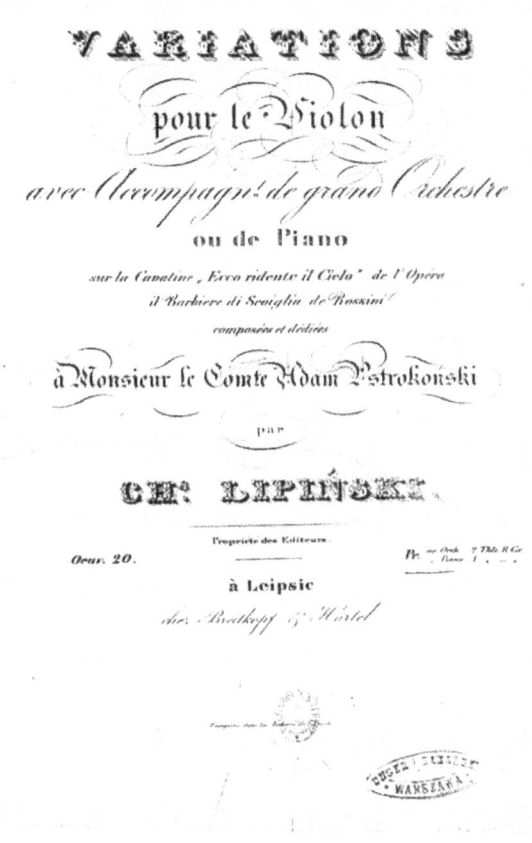

Figure 2: Cover of Lipiński's Variations. This and all subsequent illustrations provided by Maria Zduniak. Used by permission.

Lipiński's first concert, announced in this way, took place on 20 July 1821 in the Music Hall of the Wrocław University (Musikzsaal, presently Oratorium Marianum).[10] On the basis of concert reviews, filled with praise expressed in superlative terms, we can partly reconstruct the concert program during which the virtuoso performed the first and second movements of a violin concerto by Giovanni Battista Viotti. An anonymous music critic enthusiastically described the Polish violinist's virtuoso performance in a German-language Wrocław newspaper, *Breslauer Zeitung*. The critic emphasized the violinist's ease with overcoming technical difficulties, while praising—above all—the "wonderful tone that the artist 'charmed' out of his invaluable instrument and which came into a full, lively presence in the hall's beautiful interior, with its exceptionally good acoustics."[11] The reviewer also expressed a regret that the attendance was disappointing and that the number of people who came to the concert was so low. Regardless of its overall positive tone, the enthusiastic review also contained some critical statements, referring, for instance, to the violinist's apparent misuse of harmonics, that the critic derisively dubbed "cheap whistling."[12] Finally, the same review announced Lipiński's further performances to be given in Leipzig and other German towns.

After the virtuoso's departure from Wrocław (between 21 and 24 July) one more article about him appeared in the local press (*Breslauer Zeitung*).[13] Penned by Leberecht Bentley, the text was entitled "A Postscript on Account of Lipiński" ("Nachrede wegen Lipiński") and described Lipiński's performance with superlative praise.[14] The reviewer used an exaggerated tone and a lofty language, filled with verbal flights of fancy, to compare Lipiński's performance to the style of the cellist Bernhard Romberg and to the vocal talents of Angelica Catalani (both of whom were known from their earlier appearances in Wrocław, in 1816 and 1819 respectively[15]). Not surprisingly, the Polish press followed the virtuoso's travels with intense interest. The Polish newspaper *Rozmaitości* in Lwów reprinted an excerpt from the Wrocław paper informing the readers about Lipiński's concert tour in the following words:

> Karol Lipiński, traveling in the profession of his art, gave a concert in Wrocław. A local newspaper contained the following report from this event: "My efforts in recommending Mr. Lipiński did not, unfortunately, bring positive results, because only a small number of listeners attended his concert given at the Music Hall of the University. Nonetheless, this small group rewarded the musician with intense applause and cheered for him with the greatest zeal... Who would not bestow on him the honor of a first-class violinist? How rare is the assuredness and ease with which he overcomes even the greatest technical difficulties!"[16]

Several months later, on the way back to Lwów while returning from concerts in Dresden, Leipzig and Berlin, Lipiński again stopped in Wrocław and received a friendly welcome. A proof of this positive attitude may be found in a laudatory article written on this occasion by Karl Schall. In addition to the article, numerous announcements informed about Lipiński's concert, scheduled for 10 November and to be held at the Music Hall of the University.[17] The program included a Violin Concerto by Viotti and the Variations in G minor (Op. 5?) by Lipiński, among other works. In a review of the concert, an anonymous music critic concluded that, by the time this concert took place, a group of enthusiasts of Lipiński's art emerged in Wrocław; it was this group of "fans" of his talent that so enthusiastically welcomed the virtuoso.[18] The reviewer also expressed a wish that another concert of chamber music would be organized with Lipiński's participation, since the virtuoso had revealed his abilities as an extraordinary chamber musician in private performances of a range of quartets and quintets by different composers. These performances were held during musical soirées, exclusive social gatherings primarily focused on music making.

It is significant that the same review also appeared in Lwów periodicals—it was printed in Polish translation as early as 24 November 1821.[19] Another proof of Lipiński's great popularity and a widespread recognition of his talent in Wrocław took the poetic form of a sonnet, entitled "Homage" ("Hołd") and written by a well-known Silesian poet, Karl Holtei. The identity of the author was not fully disclosed, but merely suggested through his abbreviated signature of an "H." The sonnet appeared in a local newspaper several days after the performance:[20]

> Wie heißt der Mann, der aus vier armen Seiten
> So mächt'ge Worte weiß hervorzulocken,
> Daß in Begeisterung die Puls' uns stocken,
> Und alle Herzen Opfer ihm bereiten?
>
> Daß uns geschieht, als ob aus blauen Weiten
> Die Töne niederschwebten zart wie Flocken;
> Und kräftig dann, als ob mit allen Glocken
> Geläutet würde: für die Kunst zu streiten!?
>
> Wie heißt er wohl, der seelenvolle Meister,
> Der mir erscheint, zum Herrscher im Gefilde
> Der Musica, der heiligen, erkohren?

Der Bund'sgenosse schon verklärter Geister:
Tonkünstler feurig, fromm, stark, streng und milde?
Lipinsky ist's, im Polenland geboren!!!

Interestingly, the Polish translation of this sonnet appeared in *The Cracow Bee* (*Pszczółka Krakowska*) in the same year of 1821:[21]

Hołd Lipińskiemu (Homage to Lipiński)

What is the name of this man
Who draws such expression from mere four strings
That the Spirit, overwhelmed with feeling,
Compels all hearts to give him homage?

At times, he is distant
And seems to hide the sounds underground.
Then, suddenly, loud bells seem to strike under his bow,
A call to battle resounds - for the fame of his art.

"From what country did he arrive,
This master filled with fire? He, bold and invincible,
Who sweetens power with gentleness?

Who captures the soul with magical tones?"
"This Ally of Heavens," says Glory,
"He is called Lipiński, and he came from Poland!!!"

Indeed, it seems that Lipiński's concert of 10 November 1821 was quite extraordinary. The artist soon decided to play once more, scheduling the concert in the Music Hall of the University for the 14th of November. An announcement about this concert, signed by a local music critic, Mr. Schall, contained information about another planned event, dedicated to chamber music. As it turned out later, that additional concert could not take place because of limited time that the artist had at his disposal, due to his early departure for Lwów on 15 November. The Wrocław public welcomed the concert of 14 November (it was the third and last one in the year 1821) with such exceptional enthusiasm that the hall was filled to the last seat (it had the capacity of about 400 persons).[22] The listeners' delight exceeded all expectations and was publicly expressed in a spontaneous manifestation.[23] Furthermore, Lipiński's astounding success was reflected in a wide array of press reviews published in Poland. Remarks about this subject, or reprints of his Wrocław reviews, appeared in numerous daily papers throughout the country, including *Gazeta Warszawska* (Warsaw Gazette), *Gazeta Wielkiego Księstwa Poznańskiego* (Gazette of the Grand Duchy of Poznań), *Rozmaitości* (Variety) of Lwów, and *Kurier Litewski* (The Lithuanian Courier) in Vilnus.[24] *Gazeta Korespondenta Warszawskiego i Zagranicznego* (Gazette of the Warsaw and Foreign Correspondent) published the following report that may serve as a typical example of the event's press coverage:

> Mr. Karol Lipiński gave two concerts in Wrocław. The *Neue Breslauer Zeitung* dated 12 and 17 November praised the great talent of our compatriot. One of the local lovers of true art honored him with a beautiful sonnet published in another newspaper. An even greater honor was bestowed upon him on 14 November. Below you will find the exact reprint of the article from the Neue Breslauer Zeitung (no. 182): "Honor to the one to whom it is due! Wrocław, 15 November. Yesterday Mr. Lipiński's concert—during his present visit with us (the last one, alas)—attracted numerous listeners who gave the eminent master a well deserved homage of admiration in the full sense of this word. The whole hall resounded with loud applause during the final portion of the last piece on the program, composed and performed by Mr. Lipiński (Rondo alla Pollacca), in which he unveiled the whole immediacy, charm and richness of his extraordinary talent in the most vividly articulated expressions of power and sweetness, performed with the full conviction, assuredness, and profundity of interpretation that characterize his playing.
>
> At the end of the concert, four representatives of the public approached the virtuoso to express the gratitude of all the students of the University . . . One of the delegates was Polish; after greeting his eminent compatriot with words in the native language, he presented the violinist with a beautiful silver chalice, on behalf of, and as a commemoration of, Wrocław University. The rim of the chalice was decorated with Latin inscriptions: "Music amicum manent honores immortales" (Friends of music honor immortal hands) placed around it, and "In memoriam Viadrinae Carolo Lipinski," placed inside the chalice.
>
> Prior to the presentation of this gift, the student delegate drank a toast from the chalice, offering it to the violinist's health after exclaiming, "Long live the artist!" Mr. Lipiński, who unites in himself such a great degree of perfection of his art with such an amazing humility and politeness, accepted the gift with so tender a joy, that he barely could find words to express his gratitude. The music world's celebrities and other listeners applauded again, while repeating the joyous exclamation: "Long live Lipiński!" What true friend of the art of music would not want to rejoice over this rare event, so richly deserving of being honored and worshipped? This event gave as much honor to those who were its

initiators as to the one to whom it was dedicated. Mr. Lipiński left for Lwów today; may God inspire him to come and visit us again.[25]

Towards the end of his stay in Wrocław, in the company of his wife, Regina, Karol Lipiński paid a farewell visit to the Kapellmeister of the Cathedral, J. I. Schnabel, a well-respected composer and a distinguished organizer of local musical life. A commemoration of their encounter was preserved in the personal album of the Schnabel family. The Lipiński entry was dated 15 November 1821 and consisted of two inscriptions. Karol Lipiński wrote a polite sentence in German: "Ein in Ihrer schätzbaren Gesellschaft, wenigen zugebrachten Augenblicke, werde ich immer unter die angenehmsten meines Lebens zählen." In addition, his wife wrote in Polish: "Remember us" ("Pamiętaj o nas").[26]

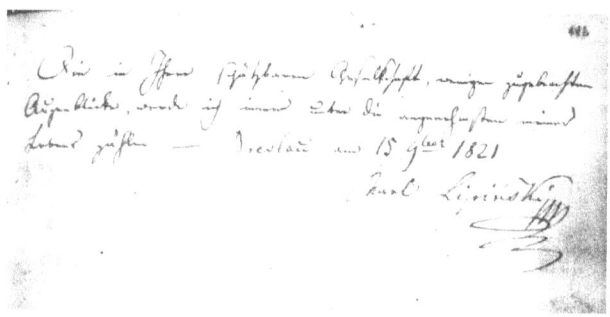

Figure 3a: Lipiński's inscription in Schnabels' Album.

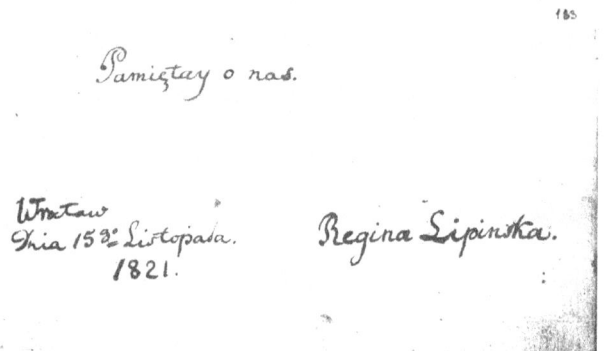

Figure 3b: Lipiński's wife's inscription in Schnabels' Album.

Meanwhile, Lipiński's fame was spreading quickly. His artistic reputation also grew in Wrocław, as shown in public expressions of continuous interest in his career. This interest was revealed through a variety of announcements in the press; for instance, advertisements of the availability of Lipiński's compositions in local bookstores.[27] In February 1824, on the occasion of a Wrocław arrival of the famous violinist and composer from France, Jacques-Fereol Mazas, one notice in the press reminded Wrocław citizens about Lipiński's earlier performances.[28] By that time, as mentioned earlier, Lipiński had a sizeable group of admirers of his talent in the city. This group mostly included musicians, among whom Johann Theodor Mosewius, the founder of Wrocław Singakademie, occupied the most prominent position. From time to time, he published articles in the press, including miscellaneous notices informing the readers about career progress of the Polish violinist; he also published advertisements about Lipiński's upcoming concerts in Wrocław.[29]

In the spring of 1826, Lipiński undertook another artistic travel to Western Europe, planning, on this occasion, to visit Leipzig and negotiate matters concerning the publication of his works by well-known publishing houses, Breitkopf und Härtel, and C. F. Peters.[30] The way from Lwów to Leipzig led through Kraków, where the violinist appeared in the company of his student, Jacek Majewski. The travelers probably arrived in Wrocław on 11 June 1826. This hypothesis is based on an announcement published on 12 June in a Polish newspaper about visitors to the city. The paper reported that "recently, at the inn 'Under the Golden Sceptre' (Pod złotym berłem), located at Kuźnicza Street, two artists took residence: the artist Lipiński from Lwów and the artist Majewski from Kraków."[31] Two days later, announcements appeared about the first concert in which Lipiński was scheduled to perform. The concert was planned for 17 June 1826 and was to be held at the Music Hall of the University.

It is worth noting that this announcement was written by Friedrich Wilhelm Berner, a well-known composer, pianist, and organist at St. Elizabeth Church, who enjoyed a solid reputation in the Wrocław music world, similar to the positions of Schnabel and Mosewius. In order to bestow on Lipiński's visit an atmosphere of heightened interest, Mosewius published another announcement of the concert, written in a joyous, enthusiastic tone. It started from an exclamation: "Lipiński is in Wrocław! Long-awaited Lipiński, an extraordinarily talented, excellent violinist, is here again and on Saturday, on the 17th of this month, he will give a concert."[32] The author of this announcement also cited an overwhelmingly enthusiastic review by Bentley mentioned earlier (it was written on the occasion of a concert that took place on 20 July). Another article, penned by D. Grattenauer, was filled with boundless praise, expressed in an elaborate form typical for the period. This particular article, published on 16 June 1826 by the *Breslauer Zeitung*, suggested that Lipiński played on an Amati violin at that time.[33] For unknown reasons the announced concert was postponed until 20 June 1826; unfortunately it was not reviewed.[34]

However, a copy of the program survived and was preserved at the University Library; it provides information about the order of individual pieces on the program, arranged in a fashion typical for the period. The concert began with the Overture to Mozart's opera *Don Giovanni*. Then, Lipiński presented a Violin Concerto "of his own composition:" it was, most likely, his First Concerto in F-sharp minor, Op. 14. In turn, Garczyńska—a singer from a Wrocław theater, known only thanks to her presence on this program—sang Beethoven's song, *Adelaide*. Lipiński, in turn, played two other violin compositions of his own, Variations (unknown opus number) and *Rondo alla Polacca* (unknown opus number). These violin pieces were separated by another overture by Mozart, from *The Magic Flute*.[35] Though the concert program did not mention the name of the conductor, in all likelihood it was Friedrich Wilhelm Berner. The copy of the program preserved at the University Library provides clues about this fact in handwritten annotations.

The titles of orchestral works, added by hand, included a note stating that the new conclusion to the Overture to *Don Giovanni* heard during the concert was composed by Berner. Having arranged the pieces, he was also the most likely conductor of the whole program. Several days after this concert appearance, Lipiński announced another Wrocław concert. It took place on 26 June 1826 and was, like the previous event, scheduled for the Music Hall of the University, but it was not reviewed.[36]

Polish youth, studying at the Wrocław University at this time, publicly honored the arrival of the virtuoso through the publication of an ode by Michał Kolicki, written in Polish and entitled *To Lipiński, His Compatriots Remaining at the Wrocław University*. This ode was published on 22 June 1826.[37] The violinist, in response, expressed his gratitude to the Wrocław students for the displays of their friendship and recognition by dedicating to them a newly composed song for men's choir. Not surprisingly, this song was entitled *Compatriots at the Wrocław University*. Only the title is known since the score of this song did not survive.[38]

As was the case during Lipiński's previous travels, the Polish press greeted his artistic tour with great interest. It is understandable that the Lwów press followed the successes of their compatriot with a particularly intense attention. The Lwów *Rozmaitości* devoted much room to this subject in its editions issued on 21 July and 18 August 1826.[39] Announcements about his concerts appeared also in Russian and Prussian-occupied partitions of Poland, *Gazeta Wielkiego Księstwa Poznańskiego, Gazeta Warszawska, Gazeta Korespondenta Warszawskiego i Zagranicznego*, and *Kurier Warszawski*.[40] In the latter newspaper, indirect reports from Poznań indicated that

> the famous Lipiński who has been visiting Wrocław, where he gave the second concert on the 26th of this month, and on the 29th of the same month, was to play for the last time there, supporting one of the most accomplished local artists. He is also expected here and is awaited by many with true devotion.[41]

During the years 1835-36, Karol Lipiński undertook another extensive concert tour throughout Europe. The way back from London and Paris led through Frankfurt-am-Mein, Leipzig, Dresden and Wrocław. Lipiński must have enjoyed his great popularity among the Wrocław concert public, because the local press informed their readers right away about the successes of the Polish violinist abroad, publishing either notices about the stages of his travels, or longer reports about his performances. Authors of these press notices included Mosewius who informed the local music lovers about Lipiński's performance at the Gewandhaus in Leipzig, given on 7 October 1835. In the same review, Mosewius announced Lipiński's arrival in Wrocław and reaffirmed his elevated position in the music world, stating: "Lipiński takes the first place among the violinist whom we have ever heard and is, for us, the foremost violinist in the whole world."[42] Such public expressions of admiration as well as well-timed advertising undoubtedly influenced the growing interest with which the virtuoso was awaited in Wrocław. He arrived in town on 21 November 1836, taking up his lodgings, as usual, at the inn "Under the Golden Sceptre."[43]

The composer himself announced the first concert, planned for 26 November 1835 at the Music Hall of the University.[44] On the following day, in addition to repeating the announcement, the Wrocław press also published the concert program. It featured the following works by Lipiński: Second Violin Concerto in D major, Op. 21, known as the "Military;" *Variations on a Cavatina Theme from the Opera 'The Barber of Seville' by Rossini*, Op. 20; *Fantasy on Themes from the Opera 'Il Sommnabula' by Bellini*, Op. 23; and solo and symphonic works by other composers.[45] We should note here that while engaging in activities of a composer, Lipiński often expressed the point of view of a virtuoso violinist. This is why his compositions are so typical for the period of *stile brillant* and this is why they were predominantly written for his own performance capabilities. To put it simply, the violinist's compositions were dictated by a desire to provide a virtuosic display for his performative talent.

Breslau, Dienstag den 20. Juni 1826.

Mit hoher Bewilligung:

Großes
Vocal- u. Instrumental-
Concert

im Musiksaale der Universität,
veranstaltet von

Herrn Lipinski,
Violinist aus Lemberg.

1. Ouverture.
2. Concert für die Violine, componirt und vorgetragen von Lipinski.
3. Adelaide von Beethoven, gesungen von Frau von Garczynska.
4. Variationen für die Violine, componirt und vorgetragen von Lipinski.
5. Intermezzo.
6. Rondo alla Polacca, componirt und vorgetragen von Lipinski.

Einlaßkarten zu 20 Sgr. sind in den Musikhandlungen der Herrn Leukart und Förster, wie auch am Tage des Concerts an der Kasse zu haben. Jedes Chor-Billet kostet 10 Sgr.

Einlaß 6 Uhr.   Anfang 7 Uhr.   Ende gegen 9 Uhr.

Figure 4: Poster for Lipiński's concert of 20 June 1826.

On the day of the 1835 concert, the editor of *Breslauer Zeitung* reprinted a panegyric poem entitled *Postscript: To Lipiński*, which had originally appeared in 1821. The newspaper also issued a plenitude of additional information about the composer and his brilliant artistic career.[46] Two days after the concert, *Breslauer Zeitung* published a review by an anonymous music critic, which documented yet another extraordinary success of Lipiński. While describing the characteristics of the violinist's performance style, the critic analyzed his bowing technique, his articulation and the rich variety of tone colors, thus presenting an overall account of technical and interpretative capabilities of the artist.

The critic's delight and admiration may be best illustrated by the following quote: "Lipiński plays double stops with such breathtaking speed and in such great abundance, he articulates them so clearly and with such perfect intonation, that such passages cannot be performed with a greater precision even on the piano."[47]

Nonetheless, the reviewer also had some reservations about the program of the concert:

> Whoever heard Lipiński this time could not have come to know him well because he played only his own works. Obviously, these compositions are brilliant and present in full light his extraordinary features as a virtuoso. However, they do not provide any indication at all about his abilities as an interpreter of works by other composers, for instance, Viotti—the father of a new performance style. The above statement contains an invitation directed to the virtuoso and to the listeners alike. I hope that it would be possible to organize a second concert, during which Lipiński could expose us to, and provide an opportunity to admire, a wider range of his repertoire.

It has to be said that other reviewers of this concert were unanimous about this need to expand the violinist's repertoire. August Kahlert, a well-known poet, philosopher and music critic working for the *Schlesische Zeitung*, stated in an extensive and insightful article that he primarily valued Lipiński's inspiring interpretations, characterized by emotional intensity and exceptional warmth.[48] He also asked his readers to pay attention to the virtuosic character of the violinist's oeuvre, typical of *stile brilliant*. According to Kahlert, Lipiński's compositions, when heard in an incomparable interpretation by the composer himself, became ennobled and their virtuosic displays were less random and superficial than those by other virtuoso musicians.

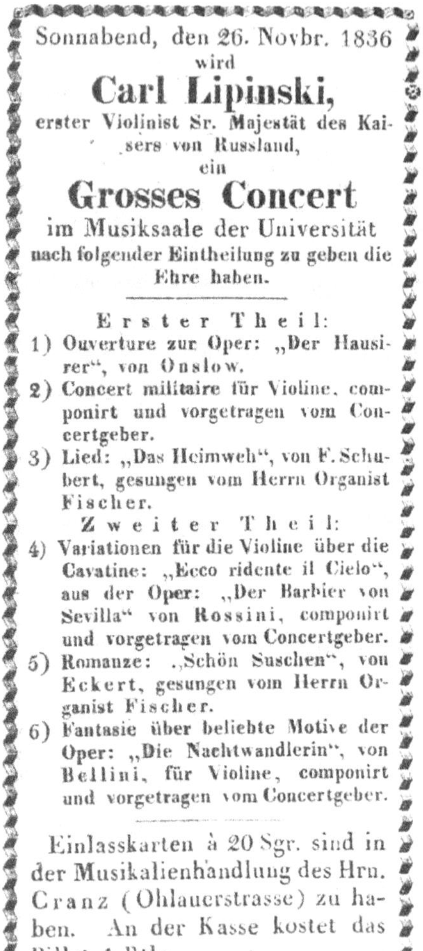

> Sonnabend, den 26. Novbr. 1836
> wird
> **Carl Lipinski,**
> erster Violinist Sr. Majestät des Kaisers von Russland,
> ein
> **Grosses Concert**
> im Musiksaale der Universität
> nach folgender Eintheilung zu geben die Ehre haben.
>
> ---
>
> Erster Theil:
> 1) Ouverture zur Oper: „Der Hausirer", von Onslow.
> 2) Concert militaire für Violine, componirt und vorgetragen vom Concertgeber.
> 3) Lied: „Das Heimweh", von F. Schubert, gesungen vom Herrn Organist Fischer.
>
> Zweiter Theil:
> 4) Variationen für die Violine über die Cavatine: „Ecco ridente il Cielo", aus der Oper: „Der Barbier von Sevilla" von Rossini, componirt und vorgetragen vom Concertgeber.
> 5) Romanze: „Schön Suschen", von Eckert, gesungen vom Herrn Organist Fischer.
> 6) Fantasie über beliebte Motive der Oper: „Die Nachtwandlerin", von Bellini, für Violine, componirt und vorgetragen vom Concertgeber.
>
> Einlasskarten à 20 Sgr. sind in der Musikalienhandlung des Hrn. Cranz (Ohlauerstrasse) zu haben. An der Kasse kostet das Billet 1 Rtlr.
> Anfang 7 Uhr. Ende 9 Uhr.

Figure 5: Poster for Lipiński's concert of 26 November 1836.

Furthermore, the critic pointed out that Lipiński's style of violin performance was permeated with Polish national characteristics. In conclusion, however, Kahlert expressed a wish that the violinist's subsequent concert programs also include works by Viotti, Bach, and Beethoven. The critic greatly valued Lipiński's interpretations of these compositions since he knew them from the virtuoso's appearances in Leipzig. Nonetheless, we should note that in Kahlert's account, this concert was welcomed with great public interest, despite the fact that its date was identical to the date of the 25th anniversary of relocating the University from Frankfurt am Oder to Wrocław celebrated in the city.

The editor of *Breslauer Theater Zeitung*, Hermann Michaelson, maintained a similar, enthusiastic tone throughout his review. Paraphrasing well-known statements usually associated with J. W. Goethe—the prince of poets—Michaelson called Lipiński a "Crowned Orpheus" and the "Prince of all violinists."[49] Buoyed by such abundant praise, Lipiński gave in to the pressure of repeatedly expressed wishes and announced an additional, second concert, setting its date for 3 December 1836.[50] On the day preceding this concert, in addition to standard announcements about its occurrence, the local press published its full program. In accordance with the customs of the time, the concert was to feature vocal and orchestral works by many composers, including Viotti's Concerto in B minor, as well as two compositions by Lipiński: Rondo, probably Op. 18, and *Variations on a Theme from The Opera 'Cendrillion' by Rossini*, Op. 11.[51] Once again, the violinist was very successful and this success was noted in reviews. August Kahlert discussed Lipiński's interpretation of Viotti's Violin Concerto in an exhaustive manner and made the following observation about this work: "The graceful and skillfully composed Rondo featured numerous technical problems. Its bravura performance was rewarded by a storm of applause."[52] In a similar vein, an anonymous critic (identified only by the initials "W.W.") stated in the *Breslauer Zeitung* that in the light of so many positive opinions about Lipiński's performance style and talent that had already appeared in the local press, he would not be able to write anything new about the concert. Nonetheless, the critic ventured to say that "the impression that the virtuoso's performance had on his listeners, compared with his first concert, was much stronger... The music hall was filled to the brim and Wrocław citizens had proven yesterday that they did not avoid expenditure if it concerned such artistry."[53]

The measure of the Polish violinist's popularity in Wrocław was provided by two subsequent concerts, organized in the city's theater, which was at that time located at the crossing of two streets, Oławska and Piotra Skargi (today's street names—MZ). The theater's auditorium could contain a larger number of listeners than Wrocław auditoriums traditionally used for concerts, such as the Aula Leopoldinum and the Music Hall at the University, or the hall of Hotel Polski on Biskupia Street. In addition, ticket prices to concerts held at the theater were usually lower and allowed wider circles of Wrocław inhabitants to participate in this event. Lipiński's two theater performances took place on 10 and 13 December 1836, with substantial audience in attendance.[54] Due to an unfortunate fact that only advertisements about the concert were published (without the concert programs) and that the theater programs from the year 1836 were not preserved, we are not able to ascertain which pieces the violinist presented to Wrocław music lovers at that time. Michaelson, while reviewing the concert for the Wrocław theater newspaper, focused his attention on the performer's virtuosity that was greeted with outbursts of enthusiasm by his listeners. In his review, written in a manner typical for its time, Michaelson made one important statement: "This virtuoso is a representative of the very nation which popularized the violin itself."[55]

Figure 6: The cover page of Lipiński's Rondo.

Around 1837, after twenty years of concert-giving activities, Lipiński decided to withdraw from an intense and exhausting lifestyle of a touring virtuoso and began attempts to secure a position of the first concertmaster at the Royal Chapel and the director of church music in Dresden. The choice of Dresden was motivated by many considerations. First, the position became available after the death of the previous concertmaster, Antonio Rolla. Second, a friendly and welcoming atmosphere usually greeted Lipiński's concerts in this town and, therefore, he expected a warm welcome for a more extended stay. While seeking to accomplish his goal, he remained in constant contact—by letter—with the director of the Chapel orchestra, Baron August von Luttichaue.[56] In order to accelerate the final arrangements, Lipiński traveled to Dresden in December 1837. On 7 December, while passing through Wrocław, he took residence at the inn "Under the Golden Sceptre," which was frequented by Poles and served him well during his previous travels.[57] At that time he did not give any public performances in the city; however, he appeared in a private concert for other musicians and his personal friends.[58] Lipiński's job-seeking efforts were rewarded with success. His Dresden engagement began at the outset of July 1839, starting the period of over 20 years during which he worked as the director of an ensemble which was regarded as one of the finest orchestras in the whole Europe.[59] The violinist was also recognized as an excellent chamber musician, actively participating in various aspects of musical life in Dresden. Concerts of string quartets (Quartett-Akademie), directed by Lipiński, enjoyed a great following and status; they were reviewed in the most glowing terms by local and foreign press.[60] The Polish violinist was especially admired for his interpretations of violin sonatas by Mozart and Beethoven, which he sometimes played with Liszt, or with another well-known pianist of the time, Charlotta Fink.[61] In his memoirs, Hector Berlioz, while recalling his stay in the capital of Saxony in 1842, had the following to say about Lipiński:

> In Dresden, I had an opportunity to renew my acquaintance with a devoted, energetic, and enthusiastic friend, Karol Lipiński, whom I had once met in Paris. It is impossible . . . for me to say how much effort did this eminent man put into assisting me. His position of the first concertmaster and the universal respect that his person and talent enjoyed, gave me a great power over the musicians in the orchestra. . .
> During my stay in Dresden, Lipiński was so helpful, so attentive, so devoted to me, that my praises for him would seem to be entirely deprived of impartiality, because they would have been ascribed to gratitude rather than to representing a true outpouring of admiration. . . He was much applauded at my concert, in my *Romance* for violin and . . . in the viola solo in my second symphony, *Harold*.[62]

During the Dresden period, Lipiński also engaged in a variety of editorial activities. He edited all the string quartets by Haydn, and, working with the organist August Klengel,[63] the six sonatas for harpsichord and violin, BWV 1014-1019, by Johann Sebastian Bach.[64] The last concert by Lipiński that was noted by the Wrocław press took place in 1840. At that time, the violinist was 50 years old and he had already been working in Dresden where he had settled with his family in 1839. New, numerous duties at the Royal Chapel in Dresden left him with comparably few opportunities to undertake many artistic travels. Despite these limitations, Lipiński visited Wrocław again while traveling from Dresden to Lwów at the end of May 1840. As usual, he stopped at the inn "Under the Golden Sceptre."[65] Wrocław press quickly disseminated information about the arrival of the violinist. Articles about his visit were published by local critics, including August Kahlert in *Schlesische Zeitung*[66] and Johann Theodore Mosewius who wrote:

> Among all the great artists who ever visited Wrocław, Lipiński distinguished himself not only by his genius and outstanding virtuosity, but—first and foremost—by his extraordinarily nice character. I express the wish of all the friends and adherents of music who ever heard this incomparable artist, when I say that we wish he would agree to give a concert. Even though the days of this and the next week are taken up by other matters, I hope that there would be, perhaps, one day during which it would be possible to arrange a concert for the local admirers of his talent, as well as for a large number of his compatriots now staying in the city. [67]

These words acquire a particular meaning when considered in their proper context, provided by the enthusiastically welcomed and applauded concerts given in Wrocław by the all-time most famous violinist, Nicolo Paganini, who appeared there in late July and early August of 1829.[68] Lipiński's visit to Wrocław in 1840 was scheduled concurrently with a well-established trade event, the Wool Market, held every year in the spring. Because of that, it was not a period suitable for concert activities and the Wrocław press often pointed out this fact to traveling virtuosi. The immensely successful concert given by Lipiński was, in this respect, a complete exception. This performance took place on 29 May 1840, in a hall at the Hotel Polski, which was filled by listeners to its full capacity. The violinist included only his own compositions on the program: Violin concerto in D major, Op. 21 (fist and second movements), a *Romantic Rondo* (an unknown work), and *Grand Fantaisie on Reminiscences from the Opera 'Puritans' by Bellini*, Op. 28.[69]

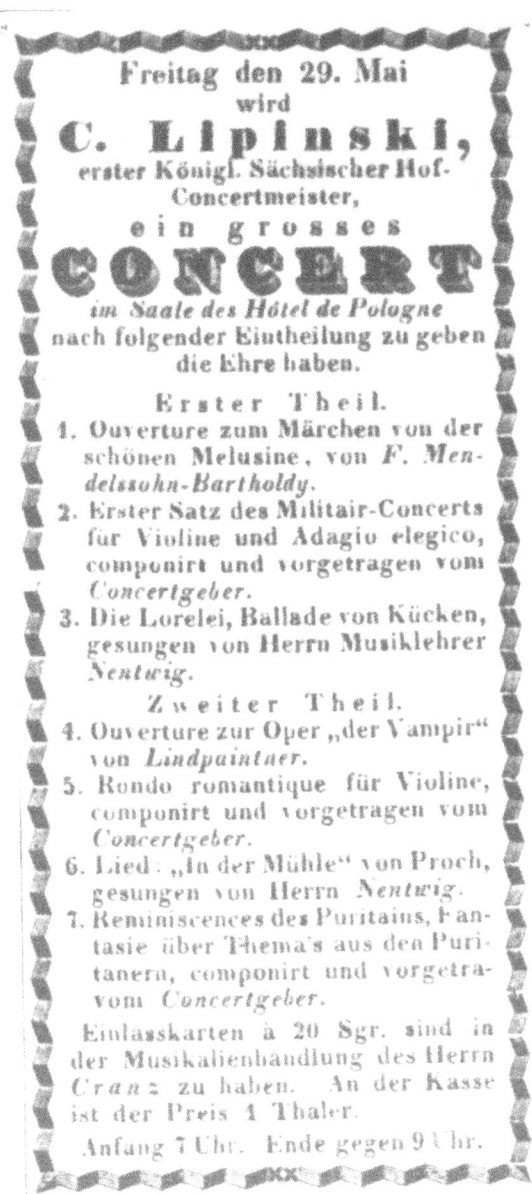

Figure 7: Poster from Lipiński's concert of 29 May 1840.

Two days after this performance an anonymous reviewer reported in the local daily:

> The hall was overflowing during Lipiński's performance. The virtuoso was greeted with an intense enthusiasm. Twenty years passed since the time he had commenced his European career in our town. Again this time, those features of his performance style that distinguished him from others from the start of his musical career, became quite prominent. He is capable of mixing perfect southern intensity with the Sarmatian fire.[70]

It is interesting to note that Karol Lipiński was recognized in Wrocław as being more than merely as a soloist. The reviewer did not hesitate to remind the readers about the violinist's accomplishments in the areas of ensemble and chamber music, writing: "In a private setting we had an opportunity to admire Lipiński as a chamber musician. In this area his abilities are equally perfect and they do not take a second place to his talents as a soloist." In another statement, however, an anonymous critic expressed some reservations about Lipiński's bowing technique, as well as about his staccato and trills. Nonetheless, the same critic admitted that the virtuoso was incomparable in the interpretation of double stops, excelling especially in passages of parallel intervals.[71] It is quite certain that Lipiński visited Wrocław again later and that it was not his last appearance in the city, because the capital of Silesia was located on the path of his travels (personal, not artistic) from Dresden, where he lived with his family, to Lwów, the city of his youth, with which he undoubtedly remained in contact. However, there are no surviving documents that would suggests that he ever again performed in Wrocław.

Numerous Wrocław fans of his talent admired the musical oeuvre of the Polish violinist. His music was introduced on the stages of local concert halls not only by the composer himself, but also by other virtuosi, local and foreign, including: Ignaz Peter Lüstner, brothers Eichhorn, Carl Müller, Friedrich Mollenhauer, August Möser, Władysław Iżycki, Jerôme Gulomy, Eduard Rappoldi, Keller, Georg Häflein, Erlekamm, and Louis L. Lüstner.[72] We may find out about the great popularity of Lipiński's music in Wrocław from a variety of announcements and notices about his life and activities, published in local press.[73]

In 1837 the violinist's Vienna successes were noted; at that time, he gave a concert for the Austrian Emperor and his family. The subsequent correspondence, dated from 1838 and reprinted from a Lepzig newspaper, brought news about Lipiński having taken over the position of the concertmaster of the Royal Chapel in Dresden.[74] Another report concerning his activities associated with this position was published in a letter from Dresden in 1845.[75] Many years later, the organist and the main music critic at the *Breslauer Zeitung*, Adolph Friedrich Hesse, wrote a cycle of articles about the history of music, including the activities of Karol Lipiński in his survey. While characterizing the Polish violinist's performance style, Hesse wrote that it was marked by an amazing tone and virtuosity, thanks to which the violinist's interpretations were saturated with astounding expressions of passion that distinguished him from many other virtuosi. He also pointed out that both Lipiński's oeuvre and his performance style were marked by traits of Polish national character, albeit without defining precisely what these traits were.[76]

In 1861, after 22 years of working in Dresden, Lipiński decided to retire because of health problems. He moved to his estate at Urłowo in Galicia where he started to realize the dream of his life: he bought violins from Lwów and founded a music school for talented peasant children. Unfortunately, he was not able to enjoy this charitable activity for long: Lipiński died on 16 December 1861. In accordance with his last will, his son Gustaw, the only heir to Urłowo, established scholarships named after Karol and Regina Lipiński. These scholarships were supported by the income from the estate and awarded to three talented Polish violinists at a time.[77]

During his international career, Lipiński was greatly acclaimed throughout Europe and collected an array of honors. While on concert tours, he always emphasized his Polish background. He served his homeland by promoting his own works permeated with traits of national style and by winning recognition for Polish music in the most prominent cultural centers of Europe. Lipiński received proofs of admiration and profound respect even from some of his greatest contemporaries. Nicolo Paganini gave Lipiński, in his last will, one of his most valuable violins—the instrument by the famed violin maker, Andrea Amati. Franz Liszt offered Lipiński his own portrait, grandiosely signed "Maestro di maestri." Robert Schumann dedicated to the Polish violinist his piano composition, *Carnival*, Op. 9. Hector Berlioz called him "a great artist and a wonderful man." Richard Wagner described the virtuoso in his autobiography as a "genial, eccentric Pole."

Achieving such a prominent place among great violinists was not an easy task in the era of virtuosity. In addition to possessing a fascinating technique, Lipiński had a beautiful, richly modulated tone. The displays of his musical talent, sensitivity, and inspiring abilities, dazzled and charmed the audiences who had the opportunity to witness these unique experiences in concerts. One reviewer active at the time, while describing Lipiński's performance style, wrote: "So boldly and lightly does the master overcome all the harmonic and melodic difficulties in the music—including chromatic, diatonic and other passages; thirds, sixths, and octaves; leaps from the lowest octave to the highest registers; melodic motives supported by difficult, yet charming accompaniment of arpeggiated chords—that it seems to be entirely unbelievable."[78]

Lipiński's musical personality is best characterized by his performances and interpretative abilities. He is regarded as the creator of the Polish violin school, distinct from the Italian or the French-Belgian schools.[79] He is immortalized in music history as the most talented Polish violinist before Henryk Wieniawski and as one of the greatest virtuosi active in the first half of the 19th century. The fame that Lipiński achieved in the era of virtuosity is the homage to his great talent. With his activities, he contributed to the popularizing of Polish culture, the culture of a nation that was absent from the political map of Europe.

Translated by Maja Trochimczyk

ENDNOTES

[1] Józef Powroźniak, *Karol Lipiński* (Kraków: PWM, 1970); by the same author, English translation of the previous item, *Lipiński* (Neptune City, New Jersey: Paganiniana Publications, 1986). Vladimir Grigoriev, *Karol Lipiński* (Moscow: Muzika, 1977). Collection of studies *Karol Lipiński - Wrocław 1988*, with articles by F. German, "Karol Lipiński i Fryderyk Chopin," 69–77; H. John, "Działalność Karola Lipińskiego w latach 1839–1849 w Dreźnie: dokumentacja na podstawie źródeł archiwalnych" (The activities of Karol Lipiński during the years 1839–1849 in Dresden: based on original archival documents), 34–46; P. Świerć: "Spotkania Karola Lipińskiego z innymi skrzypkami-wirtuozami" (Karol Lipiński's encounters with other violin virtuosos), 47–58. M. Zduniak and M. Passella, eds., *Karol Lipiński: życie, działność, epoka* (Lipinski: life, career, epoch) (Wrocław: Wydawnictwo Uniwersytetu Wrocławskiego, 1990). Józef Powroźniak and Zofia Chechlińska, "Karol Lipiński," entry in *New Grove Dictionary of Music and Musicians*, online edition, 2003.

[2] Symphony No. 2 in E-flat major, Symphony in C major, Symphony in B-flat major, Op. 2.

See the list of works in the book by Powroźniak, op. cit., pp. 240-248.

[3] Wacław Zaleski (Wacław z Oleska), *Pieśni polskie i ruskie ludu galicyjskiego* (Polish and Russian Songs of the People of Galicia); vol. 2, *Muzyka do pieśni polskich i ruskich ludu galicyjskigo zebranych i wydanych przez Wacława z Oleska. Do śpiewu na fortepian ułożył Karol Lipiński* (Music for Polish and Russian Songs of the People of Galicia Collected and Published by Wacław of Olesko, Arranged for Singing and Piano by Karol Lipiński) (Lwów, 1833).

[4] Published in section W4 of *Goniec Krakowski* (Cracow Messenger), no. 79 (1829).

[5] Cited from Powroźniak's biography of Lipiński, op. cit.

[6] Franciszek Liszt, *Fryderyk Chopin* (Kraków: PWM, 1960), 45.

[7] *Gazeta Wielkiego Księstwa Poznańskiego*, nos. 52, 53 (1821).

[8] *Breslauer Zeitung*, no. 112 (1821). The ticket price for the announced concert was 16 silver grosz. This well documented information about the Wrocław concert corrects earlier erroneous data contained in Powroźniak's book, op. cit., p. 62. Powroźniak stated that "Lipiński went from Poznań to Berlin." A notice published in the Berlin press on 25 September 1821 stated that the violinist arrived in the capital of Prussia only in September of that year. His concert in Berlin took place on 28 October 1821. See *Königliche privilegirte Berlinische Zeitung*, no. 115 (1821). See also Wiktor Hahn, "Koncerty Karola Lipińskiego we Wrocławiu w 1821 r.," *Śląski Kwartalnik Historyczny, Sobótka* 4 (1949): 209-210. Hahn gives a wrong date for the first concert (27 June); it took place on 20 July 1821.

[9] Powroźniak's book does not mention Lipiński's concerts in Moscow and St. Petersburg scheduled before 1821. Perhaps mentioning these events in the Wrocław press was only an advertising gimmick. The author of this article, published by *Neue Breslauer Zeitung*, no. 112 (1821) and signed with the initials "K.S.", was most likely Karl Schall, a poet and founder of this newspaper.

[10] *Schlesische Zeitung*, no. 84 (1821). Richard Conrad Kiessling also mentions this concert in *Nachrichten über Conzerte in Breslau* (1722 - 1836); the manuscript is held at the University Library in Wrocław; Call No. 2907, p. 78 r.

[11] *Breslauer Zeitung*, no. 116 (1821). All the quotations from the Wrocław press of the time are translated from their Polish version by Maria Zduniak.

[12] Powroźniak (op. cit., p. 63) erroneously associates this review with a concert held in November 1821.

[13] Karol Lipiński arrived in Dresden on 26 July 1821. See *Dresdner Anzeiger*, column 1231 (1821).

[14] *Breslauer Zeitung*, no. 118 (1821). According to R. C. Kiessling (op. cit., p. 78), the last name of the author of this article was Stöckel and "L. Bentley" was an alias.

[15] *Schlesische Zeitung*, no. 21 (1816); no. 133 (1819).

[16] *Rozmaitości* (Variety), no. 92 (1821).

[17] *Breslauer Zeitung*, nos. 176, 177, 178 (1821); *Schlesische Zeitung*, nos. 132, 133 (1821). An ad about this concert also appeared in *Gazeta Wielkiego Księstwa Poznańskiego*, no 90 (1821).

[18] *Breslauer Zeitung*, no. 179 (1821).

[19] *Rozmaitości*, no. 135 (1821).

[20] Original, German version published in *Breslauer Zeitung*, no. 179 (1821).

[21] Polish translation published in *Pszczółka Krakowska*, no. 4 (1821). I thank Dr. Maria Bąk of the Library of Karol Lipiński Academy of Music in Wrocław for locating this poem and brining it to my attention. The poem's text in Polish: "Jakże się ten mąż nazywa, / Co z czterech stron poziomych, wyrazów dobywa, /   Któremi spętana dusza,/ Wszystkie serca dla niego hołdu przymusza? (2) Co raz jakby oddalony, / Zdaje się, że już dźwięki pod ziemię ukrywa, / Nagle uderza jak w dzwony... / I do boju za sławę swej sztuki wzywa!... (3)

Z jakiejże krainy pochodzi, / Mistrz pełen ognia, śmiały i niezwyciężony, / Co moc, łagodnością słodzi, / Porywa dusze, serce, czarownemi tony?... (4) Ten niebian sprzymierzeniec, odpowiada Chwała: / Lipiński się nazywa - Polska go wydała!!!

[22] Maria Zduniak, "Sala koncertowa" (Concert Hall), in *Oratorium Marianum Uniwersytetu Wrocławskiego*, ed. Henryk Dziurla (Wrocław, 1999).

[23] *Breslauer Zeitung*, no. 182 (1821).

[24] *Gazeta Warszawska*, no. 190 (1821); *Gazeta Wielkiego Księstwa Poznańskiego*, no. 90 (1821); *Rozmaitości*, nos. 135, 136 (1821); *Kurier Litewski*, no. 140 (1821).

[25] *Gazeta Korespondenta Warszawskiego i Zagranicznego*, no. 189 (1821). C. Kiessling also noted these concerts in his manuscript, op. cit., p. 79 r.

[26] Joseph Ignaz Schnabel, *Sztambuch z lat 1803-1862*, manuscript, Warsaw University Library, Sygn. Mus. 2.

[27] *Schlesische Zeitung*, no. 145 (1821); *Schlesische Provinzialblätter*, vol. 74, (1821): after p. 280; *Breslauer Zeitung*, no. 194 (1821).

[28] *Breslauer Zeitung*, no. 29 (1824).

[29] Ibidem, nos. 177 and 179 (1825); no. 259 (1843); no. 135 (1844).

[30] Powroźniak, op. cit., p. 83. During his stay in Leipzig in 1821, Lipiński probably contacted the publishing houses Breitkopf & Härtel and C. F. Peters. As a result, n the years 1820-1825 a series of his works was published by both printers (opus numbers: 3, 5, 6, 7, 8, 9). See *Verzeichniss des Musikalienverlages von Breitkopf & Härtel in Leipzig. Vollständig bis Ende* (1902). See also Maria Zduniak, "Współpraca Karola Lipińskiego z wydawnictwem C. F. Petersa w Lipsku," in *I Ogólnopolska Sesja Naukowa nt. Karola Lipinskiego: życie, działalność, epoka,* Zeszyt Naukowy Akademii Muzycznej im. Karola Lipińskiego we Wrocławiu, no. 51 (Wrocław, 1990).

[31] *Breslauer Zeitung*, no. 91 (1826).

[32] Ibidem, no. 92 (1826).

[33] Unless Lipiński owned two Amati instruments during his career, this information seems erroneous. The virtuoso received a 16th-century violin by Andrea Amati only in 1840, in a bequest from the Paganini's estate. This fact is confirmed by an anonymous press notice preserved in a binder with documents about Lipiński, containing press clippings and letters, at the Library of the Ossoliński National Publishing House (Biblioteka Zakładu Narodowego im. Ossolińskich), Wrocław, sygn. 5982/II. Cited words come from the same paper, no. 94 (1826).

[34] *Breslauer Zeitung*, nos. 94, 95 (1826).

[35] The entrance price was 20 silver grosz. The program is preserved in *Programme von Konzerten einzelner Künstler* (1800 - 1850). Wrocław University Library, sygn. Yv 1147/1.

[36] *Breslauer Zeitung*, no. 98 (1826). Kiessling mentions both concerts, op. cit., p. 99v.

[37] "Do Lipińskiego rodacy w Uniwersytecie Wrocławskim zostający." A copy of this ode is preserved in the Library of the Ossoliński National Publishing House, Wrocław, sygn. 5982/II. Michał Kolicki, born in 1801 in Poznań, studied law for three years at the Wrocław University. The event associated with Lipiński's concert was reported by *Przegląd Poznański*, vol. 18 (1854): 159-162.

[38] "Rodacy na Wszechnicy Wrocławskiej." This work was issued by the publishing house of C. Weinhold in Wrocław, according to information from *Kompletny Katalog Śpiewów Polskich według słów i przyśpiewek. Zebrał i w alfabetycznym porządku ułożył Jan Woźnicki* (Kijów, 1908): 205.

[39] *Rozmaitości*, nos. 29, 33 (1826).

⁴⁰ *Gazeta Warszawska*, nos. 101, 102 (1826); *Gazeta Wielkiego Księstwa Poznańskiego*, no. 52 (1826); *Gazeta Korespondenta Warszawskiego i Zagranicznego*, no. 102 (1826).
⁴¹ *Kurier Warszawski*, no. 159 (1826). The last concert, announced in that review was not advertised in the Wrocław press.
⁴² *Breslauer Zeitung*, nos. 246, 256 (1836). According to Józef Powroźniak (op. cit., p. 109), Karol Lipiński did not give any further concerts in that hall after losing the competition for the position of the Kapellmeister of the Leipzig Gewandhaus Orchestra. However there is proof that he appeared in this hall on 7 and 15 October 1836. See Johannes Forner, *Die Gewandhaus konzerte in Leipzig 1781-1981*, vol. 2 (Leipzig, 1981, reprint).
⁴³ *Breslauer Zeitung*, no. 275 (1836).
⁴⁴ Ibidem, no. 276 (1836).
⁴⁵ Ibidem, no. 277 (1836).
⁴⁶ Ibidem, no. 278 (1836).
⁴⁷ Ibidem, no. 279 (1836). According to Kiessling (op. cit., p. 154 v.) Joseph Nimbs reviewed this concert.
⁴⁸ *Schlesische Zeitung*, no. 279.
⁴⁹ *Breslauer Theater-Zeitung*, no. 93 (1836).
⁵⁰ *Breslauer Zeitung*, no. 280 (1836). Kiessling also noted both concerts (op. cit., p. 154 v.).
⁵¹ *Breslauer Zeitung*, no. 283 (1836). The entrance tickets cost 20 silver gross, if bought beforehand; on the day of the concert at the evening box office, the ticket price was 1 talar.
⁵² *Schlesische Zeitung*, no. 285 (1836).
⁵³ *Breslauer Zeitung*, no. 285 (1836).
⁵⁴ *Schlesische Zeitung*, no. 291 (1836); *Breslauer Theater-Zeitung*, nos. 96, 99 (1836); *Der Breslauer Beobachter*, nos. 148, 149 (1836); Kiessling, *Chronologie des Breslauer Theaters*, manuscript. Wrocław University Library, sygn. R 2905, pp. 57r, 57v.
⁵⁵ *Breslauer Theater-Zeitung*, no. 90 (1836).
⁵⁶ *Acta die Königliche Kapelle betreffend. Min. f. Volksbildung*, no. 14433 Bl. 305; no. 14434 Bl. 297, Bl. 298; no. 14435 Bl. 133, Bl. 134, Bl. 143. Staatsarchiv, Dresden.
⁵⁷ *Breslauer Zeitung*, no. 289 (1837). At the turn of 1803-1804 the guests of the inn "Under the Golden Sceptre" included, among others, Józef Wybicki. See Zygmunt Antkowiak, *Ulice i place Wrocławia* (Wrocław, 1970).
⁵⁸ *Schlesische Zeitung*, no. 292 (1837).
⁵⁹ Hans John, "Działalność Karola Lipińskiego w latach 1839-1849 w Dreznie. Dokumentacja na podstawie źródeł archiwalnych," in *I Ogólnopolska Sesja*, op. cit.
⁶⁰ Reiner Zimmermann, "O działalności koncertowej Karola Lipińskiego w Dreźnie," in *II Ogólnopolska Sesja nt. Karol Lipińskiego: Życie, działalność, epoka*, Zeszyt Naukowy Akademii Muzycznej im. Karola Lipińskiego we Wrocławiu, vol. 62 (Wrocław, 1993).
⁶¹ *Allgemeine Musikalische Zeitung*, nos.10, 13 (1840); *Neue Zeitschrift für Musik*, no. 15 (1853).
⁶² Hector Berlioz, *Z pamiętników* (Kraków: PWM, 1966): 233, 236. The fifth letter was addressed to Heinrich Wilhelm Ernst.
⁶³ Zduniak, "Współpraca Karola Lipińskiego," op. cit.
⁶⁴ *Vollständige Sammlung der Quartetten für zwei Violinen, Viola u. Violoncello von Joseph Haydn. Neue Ausgabe. Revidirt und mit Tempobezeichnung versehen von Carl Lipinski* (Dresden: bei Wilhelm Paul (n.d.)).
⁶⁵ *Schlesische Zeitung*, no. 121 (1840).
⁶⁶ Ibidem, no. 122 (1840).
⁶⁷ *Breslauer Zeitung*, no. 122 (1840).

⁶⁸ Zduniak, "Koncerty Niccolò Paganiniego we Wrocławiu," in *Książka programowa 37. Międzynarodowego Festiwalu Wratislavia Cantans* (Wrocław, 2002).
⁶⁹ *Schlesische Zeitung*, no. 124 (1840). Józef Powrozniak (op. cit.) does not mention this concert. The list of the composer's works does not include any *Rondo romantyczne* (Romantic Rondo). It was probably the *Concert Rondo*, Op. 18.
⁷⁰ *Schlesische Zeitung*, no. 126 (1840).
⁷¹ *Breslauer Theater-Zeitung*, no. 126 (1840).
⁷² Breslauer Zeitung, no. 54 (1831); nos. 191 and 286 (1835); no. 242 (1840); no. 868 (1885); Breslauer Theater-Zeitung, no. 65 (1836). See also "Alfabetyczno-chronologiczny wykaz ilościowy wykonań utworów polskich kompozytorów w latach 1801-1914 we Wrocławiu," appendix to Maria Zduniak, *Muzyka i muzycy polscy w dziewiętnastowiecznym Wrocławiu* (Wrocław, 1984).
⁷³ *Breslauer Zeitung*, no. 127 (1837).
⁷⁴ Ibidem, no. 290 (1838).
⁷⁵ Ibidem, no. 15 (1845).
⁷⁶ Ibidem, no. 173 (1854).
⁷⁷ Dmitrij Kolbin, Roman Horak, *Spuścizna Lipińskiego oraz fundacja imienia Karola i Reginy Lipińskich*. Unpublished typescript.
⁷⁸ Cited from Powroźniak, op. cit., p. 140. *Neue Zeitschrift für Musik*, no. 29 (1839).
⁷⁹ Paweł Puczek, "Karol Lipiński—twórca polskiej szkoły skrzypcowej," in *II Ogólnopolska Sesja Naukowa*, op. cit. See also, by the same author, "Uwagi o fakturze i interpretacji wybranych utworów Karola Lipińskiego," in *Karol Lipiński: życie, działalność, epoka, Proceedings of the 3rd International Scholarly Symposium* (Materialy III Międzynarodowej Sesji Naukowej) (Wrocław: Akademia Muzyczna im. Karola Lipińskiego we Wrocławiu, Zakład Historii Śląskiej Kultury Muzycznej, 2003).

Chapter 3

Stradivari, Guarneri, and Amati: A History of Karol Lipiński's Violins

Krzysztof Rottermund

I. Introduction

Karol Lipiński (1790-1861) was one of the most distinguished Polish musicians active in Europe before Fryderyk Chopin.[1] Many of Lipiński's contemporaries considered the outstanding violin virtuoso and composer as an equal to Paganini.[2] His stellar career reached its apex when he assumed the post of the concertmaster at the Royal Court of Saxony in Dresden. He remained at this highly prestigious position for over twenty years. While working at the Saxon Court, Lipiński had an opportunity to personally meet and befriend many notable musicians and composers with whom he socialized or gave joint concerts. Here, it will suffice to mention here the names of: Robert Schumann who dedicated his *Carnaval*, Op. 9 to Lipiński; Franz Liszt (with whom Lipiński played Beethoven's Sonata in A Major, "Kreutzer," Op. 47), as well as Maria Szymanowska, Mikhail Glinka, Hector Berlioz, Nicolo Paganini and many others. Richard Wagner, who was engaged in a long-standing dispute with Lipiński, called his opponent, "a genius, an eccentric Pole."[3]

In this article documenting the history of Lipiński's violins, I will review the established facts concerning these famous instruments and correct some erroneous information while filling in the lacunae in the existing data with new information, coming from sources, which were not known, to earlier scholars. In my research, I discovered interesting, hitherto unknown, information about his most famous violin, an instrument made in 1737 in Cremona by Giuseppe Guarneri del Gesù; this was the instrument on which Lipiński played for the longest time during his life. The history of the Guarneri violin was rediscovered half a century after the death of the violinist and it was twice described in the *Zeitschrift für Instrumentenbau*, a periodical dedicated to the building of musical instruments.[4] Before we reach these newly discovered sources which present the virtuoso in a somewhat more controversial light, I should review two most important statements about this issue, made by scholars Józef Powroźniak, who wrote the most important Polish biography of Lipiński and Vladimir Grigoriev, a Russian researcher who conducted extensive studies of the life and oeuvre of the Polish violinist and composer.

Karol Lipiński

Every violin virtuoso considers the quality of the instrument on which he or she showcases their talents to be of great significance. According to a widely disseminated and generally accepted view, a good musician may give a relatively good performance even on an instrument of weaker quality. However, this view is not true. It is quite impossible, even for the best of musicians, to reach a maximum of expressive power on a bad instrument. While playing an imperfect instrument, the musician cannot fully capture and engage the minds and hearts of the public. From among the violins used by eminent musicians-virtuosi of the 19th century to give concerts, those instruments, which survived, the ravages of time undoubtedly belong among the most precious memorabilia associated with the past lives of these musical stars of the stage and the salon. Unfortunately, not too many material artifacts and memorabilia of this kind are extant to give testimony about the life of Karol Lipiński.

After his death, the histories of instruments that he had owned or played on went through numerous twists and turns of circumstance. Not much is known about them. His biographers, Powroźniak and Grigoriev, mentioned Lipiński's violins only in a few sentences in their books. While Powroźniak paid somewhat more attention to these violins than Grigoriev did, neither of the two authors provided an account of the history of these instruments from the death of their owner to the present time. Furthermore, tracing the history of some of Lipiński's instruments has been extremely difficult and, indeed, verging on the impossible, because, in contrast to the violins of Paganini which became the property of the Italian state and may now be seen in the Paganini Museum in Genoa, none of Lipiński's violins found a governmental benefactor. One reason for this neglect is obvious: there was no independent Polish state through the 19th century and no national government willing to invest in the preservation of the material documents of the Polish violinist's life.

Lipiński's career as a violinist started equivocally: during his youth, the virtuoso studied the performance of not one, but two string instruments, the violin and the cello. In his biography of the composer Powroźniak wrote that

> in his memoirs, Lipiński used to emphasize the benefits that he gained from playing the cello in his youth. He even ascribed to this experience with the cello his widely praised accomplishment of a "great" tone, which enabled him to "sing" like no other violinist while playing the higher-pitched instrument. His subsequent successes as a virtuoso violinist stemmed to a large extent from his beautiful and profound tone.[5]

While the statement about the extraordinary quality of Lipinski's "tone" is certainly true and confirmed by numerous other sources it requires some additional explanations. The wonderful and oft-admired singing quality of Lipiński's violin playing owed its existence to some other factors than his early experience with the cello. I believe that the primary importance should be ascribed here to the quality of the instruments that the violinist played on. It was a dream of every violinist, as well as Lipiński's, to possess a masterly, old-Italian instrument, preferably from the so-called Cremona school of violinmakers, such as Amati, Stradivari, or Guarneri. At one time or another, the Polish violinist was blessed by possessing as many as three such instruments, created by the three greatest violin-makers of all time. He owned the following three masterly Italian instruments from the Cremona school:

- A 16th-century violin by Andrea Amati;
- An 18th-century violin, made in 1715 by Antonio Stradivari; and
- An 18th-century violin by Giuseppe Guarneri del Gesù, made in 1737 (not in 1720 as Powroźniak claims).

Of the three Cremona instruments, two were gifts to Lipiński; he bought the Guarneri violin by himself. Interestingly, the young violinist first came in contact with a violin by Guarneri (not the one he purchased, though). As is well known, Karol Lipiński studied music with his father Feliks who directed, among other ensembles, the court orchestra of the Starzeński family in the city of Lwów in southeastern Poland. Already during these years of studies and apprenticeship in the orchestra conducted by his father, Karol Lipiński had had an opportunity to play a masterly violin made by Guarneri. This instrument, though, belonged to the Starzeński family and should not be confused with the "Lipiński" Guarneri that the violinist later used in the majority of his concerts.

In addition to the violins by Guarneri, Stradivari and Amati, Lipiński also played on other, less precious instruments, using them for shorter periods during his long career as a virtuoso performer. Unfortunately, there is almost no extant information about these less valuable violins. Furthermore, as we shall see, not all the published data about Lipiński's known Old-Italian violins is reliable and precise to the same degree.

II. The Stradivari Violin of 1715

The most famous instrument in Lipiński's possession, often described and depicted in music literature (also in Poland), was a violin made by Antonio Stradivari in 1715.[6] Lipiński received this instrument as a gift; its colorful history includes several legends. Even research publications do not contain information about the instrument's history that is exact and unambiguous. In a well-known Stradivari monograph by the Hill family, there is no mention of this instrument at all.[7] In 1970, Józef Powroźniak cited two versions of the circumstance under which this instrument supposedly came into Lipiński's possession.

The first, a more likely one, is based on the reminiscences of a certain von Krockow, who met Lipiński in Dresden in 1849. The history of the instrument that the violinist supposedly told Krockow on this occasion was reproduced in writing over 30 years after the death of the virtuoso. It was published in an English periodical, *The Violin Times* in 1895 and 1896.[8] According to this version of events, Lipiński, while visiting Milan with a recommendation letter from Louis Spohr (which he had received in 1814), went to see a famous violin teacher, a certain Mr. Salvini, who had once been a disciple of the great Giuseppe Tartini. This trip probably happened at the end of Lipiński's Italian concert tour of 1817-1818. Before Lipiński started to demonstrate his extraordinary performance capabilities to Salvini, the distinguished teacher examined his instrument. Without saying a word and without pausing to consider his actions, Salvini took the violin and destroyed it completely with a strong hit against the corner of a table. If we were to trust this account, at that time Lipiński had owned a very mediocre instrument, not deserving of his talent.

After this act of apparent vandalism, Salvini handed Lipiński the 1715 Stradivari violin and asked him to play it. At the end of the young virtuoso's excellent performance of a Beethoven sonata, Salvini reportedly said: "Your playing moves and delights everyone. You are following in the footsteps of Tartini, therefore I ask you to accept this violin as a gift from me and, simultaneously, as a commemoration of Tartini."[9] This story implies that the 1715 Stradivari violin had previously been owned by Tartini. Von Krockow's account also establishes Lipiński's credentials as an heir to the Italian school of violin virtuosity, a position that was affirmed by the gift of the precious Stradivari.

A second account of the provenance of this instrument, cited by Powroźniak, focused on a hypothesis that Lipiński received this violin as a gift from Dr. Mazurrana, another disciple of Tartini. I believe that this account is erroneous. Although Powroźniak cited statements found in the seventh edition of a book by Wilhelm Josef von Wasilewski as proof of the veracity of this hypothesis.[10] Wasilewski (1822-1896), born near Gdańsk, was a conductor, researcher, and writer about music; he studied composition with Mendelssohn and violin performance with Ferdinand David. He knew Lipiński personally and often quoted the Polish virtuoso's statements and opinions in his writings. Nonetheless, there is no mention of the Stradivari violin in the 1927 edition of Wasilewski's book; neither does any reference to it appear in its first version published in 1869. According to Wasilewski, a meeting of Lipiński with a former student of Tartini supposedly happened between 1817 and 1820 in the city of Trieste.

Apparently, Lipiński wanted to learn Tartini's interpretative art first-hand, from the last surviving student of the Italian master, who represented the so-called Padova school of violin performance. In this account, Wasilewski mentioned neither the name of Tartini's student, nor his age. Powroźniak claimed that this student was none other than Mazurrana, who was 90 years old when his reported encounter with Lipiński took place. Wasilewski's books do not confirm this identification that is absent both from the history of the violin cited above and from his memoirs that repeatedly referred to Lipiński, but did not mention, not even once, the name of Mazurrana.[11]

However, it needs to be emphasized that Mazurrana was not entirely unknown to 19th-century writers: his name appeared in a book about the most famous European violinists written by Alfred Ehrlich and first published in 1893.[12] Powroźniak seems to not have been aware of this book since he never cited it. In Ehrlich's study, we may find additional information about Karol Lipiński and his 1818 meeting with a former student of Tartini whose identity may be confirmed as that of the 90-year-old Dr. Mazurrana. The meeting took place, as rumored, in Trieste, during the Polish virtuoso's return travel to Poland. However, while identifying Tartini's student by name, this book does not mention whether Dr. Mazurrana gave the Stradivari violin to Lipiński during this meeting.

In addition, the encounter of Mazurrana and Lipiński was reported in a book by Max Grünberg.[13] Again, the account did not include the additional episode about the gift of the Stradivari violin. Furthermore, the encounter between Lipiński and Mazurrana was described by Grigoriev, who provided two distinct versions of the Italian's last name: "Madzurano" and "Mazurrano." Grigoriev used as his source a manuscript of memoirs by a Russian writer and poet, Nestor Kukolnik (1809-1868).[14] Apparently, Kukolnik had met Lipiński in Dresden and heard about the Mazurrana meeting from the Polish violinist himself. This account, again, did not include any references to the supposed gift of the Stradivari violin during the meeting of Lipiński and Mazurrano. Instead, Kukolnik focused on certain aspects of Tartini's interpretative art that, according to him, Mazurrano discussed with Lipiński. "He opened my eyes. During my whole life I thanked Mazurrano and during my whole life I followed his instructions"—Lipiński is supposed to have told Kukolnik.[15] The Pole thus received secrets of Tartini's violin technique from Dr. Mazurrana and the masterly Stradivari instrument on which he was to put his newly acquired knowledge to practical use from another disciple of Tartini, Mr. Salvini. All the available information confirms this interpretation of events.

What did this violin look like? Fridolin Hamma, an antique instrument merchant and expert, first published photographic documenttation of the Stradivari violin owned by Lipiński in 1931.[16] The same photograph was reproduced by Jalowec in 1952 and by Powroźniak in 1970.[17] Another image of Lipiński's instrument appeared in 1972 in an extended monograph documenting the iconography of several hundred known instruments by Antonio Stradivari (violins, violas and cellos) and published by Herbert K. Goodkind.[18] When compared to the photo-graphs published in 1931 by Hamma, Goodkind's imagery shows a markedly different instrument. While reviewing these two sets of photographs we may conclude that the violin had been reconstructed between 1931 and 1972; clearly, it had been fitted with a different tailpiece. Goodkind mentions several names of former owners of this violin. Tartini, Salvini, Joachim, Hill, Hamma, Wurlitzer, Canas, and several others are on his list. It is true that after the death of Lipiński his instrument had many owners, until it finally became the property of Dr. Martin Cañas from Cuba. It stayed in his possession for a long time. Grigoriev used the present tense in his 1970 monograph when he wrote: "This violin belongs to Dr. M. Cañas, known to be living in Havana."[19]

Antonio Stradivari
Violino 1715
Il Cremonese ex Joachim

Figure 1: Two photographs of the Stradivari violin (1715) owned by Lipiński. Left: reproduced in Fridolin Hamma, *Meisterwerke italienischer Geigenbaukunst* (Stuttgart, 1931); Karel Jalowec, *Italian Violin Makers* (Praha, 1952); and Powrozniak, op. cit. Right: Reproduced in Herbert von Goodkind, *Violin Iconography of Antonio Stradivari 1644-1737* (New York, 1972).

Thus, the peregrinations of the Stradivari violin, one of the most precious material documents of Lipiński's life, led this instrument to a distant country, isolated from the external world by its restrictive political system. It is not impossible that the Stradivari-Lipiński violin is still located on this distant island. This hypothesis is partly confirmed by the account of the history of this instrument published by an online directory of historical violins, Cozio.com.[20] Doctor Martinez Cañas has supposedly owned the Stradivari since 1945. According to the online source, the instrument's previous owners were (in reverse chronological order): Roger Chittolini, A.P. Malozemoff (from 1925), the Wurlitzer Collection (from 1922), Hamma & Co; W.E. Hill & Sons, Engelberg Röngen, and Richard Weichold in Dresden (since 1861). The original three owners were, of course, Lipiński preceded by Salvini and Tartini.

In 1987, on the occasion of the 250th anniversary of the death of Antonio Stradivari, a special exhibition was held in Cremona, dedicated to this most eminent representative of the Cremonese school of violinmakers.[21] The exhibition was assembled with a goal to present the most precious and famous instruments made by the Italian genius. Unfortunately, the show did not include the Lipiński violin; instead the so-called Gibson-Stradivari of 1713 represented that period. This instrument was once a property of Polish-Jewish virtuoso, Bronisław Huberman. It is possible that the organizers of this exhibition did not know the current location of the renowned Stradivari violin associated with Lipiński; undoubtedly, they would have made efforts to borrow it for this exhibition, had they known where to look.

III. The Violin by Giuseppe Guarneri del Gesù

The second masterly violin that came into Lipiński's possession was made by Giuseppe Guarneri del Gesù in 1737. The violinist bought it while already being an owner of the Stradivari instrument. Little has been known about its history. Grigoriev does not mention this violin at all, while Powroźniak describes its origins by referring to only one source —an article published in a Lwów periodical, *Strzecha* (Thatched Roof) in 1871, ten years after the violinist's death. Unfortunately, the biographer did not provide the precise title, the name of the article's author, the issue number, nor the exact date of publication. According to information contained in this mysterious article, during one of Lipiński's visits to Vienna (the exact time was not specified), the virtuoso came across the Guarneri violin in a Rechaczek antique store. He bought this violin for an extremely high price, "not sparing any sacrifice as long as he could become the owner of this jewel . . . which then became an inseparable witness of the famous violinist's triumphs and a faithful companion of his sorrows and joys."[22]

According to the account cited by Powroźniak, there was a legend associated with this violin. Apparently, its maker built this particular instrument without any proper violinmaker's tools, only with the help of one simple knife; moreover he accomplished this feat while being imprisoned for killing his romantic rival. Inside the violin's body an inscription of the letters "I H S"[23] was supposed to be carved next to the date of "1720." This information, like some other accounts cited by Powroźniak, cannot be treated seriously and has to be approached with caution.

Another, equally unusual version of history of the Guarneri violin may be found in Franz Bouffier's book about virtuoso violinists and their instruments. This book apparently confirmed the fact that Guarneri spent "a period of time in prison."[24] However, I believe that it was Giacomo Guarneri, a cousin of Giuseppe, who was imprisoned in the early 18th century and died while incarcerated. Thus, the Lipiński violin's supposed prison connection was false. It is a fact, though, that Giuseppe Guarneri placed the Eucharistic sign of "I H S" as well as the sign of the cross on the identifying tags in his instruments. It is for this reason that he earned his nickname "del Gesù" (of Jesus).

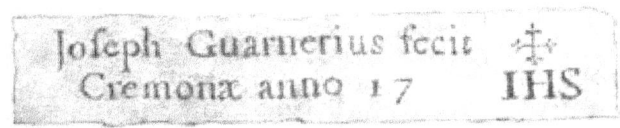

Figure 2: Guarneri's standard label used in most of his instruments.

Furthermore, Powroźniak's dating of the Lipiński-Guarneri instrument to 1720, based solely on one mention in one Polish periodical, is erroneous. It could be true only if Lipiński owned two violins by Guarneri—one from 1720 onwards and one from 1737. This, however, seems very improbable. Another option of linking Lipiński with a 1720 Guarneri could have stemmed from a possibility that he simply played such an instrument on one occasion. Both the *Zeitschrift für Instrumentenbau* (no. 22, of 1 May 1909) and the 1913 study of violin history by Willibald Leo von Lütgendorf date the Guarneri instrument owned by Lipiński to 1737.[25] In later editions of his reliable and well-researched volume, Lütgendorf included a photograph of the Lipiński-Guarneri violin. At the time when the first edition of his book appeared, however, he did not know much about this instrument and did not have its photograph available. Instead, he illustrated the Guarneri section of his book with pictures of several different Guarneri violins in the possession of antique music instruments merchants, Hamma & Co. The first ever photograph of the famous

Lipinsky Konzertgeige by Guarneri was presented to Polish readers only in my article of 2001.[26]

In 1829, Lipiński and Paganini appeared in concerts in Warsaw; their performances resulted in a famous, lively discussion, conducted in the local press, about the issue of which violinist should be awarded priority as a better performer. The voices of the critics were divided, but, as is known, neither of the two violinists was considered a winner, because of their totally different performance styles. At that time, the instruments that they performed on, also merited a mention:

> There is information here that Lipiński supposedly has a bad violin; if it were true, his talent would have been truly admirable. Instead, he is supposed to have owned a violin by the same master as Paganini, i.e. an instrument made by Guarneri.[27]

Let us, then, return to the account given by Powroźniak. He writes, again citing the article published in the 1871 issue of *Strzecha* (cited above) that the Guarneri violin owned by Lipiński was sold after the composer's death to his student, a Romanian prince Gregor Stourza (the proper form of his last name is "Stourdza"). Stourdza is supposed to have paid 600 ducats for the Guarneri instrument. Powroźniak considered this account to be false and followed it by what he considered a corrected version of events. Actually, as I was able to establish and as will be conclusively demonstrated later, the original account was not erroneous at all. In his "corrected version," Powroźniak cited a letter of one Michał Grabowski of Kołomyja, written on 19 March 1889 and sent to the editors of *Dziennik Lwowski*. In this letter, we read that Count Edmund Starzeński organized an exhibition in Kołomyja (the letter does not specify what type of an exhibition it was), which was visited by

> our eminent compatriots, Misses Bulewskis, on the way to Constantinople... Edmund Starzeński offered to Miss Jadwiga Bulewska the famous violin by Joseph Guarneri, the value of which was more than ten thousand francs, and on which Mr. Karol Lipiński himself used to perform. This violin for a long time remained in the possession in the family of Count Starzeńskis. The following inscription accompanied this gift: "The Violin by Guarneri, on which Karol Lipiński used to play long ago, I offer to Miss Jadwiga Bulewska, with a wish that she delighted her listeners with her charming tones for many years to come and that she carried the fame of the Polish name to the whole, wide world.
>
> (Signed:) Edmund Starzeński, Kołomyja, 9 March, 88.[28]

On the basis of this letter, Powroźniak erroneously corrected the information that he had cited earlier about the purchase of the Guarneri violin by the Romanian prince. Simultaneously, he proposed a new hypothesis, which was later proven to be untrue. According to this hypothesis, the son of Karol Lipiński, Gustaw, who after the death of his father was in charge of his whole estate, sold the Guarneri instrument to the Starzeński family, with whom he was linked by a close friendship, reaching back to the times of his grandfather, and the father of Karol, Feliks Lipiński. As we may recall, Feliks was at one time the court musician and conductor in the private orchestra of the Starzeńskis. Similarly, it was well known that the young, then still obscure violinist, Karol Lipiński, helped his father to direct the orchestra in which he also played on the Guarneri violin, lent to him by the Starzeńskis. Grigoriev mentions this fact.[29]

In addition, in the letter cited here, Grabowski wrote clearly that the Guarneri instrument had been in the possession of the Starzeński family for a long time. Since it had belonged to that family for generations, it could not have been identical with the instrument purportedly given to the Starzeńskis by Gustaw Lipiński. It is true, that the young Karol Lipiński had an opportunity to play on this instrument, even though he never owned it. Many years later, after the violinist had become famous in the whole Europe, the fact that he once played on the Guarneri instrument owned by the Starzeńskis increased the value of the instrument itself. Count Starzeński rightly emphasized this association with Lipiński in the letter cited above. Therefore, we might conclude that it is beyond any doubt that the famous Guarneri 1737 violin, which was for years the property of Karol Lipiński, was not the same instrument as the one once known to have been in the possession of the Starzeński family.[30]

Prior to describing the further history of old-Italian violins once owned by Lipiński, it is worthwhile to present here a small episode associated with one instrument's physical condition in the early 1910s. We do not know whether it was the violin made by Guarneri or by Stradivari that is the subject of this apocryphal story; it could not have been the Amati because Lipiński did not own it at that time. Apparently, after giving a series of concerts in Leipzig in 1835, the violinist traveled to appear in another cycle of concerts in Frankfurt-am-Mein. Unexpectedly, the planned series was limited to one event, because of the damage that the instrument sustained in the meantime. In order to repair his violin, Lipiński had to change his plans and travel to Paris. French school of violinmakers was his preferred choice, because of their expertise in repair and correction of precious instruments. Apparently, the damage had been quite serious, because the repairs, according to Grigoriev,[31] lasted for over three months. Who did the work on the violin? It is generally known that the most famous

French violin-maker after the death of Nicolas Lupot (1758-1824) was Jean-Baptiste Vuillaume (1798-1875). Lipiński, who intended to secure the services of the best possible violinmaker for repairs to his valuable Italian instrument and could have chosen him to fix the violin. Another likely choice from France was Charles-Francois Gand (1787-1845), who inherited the workshop of the great Nicholas Lupot.

In 1909, almost half a century after the death of the Polish virtuoso, the most serious, professional publication about music instruments, *Zeitschrift für Instrumentenbau*,[32] published a report about two precious instruments purchased by the well-known firm, Hamma and Co. of Stuttgart. (This company dealt with antique instrument sales, traced the provenance of and issued expert opinions about the authenticity of such masterly instruments.[33]) These two violins were: (a) a violin made by Antonio Stradivari in 1687 (at one time this instrument belonged to Jan Kubelik) and (b) the Guarneri violin that we are concerned with, previously owned by Karol Lipiński. According to the information published by the German periodical (citing as its source a Stuttgart daily newspaper *Der Neue Tageblatt*), the instrument of 1737 was among the most perfect violins ever made by Guarneri. It deserved recognition for its "large, beautiful form, and an excellent condition." The newspaper reported that, after the death of Lipiński this violin was in private possession until 1875 (the name of the owner was not given). Afterwards, the instrument was bought by a well-known German virtuoso and teacher, August Wilhelmj (1845-1908). He played on this violin for a long time, reaching a certain level of success, to which the qualities of the Guarneri instrument must have made a sizeable contribution. Similarly to Lipiński, Wilhelmj's performance style was characterized (just like the violin itself) by a "beautiful, strong tone." In 1875, Wilhelmj sold this violin to a certain violin lover and collector of antique instruments in Scotland. According to the published account, Hamma and Co. bought the violin from the Scotsman in 1909. However, what is puzzling and what undermines the validity of this account is the absence of this instrument from the catalog issued by Hamma & Co. in 1910.[34] The catalog features, for instance, the Stradivari owned by Kubelik, which was made in 1687 and purchased by Hamma at the same time as the Guarneri-Lipiński violin (as reported in 1909 by *Zeitschrift für Instrumentenbau*). This omission suggests that either the instrument was in the possession of the Hamma Company for a very short time, or that the Company served solely as the middleman in the purchase, and for this reason the instrument was not included in the catalog.

Two years later, *Zeitschrift für Instrumentenbau* (no. 32 of 11 August 1911) published another story about Lipiński's Guarneri, providing some more details, which, however, differed from those published in 1909. The new account stated that after the death of Lipiński, the Romanian prince, Gregor Stourdza, whose estate was located in Jassy, purchased the Guarneri instrument. (The periodical used a distorted form of his last name, spelled as "Stouritzer.") Prince Stourdza was a very interesting figure; biographical data about him may be found in the writings by Jalowec and William Henley. He is also mentioned in *Musik in Geschichte und Gegenwart*.[35] Gregor Stourdza (b. in 1821 in Jassy, d. in 1901 in Bucharest)[36] was an inventor and designer of several unusual string instruments, including a violin-harp ("Violino arpa") and a violin-guitar ("Violino chitarra"), which were built for him by a Vienna violinmaker and merchant of precious instruments, Thomas Zach. Several instruments invented by the prince, who at present may be found in the Museum of the Paris Conservatory, were publicly displayed during the World Exhibition in Vienna in 1873.

At the end of the 1870s, the Guarneri-Lipiński violin was purchased from Stourdza by his violinmaker, Thomas Zach. He soon sold the instrument, with the assistance of Wilhelmj, to a rich London banker, Schlezinger. (This information differs from the account of 1909 which identified Wilhelmj himself as the new owner of the violin.) In any case, in 1911, the violin was purchased from the Stuttgart firm Hamma & Co.; it must have been bought from Schlezinger in the meantime. Another, more likely possibility, as already mentioned, was that Hamma & Co. simply served as middlemen in this transaction. In any case, the new owner was a German violinist, Ernst Schiever, who lived in England for almost 30 years, having settled in Liverpool. Schiever was once the first violinist in the Count Hochbergschs Privat-Quratett. Soon afterwards, the Lipiński violin changed hands again: it was purchased for about 40 thousand marks by a "well-off German amateur" living in London, Otto Fehling. Therefore, we now know that for a period before World War I, the instrument once owned by Lipiński was located in England. The later history of the Guarneri violin owned by Lipiński, listed by Cozio.com, includes the following names of its owners (in chronological order): Hamma & Co. (Stuttgart); Alfred San Malo (since 1931); and, currently, Claude Aguttes, who purchased the violin during an auction held on 24 November 2000.

In the 1911 report, *Zeitschrift für Instrumentenbau* ended the history of the peregrinations of the famous Lipiński violin with its arrival in England and ownership by Ernst Schiever. The remainder of the article contained an unexpectedly vicious, open attack of the Polish virtuoso. In this unprecedented, anonymous criticism, the newspaper accused Lipiński of using a destructive method of treating the instrument before his public appearances. The goal of this alleged treatment was to achieve an easier reaction and better resonance from the instrument on which Lipiński preferred to give public concerts. This method was supposed to consist of warming up the instrument by rubbing it with a soft sheet of flannel for an extensive period of time. The prolonged and oft-repeated rubbing was thought to have resulted in a high degree of damage and scratching of the varnish on the instrument, through which the instrument lost not only its appearance, but also its beautiful, noble tone. It is worthwhile to cite the final section of this anonymous article:

> What is, at the end, even the best Italian instrument without the varnish that protects it and provides an enjoyment to the eye? The proof for how little did Lipiński deserve to own such a masterpiece of violinmakers' art is in his treatment of it. For such a vandal, a "Vogtland" violin would have been equally good [37]

This harsh opinion was a painful and unjust judgment. It greatly differed from a report about Lipiński's tender care of his violin, published by Franz Bouffier over 20 years earlier:

> Until his last hours, his (Lipiński's - K.R.) thoughts remained with his art, and even two days before his death, during a conversation with a friend, he gently took the violin in his hands to play for him the pizzicato melody from Olympia.[38]

It is simply improbable that Lipiński could have applied the rough method of warming up the instrument for his performances that was described in the German periodical. He was too great of an artist, who knew and cherished his wonderful instrument by Guarneri too much to treat it so thoughtlessly. Interestingly, it was the same *Zeitschrift für Instrumentenbau* that reported merely two years earlier, in 1909, that the two violins purchased by Hamma & Co., were in "excellent condition." If the Guarneri instrument had been so badly damaged as the second report maintained, the damage should have been noted in the first report in the same periodical.

These tendentiously presented and false statements, showing the Polish virtuoso in an ambiguous light, have to be read in the context of an extensive anti-Polish campaign conducted in Germany at that time. Mounting Polish-German tensions permeated many areas of life. The so-called "school-strikes" involving Polish children refusing to speak German as the only language allowed at school and being punished for that disobedience (especially at the school in Września) had recently taken place.[39] Contemporaneous musical-political events in Gdańsk / Danzig involved a ban of public performances of gramophone recordings of some well-known Polish patriotic songs.[40] The *Kulturkampf*, the "Prussian expulsions" ordered by the Chancellor Bismarck, the activities of a German nationalistic groups Hakata, and other events of this kind before World War I reveal the prevalence of anti-Polish sentiments in German lands.

Finally, the failed revolution of 1905-1907 in the Polish Kingdom had an impact on attitudes of Poles living in Polish lands annexed by Prussia and now a part of the German Reich. Anti-German demonstrations took place in Polish lands, for instance during the 1910 unveiling of the Grunwald Monument in Kraków (Galicia, part of Austro-Hungarian Empire), celebrating the 500th anniversary of the victory of joint Polish-Lithuanian forces over the Teutonic Knights.[41] Therefore, the German periodical's hostile and biased interpretation of the supposed treatment that Lipiński subjected his beloved instrument to should be seen as a part of the anti-Polish campaign, connected to the negative attitude of the German government as well as parts of German society to Poland and everything that was of Polish origin.

IV. The 16th-Century Violin by Andrea Amati

In 1840 the Polish virtuoso acquired his third old-Italian violin, the oldest of the three and made by Andrea Amati. By that time, he had been the proud owner of two excellent instruments, the Stradivari (since about 1817-18) and the Guarneri. He received the Amati in a bequest from the estate of his colleague, Nicolo Paganini, who died in 1840. The Italian virtuoso's last will designated eight of his best instruments as farewell gifts to eight of the most distinguished and talented—in Paganini's opinion—violinists of the world: Louis Spohr, Josef Mayseder, Bernard Molique, Charles de Beriot, Heinrich Wilhelm Erns, Ole Bull, Henri Vieuxtemps, and Karol Lipiński.[42] During Paganini's lifetime, Lipiński was his rival to fame and, simultaneously, a personal friend. Soon after receiving the bequest, Lipiński gave his first concert on the Amati violin; this event, held in Dresden, was dedicated to the memory of the great Italian.

The maker of the violin discussed here was none other but Andrea Amati, the founder of the first eminent violinmakers' family of Cremona, a family of artisans who finalized and perfected the model of the old-Italian violin. In 1563, Andrea Amati was commissioned to build 24 instruments for the French court of King Charles IX. The group of 24 violins that Amati made for the court and known as the French Royal Collection was evenly divided into 12 larger and 12 smaller instruments. All these instruments featured, in their bottom part, an inlaid image of the Bourbon emblem - a sun with lilies on both its sides. Lipinski's Amati was one of the instruments from the collection, which was preserved in the Royal Treasury until the French Revolution. Sadly, most of the instruments were destroyed at that time.[43] Eight instruments survived; the one reproduced above is held in the collection of the Palazzo Communale museum in Cremona.[44] On the basis of the description of Lipiński's violin by Józef Reiss (cited at the end of this chapter), we may surmise that Lipiński's Amati violin belonged to the group of "smaller" instruments that Andrea Amati made for the Royal Collection.

Unfortunately, we do not know what fate befell that instrument after its association with Paganini and Lipiński. A shadow is also cast on the issue of the Paganini bequest of the Amati violin, due to the existence of conflicting statements and accounts about its history. A Poznań journalist, musician and social activist, Maksymilian Braun,[45] claimed that the Amati violin had a "romantic history" which was supposedly told to him by Paganini himself. Braun claimed that Lipiński never actually received the instrument.[46] Powroźniak debunked this myth, perpetuated by an otherwise distinguished and well-respected musician and activist, who in 1823 had conducted an orchestra that accompanied Lipiński in concerts.[47]

V. Other Violins Associated with Lipiński

After retiring, Lipiński left Dresden and settled in the village of Urłowo in Galicia, where he purchased an estate for his family. He continued to maintain contacts with the Starzeński family in Lwów. His letter, dated 17 September 1859 and addressed to Count Adam Starzeński, contains interesting details about the history of two other violins, only loosely connected to Lipiński:

> The Most Enlightened Sir,
>
> > The violin of Thibout arrived in my hands in the best possible shape, and for this gift I thank you most sincerely. This instrument is very attractive in its appearance. As far as Ehrlich is concerned, I will write to him today, asking him to begin making the instrument. However, it seems to me that before the end of the year this cannot be promised with much exactness; it is more important to have this violin finished exactly as I would desire. As far as the sending of this violin is concerned, I will do so in ways that you advised me to follow.[48]

From the content of this letter one may surmise that Lipiński had received a violin by the famous French violinmaker, Thibout. The violinmaker at question could have been Jacques-Pierre (1779-1856) or his son, Gabriel-Adolphe (1804-1858). Because Lipiński, being of advanced age, did not give concerts anymore and dedicated his time to running his own violin school for poor, gifted peasant children, it is highly likely that the Thibout violin was designated for one of his pupils. In the case of the violin ordered from Ehrlich, the order may have been taken by a German violinmaker active in Dresden, Wilhelm Ehrilich (1820-1887), whom Lipiński is supposed to have known personally. The instrument was made on commission from Count Starzeński.

VI. Remarks on Lipiński's Performance Style

After reviewing the provenance and subsequent history of Lipiński's most famous violins it is worthwhile to discuss the issue of his performance style and its connections to the instruments that he owned. His contemporaries often spoke about his "great tone," which was his aesthetic ideal. Robert Schumann, while calling the Polish violinist "a great violinist of our times," pointed out his "enormous sound."[49] Similarly, Wasilewski suggested that "vibrato and great tone were the twin emblems of Lipiński's style. He played everything with this great tone of his."[50] The second statement may be perceived as a kind of accusation. Was his "great tone" a mere performance manner frequently used by Lipiński? Or, perhaps, was it the tone quality of the instrument itself?

It seems that the answer should be: "Both." It is certain that the "great tone" depended on the technique and style of performance used by the instrumentalist. However, the type and quality of the instrument itself on which this performer played was a factor of equal importance in creating the final effect. Therefore, Lipiński, who adhered to the ideal of a "great tone," chose to give most of his concerts on the instrument by Guarneri that was characterized by the expansive tone quality that he admired. The majority of instruments from Guarneri's "golden period" (to which the Lipiński instrument also belongs) were marked by this "great tone." In contrast, the violins by Stradivari did not have such an expansive, voluminous sound as those by Guarneri. Therefore, it is quite possible that Lipiński used his Stradivari instrument for solo performances much less often than he played on the Guarneri. It is known, though, he preferred the Stradivari for chamber music concerts.

Finally, the Andrea Amati violin received in bequest from Paganini was probably never used in Lipiński's public appearances; the only exception was the Dresden concert dedicated to the memory of the Italian virtuoso and held soon after his death. It would have been impossible to create a "great tone" on the Amati violin, because, as Józef Reiss writes,

The Andrea Amati model is small, has a great curvature, and therefore cannot be used to create a great and profound tone; instead the tone of the violin is soft, tender, bright, filled with sweetness, shining like silver, with a flute-like quality and a soprano-like timbre."[51]

Because of their delicate, silvery tone quality, Amati instruments did not sound well in huge, cavernous concert halls. However, they were perfectly suitable for performances of chamber music that Lipiński cherished and so willingly participated in.

VII. Conclusion

In conclusion, to return to the travels of the many masterly violins and their adventures,[52] it is appropriate to cite Józef Reiss again. The old-school instruments too often find their end in the holdings of affluent collectors who remove them from the public domain of concert performances. In this context, Reiss's statement from 1924 did not lose its validity after eighty years:

> The largest number of original old Italian violins is found in the hands of private collectors in England; from there these instruments will not find their way too easily and too quickly to the continent. Their owners jealously protect their treasures and keep them as carefully as relics of saints, as the most precious jewels or antique china. Therefore, these precious instruments remain hidden in costly boxes or in beautiful, stylish display cabinets, only to provide enjoyment to the eye by their beautiful shape and workmanship. They are not played upon because they are in the hands of people who do not know how to play; they rest, as if condemned to eternal silence![53]

Much is happening nowadays in the world of antique instruments.[54] It is not impossible, therefore, that the violins once used by Lipiński with such great success and during so many concerts, might resurface in the catalogs of one of the great auction houses, especially his Amati, the location of which remains unknown today.

Translated by Maja Trochimczyk

ENDNOTES

1 This article was originally published as "Karol Lipiński i jego skrzypce" (Karol Lipiński and His Violins) in *Muzyka* 46, no. 2 (2001). Reprinted by permission. Karol Lipiński was born on 30 October 1790 in Radzyń Podlaski and died on 16 December 1861 at his estate of Urłowo in Galicia.

2 Józef Powroźniak, *Karol Lipiński* (Kraków: PWM, 1970); Vladimir Grigoriev, *Karol Lipiński* (Moscow: Muzika, 1977).

3 Lipiński's musical contacts with famous musicians of his time began during his childhood in Lwów/Lemberg, when he studied with Austrian composer, Ferdinand Krernes. Since 1811, the young musician was the concertmaster and later also conductor of symphonic concerts in Lwów. After his promotion to the conductor, Stanisław Serwaczyński, later a teacher of Henryk Wieniawski, became a concertmaster. In 1820, during a trip to Berlin, Lipiński met Schumann and Spohr. Most of his musical encounters took place during his work for the Royal Chapel at Dresden, where he was since 1840. (Translator's note).

4 *Zeitschrift für Instrumentenbau* no. 22 (1 May 1909), no. 32 (11 August 1911).

5 Powroźniak, *op. cit.*, 19.

6 See, for example, Karel Jalovec, *Violin Makers* (Praha, 1952); Powroźniak, op. cit.

7 W. H. Hill, A. F. Hill, A. E. Hill, *Antonio Stradivari: His Life and Work* (New York, 1963).

8 *The Violin Times* of 15 December 1895 and 15 January 1896.

9 Cited from Powroźniak, *op. cit.*, 49.

10 Wilhelm Josef von Wasilewski, *Die Violine und Ihre Meister* (Leipzig, first ed. 1869, second ed. 1927), 138.

11 Wilhelm Josef von Wasilewski, *Aus siebzig Jahren. Lebenserinerungen.* (Stuttgart, Leipzig, 1897).

12 Alfred Ehrlich (Albert Payne), *Berühmte Geiger* (Leipzig 1893) 122-123; second enlarged edition, 1902.

13 Max Grünberg, *Meister der Violine* (Stuttgart, Berlin, 1925), 170-171.

14 Glinka composed music to some of his poems.

15 Grigoriev, *op. cit.*, 21.

16 Fridolin Hamma, *Meisterwerke italienischer Geigenbaukunst* (Stuttgart, 1931).

17 Jalovec, *op. cit.*; Powroźniak, *op. cit.*

18 Herbert K. Goodkind, *Violin Iconography of Antonio Stradivari 1644-1737* (New York, 1972).

19 Grigoriev, *op. cit.*, 20.

20 See Cozio.com. http://www.cozio.com/Instrument.aspx?id=497.

21 Charles Beare, *Antonio Stradivari. The Cremona Exhibition of 1987* (London, 1993).

22 *Strzecha* (Lwów, 1871): 374. Cited from Powrozniak, 51.

23 A widely used Latin symbol of Christ originating as an medieval abbreviation of the name of Jesus: IHESUS. This inscription was first found in an abbreviated form on a gold coin in the 8th century: DN (Dominus-Lord) IHS (Ihesus-Jesus) CHS (Christos- Christ) REX REGNATIUM (King of Kings).

24 Franz Bouffier, *Die Violine und ihre Virtuosen* (Berlin, 1890), 12.

25 Willibald Leo von Lütgendorf, *Die Geigen- und Lautenmacher vom Mittelalter bis zur Gegenwart* (Frankfurt-am-Main, 1913), vol. 2, 318.

26 A monographic study of the history of the Guarneri family written by the Hill family, distinguished specialists in the area of early string instruments, included a mention that Lipiński owned a Guarneri, but there were no other details about this subject. See W. H. Hill, A. F. Hill, A. E. Hill, *The Violin Makers of the Guarneri Family* (London, 1931); reprinted by Dover Books (New York, 1991).

27 See Hill, Hill, & Hill, *op. cit.* See also Jane Holloway, Jennifer Laredo Watkins, eds., *Giuseppe Guarneri del Gesù ugrave;* (London: Peter Biddulph, 1998).

[28] *Powszechny Dziennik Krajowy*, no. 140 (1829), cited after Reiss, *op. cit.*, 201, note 1.
[29] Powroźniak, *op. cit.*, 52.
[30] Grigoriev, *op. cit.*, 9. Powrozniak could not have known the book by Grigoriev, published seven years after his, but he knew its copyediting typed manuscript, which he cited several times in his own book.
[31] Grigoriev, *op. cit.*, 48.
[32] *Zeitschrift für Instrumentenbau*, no. 22 (1 May 1909): 833-835.
[33] The firm Hamma & Co. in Stuttgart is still in business. Founded in 1864 by Fridolin Hamma (1818-1892) it was subsequently directed by his sons, grandsons, and great grandsons. Among these, Fridolin II (1881-1969, grandson), and Walter (b. 1916, great grandson of the founder), were the authors of important books and catalogs about Italian and German violin making; both were eminent experts in the history and building of antique instruments.
[34] *Herrvorragende und berühmte alte Geigen im Besitz von Hamma & Co. Handlung alter MeisterInstrumente Stuttgart* (Stuttgart, ca. 1910).
[35] Jalowec, op. cit., 313; William Henley, *Universal Dictionary of Violin and Bow Makers* (T. V. Brighton, 1960), 105; *Die Musik in Geschichte und Gegenwart*, vol. 13 (Kassel: Barerenreiter, 1965), column 1546, entry on "Streichinstrumentenbau").
[36] Gregor Sturdza, the son of Moldavian prince Michael, the ruler of Moldavia, came from an aristocratic family with roots reaching back to the 15th century. Several historical accounts discussed the rule of his father; see *Michel Stourdza et son administration* (Brüssel 1848) and *Michel Stourdza, ancien prince regnant de Moldavie* (Paris, 1874).
[37] *Zeitschrift für Instrumentenbau*, no. 32 (11 August 1911): 1203.
[38] Bouffier, *op. cit.*, 21.
[39] Września School Strike took place in 1901; 118 children protested teaching religion in German. The strike was documented on the oldest Polish film, made in 1908 and discovered in 2001 in a Parisian archive by Prof. Małgorzata Hendrykowska and Marek Hendrykowski. The film *Prussian Culture* was made in Warsaw and funded by Mojżesz Towbin, a Polish-Jewish film distributor and producer. According to Hendrykowska, the film is a documentary about the Prussian methods of fighting Polishness in Wielkopolska Province, and features: children's protest against Germanisation in schools, i.e. their strike in Września, the punishment of their parents by the German authorities, and the fight for Polish ownership of land, symbolized by Drzymała's wagon (this famous farmer was not allowed to build a permanent home on his own land, so he lived in a wagon on wheels). The film was banned by Tsarist government after its 1908 premiere, but was shown in Italy and France, with French subtitles, as *Les Martyres de la Pologne*. (Translator's note).
[40] See Krzysztof Rottermund, "Gnieźnieński epizod z 1907 roku," *Ruch Muzyczny*, no. 14 (1997) and *Kurier Berlinski- Polonica*, nos. 1-2 (2000). The anti-Polish campaign was in part motivated by the infamous "Bismarck directive" the existence of which, long suspected, was revealed by the German government to Polish foreign ministry officials after 1989. The "directive" instructed everyone writing for the media "write nothing or bad things only about Poland."
[41] This event had two musical aspects: (1) Pianist Ignacy Jan Paderewski sponsored the creation of the monument and provided funding for it; (2) composer Feliks Nowowiejski wrote music for the patriotic, anti-German song, "Rota" (The Oath), that later functioned as a national anthem; see Chapter 8 by Krzysztof Szatrawski.
[42] These names are cited by Powroźniak and by Józef Reiss in *Skrzypce i skrzypkowie*
(The Violin and Violinists) (Kraków: PWM, 1955). Grigoriev adds to this list the name of Apolinary Kątski, who was for a time Paganini's student; see Grigoriev, *op. cit.*, 61.
[43] Reiss, *op. cit.*, 45.

44 See: http://www.rccr.cremona.it/doc_comu/mus/engl_vio_carloix.shtm.
45 Maksymilian Braun (1800-1892) was a distinguished activist and music life organizer in Poznań. He played in the string quartet of Prince Antoni Radziwiłł; in 1840 he initiated the creation of the first music society in Poznań; he was a co-founder of the "Harmonia" Society in 1884 and of the Towarzystwo Przyjaciół Nauk (Society of Friends of Science). He wrote reviews and articles about music, conducted and composed. His brother, Augustyn Tomasz (1789-1861) was a violinist, conductor and composer active in Warsaw, Odessa, and Lwów.
46 See Powrozniak, *op. cit.*, 148.
47 Ibidem. See also Barbara Zakrzewska-Nikiporczyk, entry "Maksymilian Bruno," in *Wielkopolski słownik biograficzny* (Biographical Dictionary of Wielkopolska) (Warsaw, Poznań, 1981).
48 Dmitrij Kolbin, "Lipińskiana w Lwowie," in *II Ogólnopolska Sesja Naukowa Karol Lipiński, życie, działalność, epoka* (Wrocław: Wydawnictwo Akademii Muzycznej we Wrocławiu, 1993), 159.
49 Robert Schumann, *Gesammelte Schriften über Musik und Musiker* (Leipzig, 1883), vol. 2, p. 145.
50 Wasilewski, *op. cit.*, 173.
51 Reiss, *op. cit.*, 44.
52 For instance, you may read about the extraordinary fate of the Stradivari-Gibson violin, once owned by Huberman, is described in my articles: "Bronisław Huberman i jego skrzypce" (Bronisław Huberman and His Violin), *Ruch Muzyczny*, no. 11 (1997); "Pechowe Skrzypce Bronisława Hubermana," *Ruch Muzyczny*, no. 20 (1997); "Bronisław Huberman i historia kradzieży słynnego Stradivariusa," *Gazeta Antykwaryczna*, no. 1 (2001).
53 Józef Reiss, *Skrzypce, ich budowa, technika, i literatura* (Warsaw, Kraków, 1924), 11.
54 For instance a rich collection of string instruments and various musical memorabilia from the estate of Yehudi Menuhin was sold by Sotheby in London. See Krzysztof Rottermund, "Instrumentarium Yehudi Menuhina," *Ruch Muzyczny*, no. 1 (2000); and "Instrumentarium Yehudi Menuhina at the London Auction," *Gazeta Antykwaryczna*, no. 3 (2000).

A Romantic Interlude II

Fig. 3: A postcard of a peasant newlywed couple in Cracovian costumes from the Małopolska region, with a patriotic couplet: "In a quiet village, with the grace of God / We will live, far from the world, unknown, / In the home country, we will be happy / it is sweet to live and die for the homeland." Kraków: Wydawnictwo Salonu Malarzy Polskich, 1901. With handwritten inscriptions in French. The postcard was dated 11 March 1902 and sent from Kovno (Lithuania, then Russia), to Barcelona, Spain. Maja Trochimczyk Collection.

Chapter 4

True Virtuosity and Ungraceful Music: Henryk Wieniawski's Activities in Germany and His Attitude towards Joseph Joachim

By Martina Homma

The term "virtuoso" relates to a cultural phenomenon that until today has had a profound impact on the music world through its ambivalent, irrational and emotionally charged reception. The notion of virtuosity, narrowed in time to the manual/physical dexterity of traveling instrumental virtuosos and brilliant singers, who became ubiquitous in the flourishing concert life of European bourgeoisie from the beginning of the 19th century, was often illustrated by its most famous representatives: Liszt, Thalberg, Paganini and Kalkbrenner.

However, during the 16th and 17th-centuries in Italy, the word "virtuoso" continued to describe, in a general sense, a person who was rich in "wirtu," that is someone who possessed intellectual, psychological, ethical or artistic "virtues," such as extraordinary capabilities and talents. At the end of the 17th and the beginning of the 18th centuries in Germany and France, the notion of "Virtuos/Virtuose" (borrowed from Italy) related to a musician who was characterized by an unusual scope of knowledge and abilities in the areas of musical theory, composition and practice.[1] Today, we could refer to such a person as "an expert professional." A narrowing of the definition of virtuosity to purely instrumental talents (i.e., referring solely to the instrumental technique) began around 1730. At the end of the 18th century, numerous writers about music criticized this transformation of the term, pointing out the existence of a "true virtuoso" who differed from those with mere technical capabilities. Basing their arguments on 18th-century aesthetics and citing Carl Philip Emmanuel Bach and Leopold Mozart, these writers demanded that "true virtuosi"—as excellent and sensitive interpreters— had to reveal their empathy with the spirit of the music they played.[2]

Furthermore, the image of the virtuoso is closely linked to the notion of "genius." Christian Friedrich Daniel Schubart, writing in 1784, expected that a soloist would present "fantasias of his own and composed by others" and that in "both cases the music has to be marked by genius."[3] According to this writer, a manually-dexterous ("virtuosic") ability to play an instrument was of secondary importance: "In principle, the mere capability to play an instrument well is not a merit at all." This revealing opinion appeared in 1797 in a *Textbook of Aesthetics* by Johann Heinrich Georg Heusinger.[4]

In his *Lectures on Aesthetics* (Vorlesungen über die Ästhetik) of 1818, Hegel postulated that the performer be an "obedient medium" in his attitude towards the music. The virtuoso musician had a duty to "fill the work with the fullness of spirituality, in accordance with the thought and conception of its composer."[5] The virtuosity of such "spiritualizing" of music was limited to finding proper solutions to difficult compositional tasks in technical terms. For Hegel, when considering performance in spiritual terms, musical genius may only consist in the interpretation that reaches the true spiritual heights of the composer while bringing this spiritual content to life. Thus, virtuosity associated with "the difficult task of composing in its technical aspect," was differentiated from genius, reaching the spiritual level of the composer's inner life. Here, composition—there, composer; here—technical aspects, there—spiritual heights. While emphasizing the music's "spiritual aspects" and "spiritual heights reached by a composer," German music writings of the early 19th century articulated a profound transformation in the understanding of the very nature of music. In his influential study, *The Idea of Absolute Music* (*Die Idee der absoluten Musik*), Carl Dahlhaus presented this transformation in detail, dubbing it a "paradigm shift" in music theory.[6]

The notion of "absolute music" was propagated and publicized through the writings of a highly influential music critic, Ernst Theodor Amadeus Hoffmann. In his 1813 review of Beethoven's music, Hoffmann contrasted the "so-called virtuoso" with the "true virtuoso," expecting of the latter much more than the "expressive empathy" for the music, i.e., nothing less than leading the listener on the path to forgetting about themselves through an "introduction into the enchanted kingdom of sounds."[7] The writer believed that "many a so-called virtuoso rejects Bach's compositions for piano, in which to accusations of the type 'extremely difficult' he also adds 'and ungraceful to the highest degree' (Höchst undankbar)." With this catch-phrase, the eminent music critic (and a professional performer!) referred to the conceptual dualism of "graceful—ungraceful." These aesthetic categories are well-known to each educated musician, who is initiated to this way of thinking in their childhood music lessons. However, from the point of view of aesthetics and musicological methodology, these concepts are treated with a certain disdain. They are reduced to the lack of "understanding" between the musician's hand and the keyboard, the musician's hand and the bow with strings, and so forth. Considered "extra-musical," this duality has often been ignored in theoretical accounts of performance practice; a gap that my article is partly designed to fill.

For a very long time, musicians believed that "graceful" is what "sounds difficult" but also what "fits the hand." For a pianist, these traits may be found in Toccatas by Kisielewski or Khachaturian, but not in, for instance, the Toccata by Robert Schuman, "which fits the hand only with difficulty." Interestingly, this very work stimulated speculations (based on some physiological arguments) about the subject of "the sick-arm syndrome and the toccata."[8] Similarly "ungraceful" in common knowledge is Schumann's Violin Concerto composed for Joseph Joachim with the hope of being often played by the virtuoso. It is worth noting that this Concerto was composed as a "late work" almost simultaneously with Henryk Wieniawski's Violin Concerto No. 1 in F-sharp Minor. The latter composition is interesting, from the point of view of the "gracefulness" controversy because it was an early work by a young, ambitious violin virtuoso. As such, it is a composition saturated with difficulties which, in their full scope and range, are not "graceful" and appealing for any performer. For this reason performances of Wieniawski's Violin Concerto in F-sharp Minor are rare until today. Similarly, the "ungraceful" solo part of Schumann's Violin Concerto has inspired many musicians to engage in revising this work, so as to make it more attractive. Such efforts would not have been undertaken (because of the near-universal acceptance of the principle of faithfulness to the work as conceived and written by the composer), if not for a truly adventurous history of the reception of this concerto.

The premiere of Schumann's Violin Concerto during his lifetime did not happen; it was made impossible by several people particularly close to the composer: Joseph Joachim, (the work's dedicatee), Johannes Brahms and Clara Schumann. In fact, the actual first performance of the Concerto took place almost 100 years after its composition, in 1937. This event occurred under difficult circumstances, not devoid of anti-Semitic overtones. The performance was ideologically charged by: its purposeful opposition of Schumann's work to the Violin Concerto of Felix Mendelssohn, by its attack on Yehudi Menuhin, the soloist of the American premiere of the Concerto and by an attack on Joseph Joachim, who was blamed by *Neue Zeitschrift für Musik* at the end of the 1930s for preventing the publication of Schumann's Violin Concerto back in the mid-19th century.[9] What was the problem with this work, according to this eminent violinist? In 1898, after the death of Brahms and Clara Schumann, Joachim presented his reasons for not publishing Schumann's Concerto. He explained that towards the end of Schumann's life his initially richly flourishing compositional imagination was distorted by morbid reflections. Therefore, the music could not be considered beautiful; it was extremely difficult to play, and did not guarantee a delivery of the expected, positive impression on the public.

"Difficult to play and without making a proper impression on the public"—this is an important, if not revelatory, justification for a decision to withhold the work from publication, especially that it came from such an eminent violin virtuoso and the composer's personal friend. Clearly, Joachim took the side of those who adhered to the ideology of "graceful music"—i.e., music which makes a good impression on the public. He argued as a performer, focusing on the "graceful" versus "ungraceful" aspects of a difficult work of music. It is highly significant that such arguments were presented by this violinist in particular, because he was known for his dislike of virtuoso effects and praised for his faithfulness to the work and for the subordination of an instrumentalist's ideas to the intentions of the composer. This violinist's "classical" ideals were often contrasted with and opposed to Wieniawski's virtuosity (for instance by Max Grünberg and Andreas Moser, as discussed below). We may conclude that music that was "ungraceful"—i.e., that kind of music in which it was hard to perceive the level of technical difficulty along with its virtuosic overcoming, a music permeated with contrasts and competition between the soloist and the orchestra (often without a clearly recognizable "winner")—was, in the long run, not favorably accepted in concert life. It is interesting to note that its opposite, i.e., a completely "graceful" music, was similarly rejected: music that was too "graceful" and avoided creating any contrasts between the parts of the soloist and the orchestra, in order to assign an unquestionable advantage to the soloist, was considered too simplistic to become "classical."

The personalities of virtuosos, who created spectacles for the audiences from the music's obvious technical difficulties and from the overcoming of these difficulties by their unique and astounding dexterity, was criticized quite early by a number of music writers. In the first half of the 18th century, Mizler wrote: "Our virtuosi only attempt to amuse us and to, through their astounding performance capabilities, bewilder and delight us."[10] The focus on what was attracting attention or surprising the listeners in a performance was also noticed in the music of Ludwig van Beethoven. In a review of his Violin Sonata, Op. 47, published in *Allgemeine Musikalische Zeitung*, Wieniawski was accused that "for a certain time he has become capricious, and started to treat in the most cavalier fashion the most precious gifts of nature and of his own hard work, doing so in order to appear completely different from other people."[11] Thus, by succumbing to the twin poles of "enchantment and bewilderment" a virtuoso was a suspect: suspect as a musician, as a master of his/her instrument, and as an artist. These suspicions arose long before a virtuoso's concert appearances became perceived as competing with the displays of circus tricks, exotic animals, and other curios. In a literal sense, the terms "enchantment and bewilderment" indicated that in a performance by a virtuoso (for which, appropriately, a higher ticket price was demanded and paid) the public sought "what was sensational, what was suitable for being perceived because of breaking records of some kind or another." (These were the expectations of the majority of audiences in the first half of the 19th century). In this respect, a virtuoso resembled today's professional athlete, competing in races and fights. We should also note that the concept of "measured and measurable" capabilities fits well within the framework of international performance competitions, ever increasing in number.

In the second half of the 18th century (i.e., in 1785) Carl Stamitz announced before his concert in Hamburg, in an ad published in *Geschichte des Musik und Concertwesens in Hamburg* by Sittarda, that the concert was to include an astounding "performance of a duet by only one violinist."[12] In subsequent decades virtuoso performances became more and more acrobatic. Franz Clement, the soloist at the premiere of Beethoven's Violin Concerto, advertised his concert with announcements that he was to play a sonata on one string and on "upturned" violin.[13] These types of performances were consequently written about in the context of "musical espionage" directed at discovering the secrets of Paganini's art, attempts at rational explanations of the unusually "acrobatic" characteristics of his hand, or, in contrast, attempts to irrationally define his art as demoniacal.[14] For later writers, the virtuoso-violinist Paganini had the honor of elevating "enchantment and bewilderment" to the level of an aesthetic category and technical-compositional element, shared by such "great" musical figures as Schumann, Liszt, Chopin or Brahms. Thus understood, virtuosity reached a level of integral characteristics of a compositional style. In the case of Liszt, it was not a "display" or "trick" but rather a necessary element in the complex fabric of the music.[15]

Thus defined, virtuosity is not a passive servant of a composition because its breath decides upon the life or death of the musical work depending on it for its very existence. Virtuosity is essential in every case of a solo recital, for instance the Wieniawski solo concerts mentioned earlier. In these cases, the music's reception, especially from the musicological point of view, particularly in Germany, is still overshadowed by the controversy about the nature of the "true" virtuosity, a controversy that stands in the way of a balanced, analytical study of a given oeuvre. Writing in this vein, Franz Liszt expressed in a letter to Franz Brendel (of 3April 1853, cited earlier) his reservations towards Wieniawski and his type of virtuosity which, for Liszt, really was not a "true virtuosity." Liszt saw Wieniawski as an exceptional virtuoso, but not in the literal sense of the word, because the term "virtuoso" was derived from the word "virtu" and this word should not be used too much.[16]

By the time that Liszt criticized Wieniawski, the professional music press in Germany had already for several years expressed interest in the 11-year-old child prodigy from a distant country. The *Allgemeine Musikalische Zeitung* published reports at least twice a year about the progress and successes of the young Polish violinist and his younger (by two years) brother, Józef. Already at the beginning of 1847, the *Allgemeine Musikalische Zeitung* published an account of "Henri Wieniawski's" final examination in Paris. He was a "rare phenomenon"—a music critic claimed with conviction—"I have never heard Rode's Concerto played so beautifully."[17] In December 1847, the same publication mentioned that "this wonderful, talented boy," Wieniawski, was making "astounding progress."[18] In the spring of the following year, in March 1848, the *Allgemeine Musikalische Zeitung* published a notice about Wieniawski's composition that he presented in concert: "the applause was as great as the performer was young. The musician is only 11 years old (actually he was already 12). His nine-year-old brother, Józef, turned out to be quite a good pianist."[19] Two months later, the *Allgemeine Musikalische Zeitung* reported that: "Young Henri Wieniawski of Warsaw ... is now the talk of the town, delighting the whole St. Petersburg with his violin playing."[20] In the summer of the same year, Henryk Wieniawski received the most extensive review up to date written in German. For this reason, the review deserved being cited here in its entirety:

> Our third guest, violinist Wieniawsky, is a 12-year-old boy who received the first prize in the Paris Conservatory. In any case, he is possessed of a true talent, deserving our attention. His technical capabilities are highly advanced; his strong and bold bowing technique is particularly vivid in staccato; and his intonation is mostly excellent. More notable than these trait is the fact that these technical capabilities, though easy to perceive in and by themselves, are presented in interpretations filled with good taste, at times even spiced up with intensity and permeated with the impetuous passion that seems to indicate a true genius. Since he still continues to play on a small instrument, his tone does not have a sufficient volume or power to be well-heard even by a medium-sized

audience. He gave four concerts and was very well liked. I have to mention here his own compositions, some of which were heard here, mostly with the accompaniment of an orchestra. These works also testify to his extraordinary, well-developed talent.[21]

While there was some complaining in the various reviews about the weaknesses of the violinist's intonation, he was invariably called a "talent, truly deserving of our attention."[22] In addition to having the "most charming" sound ("already developed so well"), the child was praised for his bowing technique in staccato ("the bold and certain bowing was particularly confirmed by the quality of his staccato").[23] These remarks are even more significant because on other occasions, young Wieniawski was criticized exactly for his staccato, which was singled out as his weakest side.

Similar reviews accompanied the beginning of the young Wieniawski's career in the German territory; with its subsequent stages noted in Dresden, Leipzig, and Weimar in 1848 and 1849, after his return from St. Petersburg. In Dresden, where his compatriot, Karol Lipiński was active as the concertmaster of the Dresden Opera, the 13-year old violinist performed in December 1848. He later appeared in this town on several distinct occasions. He gave concerts in the spring of 1854, in October 1858 (on the 15th and 20th), and at the end of 1877. Furthermore, Lipiński had written a recommendation letter for the 13-year-old Wieniawski addressed to Franz Liszt in Weimar.[24] For the young violinist, this town was an important stage in the early part of his career. Getting in touch with Franz Liszt during the many weeks of their stay in town during the early 1849 was important both for Henryk and his younger brother Józef, who had just completed his piano studies at the Paris Conservatory and who frequently consulted with the master of the piano. It is important to note that in the same year (1849), Joseph Joachim was appointed the concertmaster of the Weimar orchestra. Wieniawski visited Weimar again at the turn of spring and summer of 1853 (from April to June). He gave a concert on 15 April 1853, and initiated personal contacts with Joseph Joachim as well as Johannes Brahms. Four years later, Wieniawski played in Weimar on the occasion of Liszt's birthday, on 21 October 1857. A concert planned for the following year (during a stop-over on the way to Dresden, according to a proposal made by Liszt on 15 September 1858) unfortunately did not happen.[25]

In Leipzig, Wieniawski's partner in music conversations was Ferdynand David, active as a concertmaster in the Gewandhaus Orchestra since 1835 (Wieniawski's birth year). Since 1843, David was also a lecturer in the Conservatory founded by Mendelssohn. As a violinist, David was intently preoccupied with the solo violin music by Johann Sebastian Bach. Wieniawski's first Leipzig concert took place in the early 1849. However, he did not appear again in Leipzig, Dresden, nor Weimar at the end of the decade, nor through 1854. According to a 1853 review published in *Neuer Zeitschrift für Musik*, German music critics saw in the 18-year-old violinist a promising, but not fully developed talent.[26] After staying in Kraków until April 1853, Wieniawski's focus on Leipzig was related to his need for a publisher of his compositions, written until that time. He dedicated to David, his older and well-established colleague, a collection of etudes written in 1854 and entitled *L'école moderne*.

Wieniawski succeeded in the publication of his Concerto in F-sharp Minor which was printed with a dedication to the Prussian king and premiered at the Leipzig Gewandhaus on 27 October 1853. This was the period when the orchestra, directed by Felix Mendelssohn, entered into a phase of its great flourishing and development. After several concerts, scheduled between 1853 and 1855 (including a performance in October 1855 with Ferdynand David as a conductor),[27] more than ten years had to pass before Wieniawski again appeared at the Gewandhaus (on 10 October 1867); he performed there another nine years later, on 16 October 1876.

Residents of central Germany, living in such culturally well-established towns as Leipzig, Dresden and Weimar, had an opportunity of hearing Wieniawski perform about four to six times within their lifetime. This is a much greater frequency of concert appearances, when compared to Wieniawski's occasional performances in other German cities, such as Frankfurt am Main, Cologne, or Hamburg.[28] Apparently, he visited other towns and cities just once. Most frequently, these visits took place during his nearly two-year concert tour, during which he gave over 120 concerts. The tour preceded the 20-year-old violinist's 1855 return to his home town of Lublin. The list of once-visited towns includes, for instance, Aachen, with five concerts given in October and November 1853; Munich with numerous concerts given in December 1853 (on the 5th, 12th and 17th of the month) in the great concert hall Odeon (he also gave two other Munich concerts on 8 and 11 August 1855). Moreover, he performed in Augsburg on 28 and 31 December 1953, in Nuremberg on 11, 13 and 17 January 1854, in Würzburg in 1854 (early in the year and twice in September, on the 9th and 13th of the month). He played twice in Bremen, on 27 February and 6 November, 1855, and gave individual concerts in such places as Ansbach (15 January 1855) and other provincial towns that he visited after his extensive cure at the Heidelberg spa (October-November 1854).[29]

During his German concert tour of October and November 1877 Wieniawski also visited less known cities, such as Kilonia, Koblenz, Stuttgart, Mannheim, and Karlsruhe. In 1875 and 1876 he appeared in Barmen, Güstrow, Schwerin, and Kassel. Of the neighboring countries, Wieniawski frequently performed in Austria, Holland and Belgium, as well as in the East. These latter tours should be considered independently from Wieniawski's concerts in Russia and include five concerts in 1854 in Königsberg (later revisited in 1857), three concerts in May 1854 in Danzig (with a return in December 1878),[30] and a visit to Wrocław in 1848 (plus numerous concerts given there in 1855). Wieniawski appeared particularly often in Poznań (Posen), for instance performing in a series of concerts with his brother in 1854. The attraction was undoubtedly the Posen Trade Markets. It is in Poznań that the Wieniawski brothers performed their joint composition, *Grand Duo Polonais*, Op. 8, based on a song by Stanisław Moniuszko. They repeated this work during their subsequent concert appearances in Poznań, in 1857 and in October 1878.[31]

Fig. 1: Cover of Wieniawski's *Souvenir de Moscou*, Op. 6.
New York: Carl Fischer, 1906. Maja Trochimczyk Collection

In 1854, Wieniawski gave the greatest number of concerts in one German city, Berlin, then frequented by the best-known virtuosi participating in contemporaneous musical life. Between February and

April that year he gave 15 concerts. The 13-year old virtuoso had first visited this city in 1848, on his way to Paris.[32] During his second 1854 concert, held on 19 March, the public included over 1600 people. After the concert, the Wieniawski brothers were called back for 15 encores, as the *Revue et Gazette Musicale* reported in Paris. Soon afterwards, the same newspaper wrote about Berlin performances of Henri Vieuxtemps and Jenny Lind.[33] Almost eight years later, between October and December 1857 prior to his travel to Holland, Wieniawski used the opportunity of touring with other artists represented by his manager, Ullman, to give a series of eight concerts in Berlin.[34]

The evaluation of the musical talents of great instrumentalists is usually conducted in accordance with criteria, which even today continue to be valid, and which were formulated in the context of 19th century discussions about the characteristics of a "true virtuoso." The interpreter of music was perceived to be "empathetic" and "obedient" to the music in his/her subordination to the musical text. It was someone who placed his/her own personality in the shadow and present him/herself as a true "servant of the work." Other traits included the interpreter's capability of introducing the listener into the state of forgetfulness about quotidian matters. A great musician would play "adagio filled with expression," and with a "beautiful tone." This criterion of being able to play a fully expressive and captivating "adagio," a well as having a captivating "tone," coupled with the rejection of "effects" that have a certain, obvious impact on the public appears in writings about performance as late as 1925.

In a book entitled *The Masters of the Violin (Meister der Violine)*, Max Grünberg used these criteria to divide violinists into two groups, those he singled out for praise, and those that he criticized.[35] For instance, Grünberg praised Louis Spohr for the fact that, for him, performance technique was not "a self-standing goal, but only a means of bringing to life the black dots of notes on paper transformed into living sounds."[36] In contrast, the decisive fault of a virtuoso was failing to understand and focus on "the spirit of foreign works," that the writer complained about to his teacher, Franz Eck.[37] Apparently, according to Francois-Joseph Fétis whom Grünberg cited with relish, the great Paganini suffered from this weakness. In performing concerti by others, such as Kreutzer's Concerto, he was not too convincing and his interpretation did not go far beyond being mediocre ("en jouant un concerto de Kreutzer et un de Rode il ne s'y éleva point au-dessus du médiocre.")[38]

For Spohr, even the increasing of the visual attractiveness of performance was suspect as being too superficial. He named as faults of the "northern Paganini," Ole Bull (1810-1880), the techniques that are today a common practice of "sustaining the tension."[39] These techniques were: to continue holding the bow in place at the end of a long pianissimo, or to keep the bow suspended above the violin for several seconds after ending the final phrase. In France, however, Hector Berlioz approved of the same "effect" as a positive and desirable action that accomplishes its objective of capturing the attention and emotions of the public. Nonetheless, the effect's rejection frequently recurs in German music literature dedicated to the subject of virtuosity. Max Grünberg, in his monograph about the *Masters of the Violin* cited above strongly criticized Apolinary Kątski, a competitor of Wieniawski older by 10 years ("Apollinair de Kontski"), who had studied with Paganini himself. According to Grünberg, Kątski was "all in the style of Paganini, directed entirely towards effects and without a tad of good taste. He possesses the manner of Paganini, but not his soul."[40] The opinion of Reiss was even more critical.[41]

In contrast, Grünberg's opinion of Joseph Joachim was uniformly positive. This violinist was repeatedly contrasted with Henryk Wieniawski and played a significant role both among his German colleagues as well as in Wieniawski's own biography. Joseph Joachim was a child prodigy and as a 13-year-old youth performed with Felix Mendelssohn in London. As a 19-year-old, he became the director of the violin class at the Leipzig Conservatory. Later he was active as the concertmaster of the Weimar Court Orchestra and since 1868-69 served as the director of the Berliner Higher School of Music (Berliner Hochschule für Ausübende Tonkunst). According to the distinguished music critic Ernst Hanslick, Joachim was "a complete musician who transcended the most brilliant virtuosity;" that is a musician who by overcoming the most astounding virtuosity rejected it for something greater.[42] Grünberg appraised Joachim's talents in the following way:

> During the times that virtuosity is in its greater flowering and all possible lack of taste and all interpretative liberty seems acceptable, Joachim placed the creator of a work above the performer, *the musician above the virtuoso* (italics by MH) and made into law the principle of inviolability of the work of music in its reproduction.[43]

Moreover, in Joachim, "the sense of dignity" is unchanged and has become for him the "guiding star of his life" and a principle for an artist that serves his vocation "as a priest in his holy of holies."[44] As we see from these words, the "religion of art" of the early German romanticism had a long and lasting impact.

What became defined as a "measuring rod" for the quality of performance in Grünberg's study was not what was fast, what was technically difficult, or what was attractive in terms of sound effects. According to this school of thought, the true master reveals his greatness in the slow and expressive Adagio.[45] Already at the end of the 18th century in Germany statements against evaluating the quality of virtuoso musicians on the basis of their performances of fast movements were published frequently. A true expert would have had a different criterion for measuring the greatness of a virtuoso. These criteria included: the way of playing, the expressive perfection, and the sensuality of the presentation. Here the expert would also declare his preference for a fully expressive Adagio. Similarly, in *The Masters of the Violin*, Grünberg placed a great emphasis on the value of the tone and the quality of expression in the slow movements. He extensively considered the theme of a captivating Adagio already in the discussion of Franz Benda's musicianship. Among younger violinists, contemporaneous to the writer (i.e., those active between the two world wars), particular praise was reserved for Bronisław Huberman, due to his warm and richly modulated tone.[46]

Fig 2: A Polish postcard with a folk fiddler, based on a painting *Zapomniany ból / Schmerzvergessen / Oubliant la doleur (A forgotten sorrow)*, by Banat. Maja Trochimczyk Collection.[47]

Among violinists active in Germany, with whom Wieniawski was often compared, the names of Heinrich Ernst or his contemporary Ferdinand Laub (1832-1875) are the most common. Nonetheless, the comparison of Wieniawski's style with that of Joachim reveals the strongest traits of the "graceful/ungraceful" debate. Bieziekirski, for instance, reports about their competitive performances in Paris, perceived almost as a "duel" there and witnessed by the elite of violinists active in France at that time. The challenge for both musicians and the ground for comparison of their performance styles was Mendelssohn's Violin Concerto, a brilliant work in the repertoire of Joachim, and a showpiece selected by Wieniawski for his Paris appearances. Lambert-Joseph Massart, with whom 8-year-old Wieniawski started his violin education at the Paris Conservatory, stated during the rehearsal of the Andante from this Concerto: "C'est délicieux, eh bien! Celui-la va enfoncer Joachim!" (This is delicious...Well, here is the one to defeat Joachim").[48] Unfortunately, Wieniawski was not well disposed musically during the concert when the "musical duel" was actually held. (There is a certain discrepancy about this fact, however, in the reports of the *Revue et Gazette Musicale* and the account by Bieziekirski).[49] According to Massart, the difference between Wieniawski and Joachim in the performance of the slow movement was as significant as that of different weapons in the duel.

The performance style of both violinists was also directly compared in St. Petersburg. Ivan Turgenev reported about this issue in a letter to Paulina Viardot. According to Turgenev, Wieniawski played Bach's *Chaconne* so well that the listeners really wanted to hear it, even after the "incomparable Joachim."[50] The points of contact between the careers of Joachim and Wieniawski (who was his junior by four years), are located in decisive turning points in the younger violinist's professional career: his childhood studies and the outset of the final stage of his musical activities. As child prodigies, both violinists had the same teacher, Stanislaw Serwaczyński, who taught Joachim in Peszt and Wieniawski in his native Lublin. Serwaczyński was at the time the concertmaster of the Lwów Opera and frequently visited Lublin to give concerts and spend time with his family (his father, Michal Serwaczyński, was a violinist and the director of the Lublin orchestra). Under the influence of the "Polish Paganini," Karol Lipiński, Serwaczyński transmitted to his students Lipiński's musical ideals: a singing quality of his "cantabile" tone and a excellent bowing technique. These ideals strongly influenced the two students, as it was reported by Joachim himself.[51]

Wieniawski's visits to Weimar, Hanover, London, and Berlin provided him with opportunities for personal contacts with his four-year-senior colleague. His first concert in Hanover, on 24 February 1855 took place during Joachim's initial years there as the Royal Kapellmeister. Repeated Hanover performances by Wieniawski were scheduled for 22 January 1867 and 23 November 1877. During the Polish violinist's subsequent concerts in Hanover, Joachim was already active in Berlin where he lived since 1866. Young Wieniawski's concert appearances in that city, however, took place when Joachim was not at all a well-established authority there. A meeting of both violinists that gives cause for reflection took place in the early 1859 in London. The musicians were opposed in the public opinion because of representing two, diametrically different performance traditions: a Belgian-French tradition (Wieniawski) and the German tradition (Joachim). The most eminent virtuosi of the time met in London to perform a Beethoven string quartet. Joseph Joachim and Heinrich Ernst (1814-1865) played the first and second violin respectively, while Alfredo Piatti (1822-1901) played the cello and Wieniawski—the viola.

Joachim, as many others, considered the singing tone in the Adagio as the most important criterion for evaluating the quality of a violinist's musicianship. He was very enthusiastic about the *cantabile* tone in the slow movements played by Ernst: "I have never heard anything like that again. Ernst was the violin who surpassed all the other violinists that I have ever heard during my entire my life."[52] In Wieniawski's performance style, Joachim admired particularly the joy of the risk, his acrobatic leaps and the technique of his left hand (fingering). In his *School for Violin* which was published at the beginning of the 20th century in Berlin, with Joachim's own introduction as well as with Joachim's biography penned by Abraham Moser, the great violinist included an example from Wieniawski's Second Violin Concerto in the closing section of the second part in the chapter on chromatic scales ("Chromatische Tonleitern;" p. 208 in *the School for Violin*).[53]

In terms of personal contacts between Wieniawski and Joachim, different reports appear in older German books about the art of playing the violin (such as Andreas Moser or Grünberg cited earlier) and in Polish and Russian monographs about Henryk Wieniawski.[54] The latter studies describe in a particular fashion events surrounding Wieniawski's Berlin concert of 1878 and vividly paint the picture of the starting point of the decline in Wieniawski's concretizing activities. The Polish violinist, suffering from short breath (as reasons asthma and heart problems are frequently cited) had to interrupt his performance after the first movement of his own Violin Concerto in D minor. According to the reports, Joachim then took the violin from the hands of his friend, in order to continue the concert in his stead. In the opinion of Moser, Reiss and Grigoriev, this was a gesture of the predominant human (or, superhuman and artistic) quality that characterized this subtle, international musical friendship.⁵⁵ *Neue Berliner Musikzeitung* published a detailed report about this incident in October 1878.

In the following section of this chapter, I would like to focus on the differences pointed out by other authors, especially pre-eminent in the book by Grünberg where they reveal the essence of a Polish-German understanding of virtuosity while showing clearly their anti-French tendencies. According to Grünberg, Wieniawski did not reach the heights of a proper attitude towards Joachim and his art. However, Alfred Fischoff reported that "Wieniawski was too great of an artist to not notice the enormous importance of Joachim as the exemplary interpreter of classical works of music." In Fishoff's report, Wieniawski accused Joachim of being too one-sided, even expressing a suspicion that Joachim strove after these goals purposefully, i.e., because he was aware of the fact that he did not possess traits essential for a truly outstanding virtuoso. In a equally unjust and malicious evaluation, Joachim, who certainly was not unaware of these types of statements, had an opportunity for noble revenge. Wieniawski was gravely ill with heart problems and because his financial circumstances were not too good, he organized the Berlin benefit concert and ensured the presence of Joachim to guarantee success.

When the sudden weakness of heart forced Wieniawski to interrupt the concert after the first number, and threatened with ending the whole evening without its full program, Joachim spontaneously agreed to replace Wieniawski and complete the concert in his place, performing the whole Wieniawski Concerto among other pieces. He played with his usual mastery and saved the day for his sick colleague, ensuring that he would receive the income from the event. Here it is important to emphasize that Joachim clearly did not perform the whole program planned for the evening by Wieniawski. He apologized for not playing the Concerto in D Minor (this apology was much more interesting than the issue that Joachim failed to wear proper evening clothes at this concert, an item pointed out by other reviewers). Moreover, in the press, significant attention was paid to Wieniawski's financial troubles, associated with his "play" in the double sense of the word, as a musician and as a gambler in casinos. Only seemingly, this aspect, atypical for a romantic musician, was not without influence for the public perception of the interactions of the two great virtuosi during the 1878 concert.

Among German towns in which Wieniawski gave concerts there are well-known musical centers such as Leipzig, Weimar, Dresden, and Berlin. A sizeable group of locations consists of elegant resorts: Homburg (1856, 1859, and 1864), Ems (1853, 1859, 1864, and 1865), Kreuznach (1853, 1864, and 65), Salzbrunn (1855 and 1857, when in July Wieniawski was close to dueling one of the spa's employees), Schlangenbad (1864), Karlsbad (1853 and 1872), Marienbad (visited in 1853 and in 1870 with his pregnant wife), and most of all, Wiesbaden (1853, 1856, 1858, 1859, 1863, 1864, 1865, and 1877) and Baden-Baden, regularly visited in almost every season for 25 years (1853, 1854, 1856, 1857, 1858, 1859, 1863, 1864, 1865, 1866, 1872, 1877, and 1878).[56] In these resorts, the public was the most affluent and financially without compare. The revenue potential for musicians was astounding. Wieniawski's honorarium for his 1859 Baden-Baden concerts equaled 1,500 francs and the amount of money he earned concretizing allowed him to visit local casinos. There are detailed accounts of gambling passions and extended periods of uninterrupted gambling sprees of Wieniawski and his colleagues, Leopold Auer, Mikholai Rubinstein, in the Wiesbaden casino. As well known are complaints of the father about the financial plight of his sons: "Did they earn little this summer in London and Constantinople? … And how do I ask where it all went?…There is nothing left. Everything was spent. And then, with curiosity, they peek into my pockets."[57] In this context, it seems that Wieniawski's behavior deserved a mention by such an ethical author as Grünberg about the "income" saved by Joachim for Wieniawski in Berlin.

Let us return to the violin, to music and Wieniawski's repertoire. Fischoff's report of Wieniawski's offhand remark about Joachim's "classical chicanery" should not be overestimated in the overall review of Wieniawski's attitude towards the German violin master. The same Fischoff reported in *Neues Wiener Journal* that Wieniawski was one of

> the most amusing and witty people, even more, one of the most brilliant satirical minds, that I have ever encountered…Nobody may feel safe that they will not become the subject of his jokes…Un ami pour un calembourg![58]

The fact that Wieniawski was quick witted and sharp-tongued was often commented upon. His stinging response during a toast to the impartiality of the German press, given at a reception organized for his early Parisian teacher (Lambert-Joseph Massart), transformed Hector Berlioz into Wieniawski's bitter enemy and opponent.[59] The fact that Wieniawski, in a decisive moment, could not constrain himself in the presence of his sovereigns and of their subjects, resulted in his expulsion from Warsaw, harmed his chances at retaining a well-paid position in St. Petersburg, and led him to exile, so he spent many years living as an émigré abroad. Therefore, even if Wieniawski's attitude towards Joachim was not as critical as it would have appeared on the basis of his statements quoted above, we may be certain that other colleagues-virtuosi were much closer to him. For instance, Pablo Sarasate, to whom Wieniawski dedicated his Violin Concerto No. 2, shared a number of "national traits" with the Polish virtuoso and was treated far more favorably.

While talking to his close personal friend, Biezekirski, in Russia, Wieniawski is reported to have said the following about Joachim:

> Once Joachim asked me: could you explain to me the phenomenal success of Sarasate in Germany? I responded: "You are, no doubt, the pride of Germany, but what is your repertoire? It consists of violin concerti by Beethoven, Mendelssohn and Spohr, the sonatas b Bach, and, more recently, one concerto by Bruch. And this has been going on for the past 35 years. In Germany there are over 500 concertmasters and all of them want to imitate you, therefore together you have presented the same limited repertoire for the past 35 years. What is the result of this? Something very solid and very, very boring.[60]

Incidentally, Wieniawski must have felt quite offended by one reviewer in St. Petersburg (with the *nom-de-plume* Quasimodo) who accused him —just like he accused Joachim—of having a limited and one-sided repertoire. Quasimodo's mocking remark about Joachim reflects his views on virtuosity: "The Temple is transformed into a circus arena at the moment that a circus performer appears in it."[61] This statement also expresses what in, the first half of the 19th century, the adherents of the "sacred art" beliefs thought about virtuosity: it seemed to them to be something belonging in the circus, not in the temple of music, the concert hall. Interestingly, expressions of this kind have recurred about 30 years ago (in 1977) in Friedhelm Krummacher's analytical study, one of few such projects of which it would have been possible to expect a recognition of Wieniawski's talent and the quality of his oeuvre. The title of this text, *Virtuosity and the Composition of a Violin Concerto* and the subtitle "The issues of the genre from Beethoven to Brahms," indicates however, that expectations of honoring the phenomenon of virtuosity were too far fetched. In this study, the term "virtuosity" was endowed with a completely negative significance.

Thus, all "virtuosic" violin concerti remained suspect and were assumed to be inferior because they lacked what the author of the study elevated to the level of a primary criterion of musical quality, i.e. "symphonic development." According to Krummacher, the priority of "symphonicism" in the genre of the violin concerto, was a obvious; it was a fact that "does not leave any room for discussion."[62] Therefore violin concerti by such virtuosi as Viotti, Vieuxtemps and Wieniawski became associated with ambiguous compositional values and deficient in quality.

While the "great, masterly works" also happened to include virtuosic passages (these works included concerti by Beethoven, Brahms, Mendelssohn, but not Schumann, Dvorak or even Tchaikovsky), the presence of virtuosity had to explain away and justified. Krummacher found the justification for virtuosity by "legitimizing" it through thematic connections or motivic links. Such passages had to be "justified" or else, the works in which they occurred were threatened of falling out of good graces of the scholar.[63] Such a motivational connection, i.e., a form of legitimizing virtuosity by finding its merit in compositional techniques of a symphonic kind, may be very easily traced in Wieniawski's Violin Concerto in D minor. However, the dislike for instrumental virtuosity, justified in the discussion cited at the beginning of my study and dealing with the concept of a "true virtuoso" and the art as "sacrum" continues to this day and continues to hinder a serious, in-depth analytical recognition of the quality of Wieniawski's own music.

Translated by Martina Homma and Maja Trochimczyk

ENDNOTES

[1] Wangermée, Robert: "Tradition et innovation dans la virtuosité romantique," *Acta musicologica* XX, 5-32.

[2] According to Johann Abraham Schulz in Sulzer, *Allgemeine Theorie der schönen Künste*, 1774; cited by Reimer, Erich (1997) in "Der Begriff des wahren Virtuosen in der Musikästhetik des späten 18. und frühen 19. Jahrhunderts," *Basler Jahrbuch für historische Musikpraxis* 20, 1996, edited by Peter Reidemeister (Winterthur, 1997), 61-71; quoted from pp. 62-64.

[3] Schubart, Christian Friedrich Daniel: *Ideen zu einer Ästhetik der Tonkunst*, 1784, (Wien, 1806), quoted by Reimers, ibidem, 65.

[4] Heusinger, J(ohann) H(einrich) G(eorg): *Handbuch der Aesthetik I* (Gotha, 1797), 180.

[5] Hegel, Georg Friedrich Wilhelm: *Vorlesungen über die Ästhetik* III, Frankfurt am Mein 1970 (*Werke*, edited by Eva Moldenhauer and Karl Markus Michel, vol. 15, 219 f.); quoted by. Reimer (ibidem), 67.

[6] Dahlhaus, Carl: *Die Idee der absoluten Musik* (Kassel 1978).

[7] Hoffmann, Ernst Theodor Amadeus: "Deux Trios (...) par Louis van Beethoven," *Allgemeine musikalische Zeitung* 15 (1813): 153f, quoted by Reimer, *op. cit.*, 71.

[8] Giersch, Klaus: "'Der kranke Arm und die Toccata'. Robert Schumann und das Klavier," *Neue Zeitschrift für Musik* (1984): 594-601.

[9] See Michael Struck, *Die umstrittenen späten Instrumentalwerke Schumanns*, Hamburger Beiträge zur Musikwissenschaft 29 (Hamburg 1984), 259ff., especially 323-338.

[10] Mizler, Lorenz: *Musicalische Bibliothek* I/4, (Leipzig, 1738): 20, quoted by Reimer (*op. cit.*, footnote 2), 67.

[11] "Recension (...) Sonata per il Pianoforte ed un Violino (...) par Louis van Beethoven. Op. 47", *Allgemeine musikalische Zeitung* 7, (1804-5): 769 f., quoted by Reimer (*op. cit.*), 70.

[12] Sittard, J.: *Geschichte des Musik- und Concertwesens in Hamburg* (Altona und Leipzig, 1890): 134; quoted by Heinrich Schwab, "Vom Auftreten der Virtuosen. Berichte und Bilder aus der Kulturgeschichte des Konzertsaals" (III), *Das Orchester*, (1991): 1359.

[13] Quoted in. Robin Stowell, " Niccolo Paganini (1782-1840). The Violin Virtuoso *in excelsis?*", *Basler Jahrbuch für historische Musikpraxis* 20 (1996): 73-93 (quote from p. 73).

[14] For instance, by Carl Guhr in *Über Paganinis Kunst, die Violine zu spielen* (Mainz 1829), or by Dr. Francesco Bennatis in *Histoire Physiologique et Pathologique de Niccolo Paganini*, both cited by Stowell (op. cit.), 76 and 77.

[15] Franz Liszt, *Gesammelte Schriften* (Leipzig, 1882), vol. 4, 192f.

[16] La Mara (ed.): *Briefe hervorragender Zeitgenossen an Franz Liszt* (Leipzig 1893), 138.

[17] *Allgemeine Musikalische Zeitung* 4 (January 1847): 6.

[18] *Allgemeine Musikalische Zeitung*, 51 (December 1847): 882.

[19] *Allgemeine Musikalische Zeitung*, 9 (March 1848): 152.

[20] *Allgemeine Musikalische Zeitung* 11 (May 1848): 366.

[21] *Allgemeine Musikalische Zeitung* 28 (July 1848): 456.

[22] See, for instance József Reiss, *Henryk Wieniawski*, (Kraków, 1985), especially p. 25ff. Reiss cites an article by Arno Kleffel from *Rheinischen Theater- und Musikzeitung* (1904, No. 12) and refers to Paul Kraemer: *Das Geheimnis des Staccatos auf den Streichinstrumenten*, in: *Die Musik* 4, no. 22. Wieniawski's student Stanisław Serwaczyński stated that the development of the right hand was greatly emphasized by his teacher; from this school the approach to bowing practiced by Joseph Joachim has emerged. Wieniawski's op. 7, *Capriccio-Valse*, is here an example with its extremely hard staccato-parts. Furthermore, already in the finale of Mendelssohn's Violin Concerto was Wieniawski's staccato noticed during his Parisian Conservatoire years; see for instance, Grigoriew, *op. cit.*, 176.

[23] *Allgemeine Musikalische Zeitung*, no. 28 (July 1848): 456.

[24] Lipinski's letter to F. Liszt of January 27, 1849; see. La Mara (*op. cit.*, vol. 1, 106); see also Reiss, *op. cit.*, 29.

[25] Wieniawski's letter to Liszt of 15 September 1858, in: La Mara, *op. cit.*, vol. 2, 175, also cited by Reiss, *op. cit.*, 60.

[26] *Neue Zeitschrift für Musik* 19 (1853): 205.

[27] These concerts took place on 5 November 1853 and 30 September 1855.The *Revue et Gazette Musicale* reported on 21 October 1855 about strong applause after Paganini's "berühmter Phantasie"; cited in *Henryk Wieniawski. Kronika życia*, edited by Władysław Dulęba, (Kraków, 1967), 127.

[28] At Frankfurt he gave concerts in the beginning and end of 1854, on 9 October 1857, August 1864, 21 January 1867, and 12 October 1877. In Cologne he appeared in November and December 1854, as well as on the 20, 11, 8 and 9 December 1855; and one more time, 20 years later, on 12 January 1875. In Hamburg, while stopping over on the way to Paris, , he gave oncerts on 10 February 1855, and more than ten years later, on 7 January 1867 and in 1877, e.g., on 9 October 1877. A report from a concert in Cologne of 9 December 1854, given with Männergesangverein, appeared in the *Revue et Gazette Musicale* on 23 December 1855, as reprinted in *Henryk Wieniawski*, op. cit., 129.

[29] He visited Kiel on 20 November 1877, Stuttgart on 10 December 1877, Mannheim on 11 December 1877, and Karlsruhe on 12 December 1877.

[30] He gave concerts on 18 and 22 May 1854, as well as on 5 December 1878.

[31] In 1854 they gave three concerts at the theater (21, 22, 23 April 1854), and further concerts at the "Basar" (9, 11, 13 and 15 June 1854, and a charity concert on 26 June 1854). Further concerts were on 29 July and 6, 4, and 8 August at the Posener Theater. In 1857 Wieniawski had five concert dates in the June-July period (24 and 27 June at the "Basar", 28 June, 2 and 3 July 1857 at the Theater). Wieniawski performed again at the Basar on 23 November 1878.

[32] Two concerts at the court and four at the Royal Theater (on 19, 22, 27 February 1854 and 4 April 1854), six concerts at Krollschen Theater (1, 9, 13, 17, 21, and 23 March 1854) with greater public attendance, and one in the Gustav-Adolf-Stiftung (4 March 1854), as well as at the Berlin Opera (11 April 1854) and in Potsdam (18 April 1854).

[33] *Revue et Gazette Musicale*, 19 and 26 March 1854, in: *Henryk Wieniawski*, *op. cit.*, 105.

[34] The Berlin concerts took place on 22, 25, 27, 29, 30, and 31 October, as well as 1, and 3 November 1857.

[35] Grünberg, Max: *Meister der Violine*, (Stuttgart and Berlin, 1925).

[36] Grünberg, *ibidem.*, 75.

[37] Grünberg, *ibidem.*, 59.

[38] Grünberg, *ibidem*, 44ff; Francois-Joseph Fétis: *Notice biographique sur Nicolo Paganini*, (Paris, 1851), 79; cited by Stowell, *op. cit.*, 85: "en jouant un concerto de Kreutzer et un de Rode: il ne s'y éleva point au-dessus du médiocre."

[39] Spohr obserbed how Bull "an einer Stelle, die ihm Gelegenheit bot, durch eines seiner unübertrefflichen pp. zu glänzen, noch sekundenlang den Bogen dicht über den Saiten schwebend gehalten, um das Publikum, welches in athemloser Stille dem letzten Verklingen seines immer schwächer werdenden Tones gelauscht, glauben zu machen, es dauerte derselbe in unerhörtem ppp. noch fort." Spohr, L.: *Selbstbiographie* (Kassel, 1860-61), vol. 2, 229; cited by Schwab, *op. cit.*, 1360.

[40] Grünberg, *op. cit.*, 175.

[41] Reiss, *op. cit.*, 31-40.

[42] Cited by Grünberg, *op. cit.*, 98.

[43] Grünberg, *op. cit.*, 98.

[44] Grünberg, *op. cit.*, 95.

[45] Junker, Carl Ludwig: "Noch etwas vom Kurköllnischen Orchester," *Musicalische Correspondenz* (1791), cited by Reimer, *op. cit.*, 68.

[46] Grünberg, *op. cit.*, 178: "Von allen Geigern der neueren Zeit besitzt vielleicht Huberman den wärmsten und modulationsfähigsten Ton."

[47] The postcard was mailed on 8 June 1917, during World War I) from Kraków by K. Mroczkowska to her husband August Mroczkowski in Krasnystaw.

[48] Grigoriew, *Henryk Wieniawski*, *op. cit.*, 176.

[49] *Revue et Gazette Musicale* (28 April 1867); see Grigoriew, *ibidem.*, p. 175 and 241, note 150.

[50] I. Tourgueneff: *Lettres à Madame Viardot, publiées et annotées ar E. Halperin-Kaminska* (Paris, 1907), 197; cited by Grigoriew, 164.

[51] *Briefe von und an Joseph Joachim*, vol. 1, (Berlin, 1911), 456; quoted in Grigoriew, *op. cit.*, 16.

[52] Joachim to Moser, quoted by Grünberg, *op. cit.*, 93.

[53] This example is discussed by Grigoriew, *op. cit.*, 107.

[54] Moser, Andreas: *Joseph Joachim Ein Lebensbild* (Berlin, 1898), 290-292; Reiss, *op. cit.*, Grigoriew, *op. cit.*

[55] Cited by Grünberg, op. cit., 174ff.

[56] Quoted from Grigoriew, *op. cit.*, 168-170.

[57] *Dziennik Literacki*, 25 June 1869; cited by Grigoriew, *ibidem*, 182.

[58] Quoted in Grünberg, *op. cit.*, 173f.
[59] *Journal des Débats* (30 July 1850), see also Reiss, *op. cit.,* 31f; this episode was reported by Reiss, p. 62, and also by Grigoriew, p. 98.
[60] Biezekirski, W., *Iz zapisnoj knizki artista*, (Petersburg, 1910), 150; quoted by Grigoriew op. cit., p. 183ff.
[61] *Nuvellist* (Pseudonym Quasimodo) no. 4 (1863), 29; quoted by Grigoriew, *op. cit.*, 160.
[62] Krummacher, Friedhelm: "Virtuosität und Komposition im Violinkonzert. Probleme der Gattung zwischen Beethoven und Brahms," *Musica* (1977): 604-613; cited from 613.
[63] Krummacher, *ibidem*, 608-610.

A Romantic Interlude III

Fig. 4: A Polish postcard of a village couple in Cracovian costumes (from the Małopolska region), with a krakowiak couplet: "I do not seek the stars in the sky, nor the moon / But I constantly look at you / because you are more radiant / than the stars in the sky." Published in Kraków, Poland, ca. 1890. Maja Trochimczyk Collection.

Fig. 5: A Polish postcard of a village couple in Cracovian costumes (from the Małopolska region), with a krakowiak couplet: "If you only knew / What I think of you / you would run to me / to start kissing me." Published in Kraków, Poland, ca. 1890. Maja Trochimczyk Collection.

Fig. 6: A Polish postcard of a village couple in Cracovian costumes (from the Małopolska region), with a krakowiak couplet: "To kiss you is a true paradise, / So one more time give me your kisses !" Published in Kraków, Poland, ca. 1890. Maja Trochimczyk Collection.

Chapter 5

Polish Reception of Wagner's Music and Ideas

Magdalena Dziadek

It would not be an exaggeration to state that reflection about the art of Richard Wagner constitutes the most important chapter in Polish musical thought at the turn of the 19th and 20th centuries.[1] These reflections centered on the most significant issues considered by composers and music critics of the time: the future direction in the development of European music; the model of a "national" music; and fundamental aesthetic issues, such as the notion of the synthesis of all arts and the theory of symbols. Two generations of Polish critics participated in discussions about Wagner's legacy of thought and music; these discussions reached a climax in the years 1890-1905. The participants in this Wagnerian controversy represented two opposing worldviews, a positivistic stance and a modernist one. Critics belonging to the positivistic camp viewed the art of Wagner as a symptom of a profound crisis overwhelming Western culture.

In contrast, critics adhering to the modernist worldview welcomed Wagner's oeuvre as a promise of a new future. According to the latter view, his accomplishments would lead to expanding the borders of music far beyond its traditional limitations. Wagner offered a new hope for the renewal of musical language. A history of conflicts between the two contrasting worldviews represented by these two generations, completely opposed to each other in ideological terms, provides a rare opportunity for a detailed mapping of a gradual emergence of modern style in Polish thought about music. This style, despite widespread beliefs to the contrary, was not articulated in a vacuum, but emerged as a consequence of a continuous and active reception of European thought about culture in general, and music in particular. When viewed in this context, Polish discussions about Wagnerian art faithfully reflected the chronology of the emergence of various well-known artistic theories and intellectual fashions in this period. An equally important aspect of the reception of Wagner's ideas in Poland was an attempt to transfer Wagner's artistic and ideological postulates into the realm of Polish national art. This conscious effort aimed to inscribe Wagnerian ideals into the conceptual context of programs and manifestos postulated for the future development of Polish literature, theater and music. It is worth noting that many such programs emerged at the turn of the century.

Fig. 1: Richard Wagner. Postcard "made in Germany," ca. 1900.
Maja Trochimczyk Collection.

Polish beliefs about the essence of Wagnerian art and its role in the contemporaneous artistic landscape were subject to a spectacular transformation in the space of a mere fifteen years, from 1890 to about 1905. In this period, Wagner was almost miraculously transformed from a barely tolerated artist, a suspect character accused of leading music to its demise in decadence (as many Polish commentators thought even as late as at the beginning of the 1890s), into the greatest authority for young composers, venerated as if he were a prophet, or a "national bard" ("wieszcz").[2] It was an enormous intellectual effort, conducted in a brief period of time, to articulate such a profound transformation from one to the other extreme in the interpretation of Wagner's achievements and the assessment of his place in music history. Judged solely by the scope of this effort, critical reflections about the arts published during that time revealed a great intellectual potential.

Polish music historians have usually regarded this period, centered on the year 1900, as representing an era of stasis and stagnation, a period of an almost complete infertility of minds.[3] In this article I will demonstrate how far this supposed "common knowledge" diverged from the truth. We should note that the Polish version of the "Wagnerian frenzy," dramatically evolving around the end of the 19th century, was limited to a relatively small group of intellectuals. Moreover, the leaders of this group mostly originated outside the music world; they came from circles of progressive writers and journalists.

Despite a comparably high number of Wagnerian works produced on theatrical stages in Warsaw and Lwów between 1890 and 1905,[4] the "Wagnerian frenzy" did not become as widespread in Poland as to necessitate being considered a predominant cultural fashion. Furthermore, Wagner's compositions did not remain in the repertoire of Polish music theaters for very long. They were—one should add—crippled by an array of cuts and other simplifications; they were staged in ways that was quite divergent from the recommendations of the visionary composer. Typically, these imperfect interpretations of Wagner's music theater disappeared from operatic stages after barely a few performances.

It is quite obvious, however, that difficulties with transmitting the spark of the "Wagnerian craze" to the wider public in Poland stemmed from other factors, rather than the purely aesthetic ones. The main barrier for Wagner's reception in Poland at the end of the 19th century emerged in the area of politics. Wagnerian cult in Poland occurred at a time of growing hostility in the relations between Poles and Germans in Prussia (especially the Polish partition, Wielkopolska with its capital of Poznań). This hostility was caused—to a great extent—by aggressive and chauvinistic activities of a German nationalistic organization, HAKATA, and the enforced Germanization of Poles in the Poznań district. Anti-Prussian moods found strong support in Polish press of a national-democratic orientation ("Narodowa Demokracja," ND, or "Endecja"), which considered waging a battle on behalf of protecting Polish culture as one of the most important political tasks. The same members of Polish society who remained the most open and receptive to the program of national democracy (it was, first and foremost, intelligentsia), were also inclined to publicly demonstrate their hostility towards the "Teutonic element," both in political-economic life and in the openly manifested negative attitude towards the so-called Teutonic or Germanic arts.

Authors of memoirs whose backgrounds were in the intelligentsia class described the strength of a connection between, on the one hand, the slowness and reluctance in accepting Wagner's oeuvre and its aesthetics, and, on the other, a universal anti-Prussian attitude, permeating the Polish society of the time. For instance, Jadwiga Waydel-Dmochowska, a daughter of a prominent Warsaw attorney and a friend of the Karłowicz family of musicians, remembered the doomed fate of Wagnerian spectacles in Warsaw soon after the 1905 revolution (in 1907-1909), thus describing their plight:

> Neither the *Tannhaüser*—even with Kruszelnicka—nor the truly "un-Wagnerian" *The Flying Dutchman* was counted among the successful productions of our Opera House. Furthermore, an attempt to stage *Die Valküre* ended in a complete fiasco. It was perhaps a subconscious, instinctual dislike expressed by Warsaw toward the Teutonic element, which was symbolized by the figure of the Walkyrie.[5]

For many Polish writers and journalists active in the 1890s, Wagner became the symbol of the "Teutonic element" and the expansive German nationalism, based on brute strength and lawlessness. Polish critics depicted the composer, with tacit permission from both Russian and Austrian censors (in that period, neither country was interested in promoting friendship with Prussia), as a caricature of himself. Interestingly, the broad literary portraits of the German composer were outlined with the same range of descriptions that served to create a distorted image of Prussia's military leader, Bismarck. Such stereotypical expressions may be found, for instance, in the following text penned by Zygmunt Jarecki:

> Now, in the period of enchantment (lit. "being drunk") with triumphant chauvinism, is Wagner's music not the best expression of this attitude of the (Prussian—M.D.) nation? Wagner's music is simultaneously filled with strength, wildness, energy, and arrogance—it is a music that overturns all hitherto established rules of composing music, in the same way as the spirit of contemporary Germans destroys the rules of the preexistent ethics.[6]

When seen against the backdrop of contemporaneous journalistic writings, which could be said to represent the mood of the society as a whole, as well when projected against the background of the generally mediocre level of reception of new music at this time, the Polish cult of Wagner appeared to be a phenomenon that was both limited in scope and marked by "elite" characteristics. However, even with its limitations this phenomenon deserves our attention, since it exemplifies a certain pattern in the Polish reception of Wagner's art. After 1908, this pattern became a binding convention not only for the musicians and critics (even the most conservative critics would not refer to Wagner in other terms, but as a "genius"), but also for those members of the general public who aspired to educate themselves and reach a more elevated level of culture.

The initial contacts of Polish composers and music critics with Wagner's oeuvre may be traced back to the 1880s. At that time, Poles first articulated and developed their initial approach to understanding Wagnerian artistic concepts. Within this framework, a traditional respect for the achievements of Western European art competed with a series of objections which emerged from a confrontation between Wagner's new artistic proposals (known to Polish interpreters mostly from his writings and from the accounts by his German critics, especially Hanslick) with the system of aesthetic beliefs that predominated in Poland at that time. The core of the pre-existing aesthetic system was formed by a notion of music as a domain of feelings. Music's potential for arousing emotions in the listeners endowed this art with the power to uplift its listeners into the world of universal values, the domain of beauty, goodness and truth.

One consequence of this attitude—a very important one, if considered from the viewpoint of the attitude adopted by critics belonging to an earlier generation of positivists—was a conviction that the true value of music resided in the domain of the Ideal. This Ideal was most frequently interpreted as being of essentially Christian, or humanitarian nature. Needless to say, such ideals could have been realized only in those works of music that had the capability to stir "higher" feelings in their recipients:

> If sensations that music creates in us were only something of the kind as, for instance, nervous attacks, music would have been a supremely interesting means for conducting research into human pathologies, but it would have ceased to be an art. Fortunately, it is not so. Music contains a certain, more sublime element in itself. The aesthetic of beauty in music is not an empty illusion. [7]

Thus wrote, in 1883, Leon Piniński, one of the most eminent Galician politicians and a great lover of music, especially Wagner. The culture critics who belonged to the generation active after the January Uprising (1863-64) used the framework of idealized interpretations of music's true meaning and value as a conceptual background for a detailed system of postulates pertaining to the content and form of the musical work. They believed that adhering to these postulates guaranteed the physical embodiment of the Ideal in sound; thus, the Ideal was concealed within music. This concept of music as a medium for universal values was based on the principle that the realization of the Ideal through music took place in the process of communicating the music's content to the listener. Therefore, certain ideas were placed at the center of this theoretical system of postulates; these ideas guaranteed the selection of the best and the most efficient means of communication. Such ideas were borrowed from an assortment of notions about the nature of art that underlined classic aesthetics.

In the second half of the 19th century, their most ardent followers included Eduard Hanslick. According to this aesthetic position, a musical work should be harmonious, simple, clearly structured, comprehensive, and direct in expression. These traits summed up the ideals upheld by writers representing a classical strain in Polish thought, a predominant orientation at the end of the century. This strain of musical idealism was complemented by a universally shared conviction about the fundamental role of melody and harmony as the basic carriers of musical expression.

Obviously, Wagner's music transgresses aesthetic ideals construed in this way. Therefore, for writers from the positivist generation, despite their great respect for Wagner as a famous Western European composer, the strongest impetus in their discussions about Wagner's music was directed toward de-bunking particular traits or imperfections detected in his works. In the 1880s and 1890s, one thought persistently returned in the expressions and statements of the luminaries of Polish music criticism—Jan Kleczyński, Stanisław Ciechomski, Aleksander Poliński, and Zygmunt Noskowski. All these critics made comments about the lack of compatibility between Wagnerian art and the classical model of creativity, which was unanimously accepted as a universal truth, transcending time. For instance, Stanisław Ciechomski, a music critic for Warsaw's main daily, *Kurier Warszawski*, wrote:

> Wagner's most important accomplishment is undoubtedly his outstanding ability to use instrumental-symphonic elements in the realm of stage music. We should not forget, however, that his Muse, accustomed to enormous, misty forms of the North, could not behave well in its impetuousness and could not fit in with any measure of classical restraint. Therefore, despite the music's undeniable greatness, so many abuses were introduced, in their almost caricatural over-abundance, and so one-sided was the theoretical zeal, that, despite Wagner's intentions to the contrary, a longing emerged for deliverance by other composers, who could better rule over this wonderful and dangerous material.[8]

Of all the Wagnerian achievements, representatives of positivistic school in Polish music criticism accepted only those that adhered to (albeit in the most general outlines) the principles of classical aesthetics. Therefore, according to the vast majority of writers, Wagner was the master of "beautiful fragments." Their existence proved that the origins of his art were "inspired," and, therefore, authentic. In contrast, far-reaching musical, poetic, and theatrical ideas that permeated his dramas were viewed as "over-wrought" in the manner of purely intellectual, cerebral solutions to artistic issues: "As often as Wagner may, and wants to, follow his inspiration without constraining himself by paying attention to his own theories, that many times he is able to create wonderful musical fragments." Thus wrote Jan Kleczyński in 1883, expressing one of the longest-lasting (and most wide-spread in Poland) opinions about Wagner.[9]

The next, difficult issue, with which the earliest Polish interpreters of Wagnerian ideas had to struggle, was the question of the synthesis of the arts in Wagner's *Kunstwerk der Futur* (artwork of the future). The attitude towards such attempts of removing borders between the individual arts was generally quite negative. Critics who discussed this question—also in reference to program music—often expressed reservations concerning the expected reduction of the impact of individual arts to the minimum, when "one art attempts to take the place of another" while reaching for effects that are essentially foreign to it and, therefore, "unnatural."

Such statements appear in numerous declarations of ambiguous feelings about literature entering the domain of music in program music and in music drama, where the relative significance of music and literature shifted to the detriment of music. Opinions critical of uniting literature with music were penned by such eminent critics as: Antoni Sygietyński, Stanisław Niewiadomski, Władysław Bogusławski, and Aleksander Poliński. Let us review a statement made by a representative of the younger generation, Antoni Miller. After the Polish premiere of *Die Valküre* in 1903, he wrote:

> The principal axis of Wagner's new ideas consists in assigning to the orchestra a primary role, both in the broadening of its scope, and in enriching its range of instrumental colors. Nonetheless, as far as the musical ideas are concerned... in the libretto, we see the poet's predilection for themes borrowed from Germanic mythology. Myths and fantasy made it easier for Wagner to embody, through visible symbols, the living ideals of the whole humankind. Abstract art, even when envisioned by the boldest artists, also demands becoming more vivid by being visualized; thus endowed, it is better able to serve the music, to serve the ideals of an artistic-philosophical kind. Wagner created an idea of "mixing" all the fine arts in the temple of Melpomene. Was it a lucky

thought, or not? Because of the mutual dependence of the stage imagery on the music and the poetic content of the libretto, we have to regard this idea as a very useful one, as long as it does not transgress against particular characteristics that are typical for each of the arts thus united. In this case, the music, in regard to the image on the stage, assumes the role of a "metaphor:" it speaks with a centrifugal force, by moving outwards from within, revealing the deepest secrets of the human psyche. There also are moments when the word has an advantage over the, then, supportive domains of music and the fine arts.

When borders that the arts touch upon and the framework of the aesthetic supremacy of one of them, are being considered, these mutual relationships depend on the content of the libretto, as well as on the creative capabilities and the point of view of the author. In this respect Wagner was not a good example. He spoke more powerfully as a musician than as a poet, though the whole conception of the music drama is marked by an overpowering, Titanic mood. Expanding the scope of his poetic texts caused the expansion of the whole "Kunstwerk" and suffused the actions on the stage with a certain literary "stiffness," an impression of being "contrived" and artificial. Despite such important faults, there are several expressions of genius filled with creative inspiration that force us to pay homage to the bold idea of connecting all the arts.[10]

Music critics active in the 1880s and 1890s approached Wagner's ideas pertaining to the dramatic aspects of his works by applying conceptual frameworks borrowed from contemporaneous theater criticism, and developed on the aesthetic foundation of realism. In analytical studies based on these principles three main issues predominated:

1) the appraisal of the suitability of the choice of subjects in Wagner's libretti which seemed to the Polish writers, brought up on realistic literature, to constitute an evident breach of the basic principle of drama, that is the probability of situations and characters;[11]
2) the issue of dramatic action, which, according to many critics, was too extended and slow; therefore the majority of Wagnerian productions on the operatic stages in Warsaw and Lwów/Lemberg featured a profoundly abbreviated musical-verbal text; and, finally,
3) the issue of the role of music in the amplification of dramatic themes and characters, and in assisting the stage action.

The latter issue was most frequently connected to the concept of the *Leitmotif* and its basic function, which was considered to consist in a literal illustration of the stage circumstances or a psychological situation.

Few writers revealed an awareness of the existence of a deeper, symbolic meaning of the *Leitmotifs*. These thinkers included Leon Piniński, cited above. His interpretation of the function of the *Leitmotifs* brought to mind a well-known formulation by Maeterlinck, cited by Zenon Przesmycki in a study which was published eight years after Leon Piniński's, and entitled *Maurice Maeterlinck and his Position in the Literature of Belgium and the World*: "The symbol is an organic, internal, allegory; its roots are deeply hidden in darkness."[12]

Piniński extraordinarily well intuited the existence of the double, deep structure of the meaning of Wagnerian *Leitmotifs*, by emphasizing their mysterious qualities and the plurality of meanings. Thus, the *Leitmotifs* were thought to be "disappearing in darkness" of the consciousness of the artist.[13] As stated earlier, the reasoning used by Leon Piniński in this case had no parallels or equivalents in the whole Polish reflection on Wagner prior to 1900. Other writers, including figures of the status of Stanisław Przybyszewski,[14] remained faithful to the realistic reading of *Leitmotifs* as allegories with a single meaning. Such a simple allegory, in accordance with the second part of Maeterlinck's definition, "has roots in the light, but its top is wilted and barren."[15]

Writers of a positivistic orientation, when writing about Wagner, cherished an ambition to solve the Wagnerian "problem" in its historic context by outlining the origins and evolution of his theories. This task was easily accomplished by analyzing statements made by the composer himself and contained in his treatise *Oper und Drama*. The primary goal of this process was to define the place of Wagner's music drama in the creation of the "music of the future." It is important to note that before 1900, this role was perceived in a negative light. The main line of accusations raised against Wagner by the principal music critics of the time, including Zygmunt Noskowski and Jan Kleczyński, involved highlighting an extreme character of the intentions of the "Bayreuth prophet." He was perceived as distorting the hitherto continuous and "natural" direction of the development of music. For Noskowski and his colleagues, Wagnerian ideas brought about a serious crisis in musical creativity in the West, especially in Germany. One anti-Wagnerian statement by Zygmunt Noskowski, included in his article entitled "The Reform of the Fugue" ("Reforma fugi"), contains a claim that

> unfortunately, Wagner left after himself an extremely numerous progeny of pessimists. Yes, it is true! Due to his influence, principles of Schopenhauer's philosophy have spread so horribly and predominated so widely among even the most serious musicians. Without "this apostle of doubt" this phenomenon could not have happened in the most ideal— and of its nature optimistic—art of sound. Nowadays, there are artists

who are so snobbish that they cannot listen to any other music but the latest works by Wagner, because all other music seems too simple, too naive for them. These people appear to resemble such gourmet connoisseurs of food who, after losing their sensitivity of palate due to culinary abuses, have to stimulate their taste with ever stronger spices. . . A mixing of notions is the main characteristic of today's artistic trends. While certain creative people are lost among the dark dungeons of shallow eclecticism, others cry out, in resignation: "Alas! Invention in music is deeply exhausted."[16]

Jan Kleczyński considered the post-Wagnerian crisis in European music in a more optimistic light. He expressed trust in the correctness of the mechanism of progress, a belief characteristic of positivist thinkers, in the following words:

The progress of imagination and aesthetic concepts is slow and connected with many a step backwards. On the basis of this law, we may observe that even when a genius of the first rank will illuminate an issue with his ideas, immediately following this step forward certain difficulties arise, caused by attempts to move back the triumphant chariot. Such difficulties most frequently result from the violent pressure of the stream of culture that incessantly flows forward. This is the state of Wagnerian music which cast a blinding light on the issues of dramatic-musical truth, and which, simultaneously, brought within itself an onslaught of exaggeration and a lack of proportion of dimensions. Such traits often caused Wagner's music to be exhausting with its tedious uniformity; only new creative efforts may remove such faults from this method.[17]

In the word "method" used by Kleczyński we find an important indication allowing us to clarify the position of positivistic writers toward Wagner's significance for contemporary music. This is the crux of the matter: not an aesthetic revolution, not an ideological proposition, but a project of creating a certain technique to deal with sounds and poetic material. Positivistic critics thought that such technique could have turned out useful for Wagner's followers, on condition, though, that it be used judiciously and with reason, that is, on condition that it would remain subordinate to the timeless classical rules of musical composition. Such an interpretation of the historical significance of Wagner's artistic concepts allowed conservative critics to appreciate the influence of the creator of the *Kunstwerk der Futur* on the music of contemporary composers when this influence was carefully isolated and limited to the domain of technical means, which were mostly restricted to harmony and instrumentation. In order to illustrate the conviction, widespread in the 1890s, about the benefits that newer music may take from such controlled contacts with

Wagnerian art, we should once again cite Jan Kleczyński. In 1891, he reviewed a now-forgotten composition by Adam Münchheimer:

> The first accomplishment of this composition is that it clearly reflects its title and that its features include a straightforward formal framework and easily comprehensible themes... Wagner's influence may be recognized very distinctly here, both in instrumentation, and in bolder than usual harmonic passages. Nonetheless, this influence reveals itself in a limited fashion and does not erase the beauty of the contours of the work; neither does it harm the individuality of its author.[18]

At the time when Noskowski, Ciechomski and Kleczyński made public their views on the subject of Wagner's art, a conviction was strengthened in the milieu of Polish music critics that the ideas of the German composer continued to lose their validity every day and that his music was definitely in the process of being moved to the attic of the past. This conviction was supported by the successes of new Italian opera associated with the style of *verismo*. Conservative Polish critics welcomed *verismo* as a rebirth of the valuable classical operatic conventions; in this style, works were based on a realistic libretto and exposed the warmly welcomed element of *cantabile* singing.[19]

Unexpectedly, however, interest in Wagner resurged around 1900 among a younger generation of writers and journalists who transformed the German composer into a hero of their times. They inscribed reflections about his artistic ideas into the context of programs postulated for the future of "young" art and literature in Poland. Paradoxically, these representatives of the Young Poland movement were not concerned with Wagner's works as such; they added little to the conventions of interpreting these works established by the previous generation.[20] The Young Poland critics continued to maintain a reserved stance toward the ultra-German themes of Wagnerian music dramas[21] and toward many of Wagner's artistic solutions, particularly those pertaining to the synthesis of the arts. Despite declarations of some writers belonging to the Young Poland movement, which drew abundant inspirations from aesthetical principles of Wagner's concept of music drama, we have to agree that this concept was of secondary importance to this movement in general. It was embraced only by a minority, represented mainly (though not exclusively) by Stanisław Wyspiański. In contrast, the majority of Polish Wagner-aficionados active in the period 1898-1905 focused their attention on a reconstruction and remaking of the image of the artist, finding in him a model for a particular artistic and social stance that they wished to promote.[22] This model was fully coherent with the figure of the Hero, a construct widely popular among the Young Poland artists and symbolizing their key conviction about the value of individuality. Young Poland cherished the unique place of the Artist-Hero in the world; the artist was an eminent, unique individual who lived in the state of permanent mutiny against the "Philistine" society at large. A heroic re-interpretation of Wagner's life, which was developed in a communal effort by such authors as Cezary Jellenta, Władysław Jabłonowski, Walery Gostomski, Antoni Miller, Ignacy Matuszewski and Artur Górski, had a very peculiar dimension.[23] Here, an individual embodied the collective. The "chosen one"—the hero that Wagner became in the eyes of the younger artists—had the ability to empathize with and express the fate of the whole human kind. It is to this ability that interpretations of the essence of the creative intentions of the artist were addressed.

The basic formula in the approach developed by writers known today as the authors of the earliest programs of Young Poland in the realm of literature—programs that clearly favored social activity of a revolutionary kind—used as their motto selected words from the Promethean *Oda do młodości* (Ode to Youth) by Adam Mickiewicz. Under the pens of such authors as Jellenta or Górski, the cult of Wagner gave rise to a Promethean myth interpreted in accordance with its most fundamental version, where Prometheus is the synonym not only of freedom, but also primarily of knowledge, consciousness, and self-awareness.[24] In the eyes of the Young Poland writers, Wagner was, first and foremost, a courageous reformer, who, to borrow an expression from Nietzsche, "cast light on contemporary life and on the past with the ray of knowledge that was so strong that one could see as far as never before."[25]

It is not accidental that I cite Nietzsche's words from *Untimely Meditations*, because this book provided the ideological framework for the "Promethean" interpretation of Wagner's life and art.[26] In addition to the vision of Wagner as a facilitator to the mission of a rebirth of art that would save humanity, this interpretation consisted of a reconstruction of his personality as an exemplar of a typical romantic mutiny. This was a struggle against both with the conventions that limited the arts, and the social-civilizing limitations that delayed the universal acceptance of the *Kunstwerk der Futur*. With a particular insistence, Young Poland writers focused on Wagner's thread of idealistic activism; they justified such activism in moral categories. They assigned typically heroic features to his personality and considered him an exemplar of such virtues as: the will to goodness, the wish to make art nobler, and to thus ennoble the human kind through art (these traits are also discussed by Nietzsche).[27]

"For us, Bayreuth denotes the dawn on the day of the battle"—this sentence from Nietzsche perfectly illustrates Young Poland's approach.[28] In this interpretation, Wagner's idealistic activities were considered a counter-lever to contemporaneous disorientation of ideals and a general, spiritual decline of art. Here, the work of the "Prophet of Bayreuth" itself became—on equal footing with accomplishments of other romantic "Prometheans," such as Byron, Shelley, or Nietzsche,—"an expression of hatred of ill will in nature. . . a poeticized anger at the evil rule of the world." The words I just cited came from under the pen of Cezary Jellenta, the first Polish theoretician of "Prometheanism" who was known as a co-creator of the manifesto entitled *Forpoczta* (Forepost).[29]

The first indication of a changed understanding of Wagner's art, which was brought about by the Young Poland movement, is an article by Władysław Jabłonowski, entitled "Richard Wagner: A Poet and Thinker." This text does not yet contain a mature, precise understanding of the role that Wagner played in the shaping of the aesthetic program of new "young" art. Instead, the article is thematically connected to the discussions which took place prior to 1900. The author interpreted the art of Wagner as a characteristic product of social relations of his period and wrote about a particularly sensuous—"nervous" or "narcotic"—impact of his art on his listeners.[30] The originality of Jabłonowski's approach to Wagnerian program lies in the fact that the author sought to convince his readers about the greatness of the German composer. As Jabłonowski writes, in Wagner's work there is a hidden "clear condemnation of contemporaneous civilization based on abuse, egotistical life, and the absence of love."[31]

The particular effect that Wagner's music had on its listeners was, for the young journalist, yet another proof of the greatness of his work: it testified to the potential of feelings and emotions that were contained in the music. "We do not find one truly great work, by one genius that, with his abundant productivity, the power of emotions and feelings stimulated in us, would not shake us up too much, would not storm the soul, and therefore, would not abuse and strain our nerves."[32] After this forerunner, the Young Poland's "Wagnerian frenzy" in its fully developed form began with a series of articles by a Warsaw literary critic, Walery Gostomski. His essays, entitled "Bayreuth Theater and its Significance," "Wagnerian Drama," and "The Tragedy of An Artist," began their existence in the form of public lectures that the author gave in 1902 and 1903 at the Warsaw Philharmonic. Gostomski published these lectures in an encyclopedic monthly *Biblioteka Warszawska*, and, in 1904, also in book format, in a collection of essays *From the Past and the Present*. The first of these essays followed traditional thematic threads fully congruent with those permeating the text by Jabłonowski, discussed above. With youthful zeal, the author expressed an opposition to widespread convictions about the supposed "Philistine" character of Bayreuth celebrations. Gostomski emphasized the spiritual character of

Wagner's art, seen in a more prominent light when presented against the general background of the *fin-de-siècle* culture, touched, as it was, by a stigma of decadence. The young writer states:

> Bayreuth spectacles, repeated sometimes several years apart, attract to the distant Bavarian town a colorful and multi-linguistic crowd, consisting of representatives from almost the whole civilized world. In the hotels, there is lively agitation; on the streets you may see, passing by each other, elegant dandies and fashionable ladies, well-born aristocrats and well-gilded plutocrats. The representatives of artistic and intellectual worlds are not missing either. Thoughtful faces, nervous faces, people exhausted with an overabundance of reflections, impressions and feelings, continue to appear in front of the eyes of an attentive observer... Bayreuth became fashionable and this is to a large extent the reason for its popularity today... But how did this theater obtained this honor? An explanatory circumstance for the Bayreuth fashion is the unusual character and the originality of Wagnerian theater and of the arts cultivated there. This consideration is of particularly great significance for contemporary people, who, faced by a horrifying spiritual vacuum of the world that has become completely materialized, suffer a sickening hunger for impressions and greedily devour all the peculiar and unusual foods, that stir in them, even momentarily, a hope for satisfaction. Therein arise all these decadentisms, impressionisms, symbolisms, and other "-isms," which so predominantly affect contemporaneous culture of *fin-de-siècle* Europe. To a great extent, Wagnerian cult belongs in their number...The art of Wagner ... promises so many extraordinary, powerful impressions; it attracts with such charm that every proper modernist has to become its adherent, out of sheer duty. Numerous Wagnerian admirers of this kind continue to fill the Bayreuth theater... Therefore this cultural "tone," as long as it is an expression which predominantly rules in the so-called "good society" of the present epoch, seems to me not only to be in great conflict, but even to directly contradict the essence of Wagnerian art, particularly as it is revealed in the Bayreuth theater, that is to be the realization of artistic ideals of the master... Wagner demanded, first of all, that the stage was not a means of entertainment but rather a spiritual locus. He understood its artistic and social mission literally, by elevating music theater to the level of a true priesthood of art... The Wagnerian ideal of dramatic and theatrical arts undoubtedly belongs among the most significant manifestations of contemporary spiritual strivings. It is so distant from the existing reality that even its precise and clear definition may be posed with a great difficulty.[33]

In successive treatises, Gostomski attempted to develop his own concept of the meaning of Wagnerian art and of its superlative ideological and artistic features. This further work was based on a foundation of inspiration flowing from a different source than Nietzschean ideas, namely from the writings of a French writer about aesthetics active in the period of naturalism, Jean Maria Guyau. The French author was read in *fin-de-siècle* Poland with great interest because of his particular range of subjects and a passionate, almost devotional, literary style, which well harmonized with the engaged, enthusiastic stance assumed by the Polish journalists of the time. Furthermore, Poles were impressed with the persuasive power of the concept of the philosophy of man, formulated by Guyau on the basis of a principle of a harmonious development of human personality. Finally, Polish writers warmly received the idea of an organic integration of society and nature, which was accomplished through morality (born of the communal strivings and desires of humankind), religion (born of the commonwealth of ideas), and art (born of the shared feelings sand impressions).[34]

Fig. 2: Postcard of Kraków, "Square with the Town Hall Tower," sent to Paris on 22 October 1902, with greetings in French, including the location of Sukiennice, the Our Lady Catholic Church, and the home of the author marked with an asterisk. Maja Trochimczyk Collection.

The dependence of Gostomski's conceptions on Guyau's theory of art is revealed by his conscious use of quotations from the French philosopher. Gostomski cited Guyau when attempting to explain the overwhelming influence of the conceptual trinity of "art, idea and faith" in Wagnerian world and to indicate that intertwined principles of dramatic intensity and advanced harmonic language constitute the highest levels in Wagner's oeuvre. In a treatise entitled *The Tragedy of an Artist*, Gostomski provided the shortest definition of Wagner's artistic objectives as the "organic unity of action." In Gostomski's view, Wagner's objective was, suitably for this intrepid warrior for the Art of the Future, the "artistic ideal tantamount . . . with humanitarian ideals, and later also with religious ideals of humankind."[35] With insistence, Gostomski emphasized in all of his statements the "intensity" of Wagner's art. He coined for this state a neologism ("intensywizm") which meant Wagner's striving to express in art "all of his soul, all fullness of his fully human life"—to cite the words of scholar Henryk Markiewicz.[36] This intensity of expression produced an unusually high energy level and unified expression, which could be transmitted to the listeners, thus allowing the music to fulfill the highest purpose of Wagnerian art, which was—according to Guyau—accepted by all other creative individuals engaged in art-making: to infuse into all individuals the most sublime impressions and feelings.

Among many enthusiasts of Guyau's aesthetics who studied Wagner's works at the turn of the century, the name of Eduard Schuré should be mentioned. He penned a book entitled *Music Drama: Richard Wagner, His Oeuvre and Ideals*. In 1903, this book was published in Polish translation by Emilia Węsławska with an introduction by Władysław Jabłonowski. Let us review a quotation from this book, a fragment from the summary, the content of which was strictly correlated to the ideas considered by Walery Gostomski, and which, therefore, may serve as a motto for the type of "Wagnerian frenzy" which sought inspiration in the thought of the French philosopher of aesthetics:

> The example of Richard Wagner indicates to us, in an unexpected, though distinct, way, what creative power connected with faith and artistry may accomplish in our epoch. Well-understood reform of the opera, or the rebirth of musical drama, instead of being subject to some kind of a system, could, in contrast, become the foretelling of a true freedom. Here, we do not encounter the trampling of earlier musical and poetic forms, but a new development, growing through a closer mutual intertwining of both. The borrowing of an expressive language from a Beethoven symphony; the rhythms of prosody, being in their essence the movement of passionate speech itself, at the moment of emergence of melody from speech, with a resonance that led to the re-birth of a narrative (*recitativo*); choirs transformed into active personalities participating in the drama; even an appearance of a simple folk song—all of these innovative ideals reveal themselves in Richard Wagner's drama. They blend into each other with the flow of life. They are united into an organic whole that could not have been presented to us in opera until our times. We call this approach

to artistic creativity "liberty," because whoever speaks of liberty, that person also speaks about the full, total self-expression of a person; a self-expression that simultaneously appeals to the senses, to the soul, and to the mind. Such self-expression arouses in us the highest level of activity with its sudden, yet harmonious outbursts.[37]

A welcoming reception that greeted Schuré's book in Poland was connected to another aspect of the Young Poland's cult of Wagner, i.e., its paradoxical links to French culture. In its essence, this approach cast European culture as a controversy between the North, represented by the Germanic element with the South, represented by Romance cultures (France, Italy, and Spain). In certain social circles, especially in Warsaw, Wagner was received via French literature; Warsaw music critics were enthusiastic about its subtlety and finesse in regard to its ability to present Wagnerian ideas. A statement by Czesław Halicz is symptomatic in this respect:

> In Eduard Schuré, as in certain Belgians, with a mixture of Flemish and Valon blood, in an interesting and particular way traits of two races are interconnected: the romance face and the Germanic one. Here mysticism is connected to sensuality, inclination to metaphysical considerations with clarity and transparency of form, high-strung emotionalism with moderation and self-control. No purely French writer could have empathized so deeply with Wagner's music dramas... No German writer could have presented Wagner as a drama-writer and poet so comprehensively, clearly and elegantly, without any unnecessary digressions... This small book about Wagner explains more precisely the essence of his dramatic oeuvre than many of those massive German volumes now seemingly constituting the whole of Wagnerian literature.[38]

The most original type of critical reflection about Wagner came into being in the first, most lively phase of the Wagnerian frenzy for which the year 1905 provides the temporal limit. This was the year of the outbreak of a revolution, and at the same time, the date of publication of the first programmatic statements made by the representatives of the Young Poland in Music. The manifestos appeared on the pages of the periodical *The Lute Player* ("Lutnista"). This reflection resulted in the confrontation of the oeuvre of the German composer with the works of Polish romantic poets, such as Juliusz Słowacki, Adam Mickiewicz, and Zygmunt Krasiński. This form of literary-musical juxtaposition was the goal of literary critics representing a neo-romantic stance, especially Artur Górski and Ignacy Matuszewski. The approach resulted in the inclusion of Wagnerian ideals and their interpretations in the context of the Young Poland's cult of the three national prophet or bards ("wieszcz"). According to an expert in this subject, Henryk Markiewicz, the primary importance of such elevated cultural figures was ideological: it was the significance of "proclaiming a national-moral rebirth" through the re-discovery of the primacy of the three poets, accepted as spiritual leaders of the nation.[39]

For writers of a neo-romantic orientation, Wagner became the embodiment of a specific mission that was related either exclusively to the nation, or to the whole humankind. In the texts by Matuszewski and Górski, he played a similar role to that of Gostomski's essays. They both were able to recognize a moralistic effect in the position taken by Wagner in his aesthetics of art. However, the two writers interpreted the philosophical essence of Wagner's artistic objectives in a different fashion. This difference stemmed in part from their choices of method and the selection of the subject for comparison: Matuszewski compared Wagner with Słowacki, whereas Górski compared Wagner with Mickiewicz.

In a 1902 treatise of fundamental importance for the development of Polish neo-romantic literature, *Słowacki and the New Art (Modernism)*, Matuszewski attempted to find common denominators in the ideological and aesthetic stances of Słowacki and Wagner. The writer placed a particularly strong emphasis on the profound similarity between psychological traits of these two artists, believing that this phenomenon could impact the content and character of works by both creative individuals. Matuszewski singled out their inclination towards mysticism and their ability to place spiritual engagement within the context of humanity's progressive development. While comparing Słowacki's obscure and sophisticated masterpiece, *Król Duch* (King Spirit), with the Wagnerian Tetralogy, the critic devoted much room to the perceived aesthetic kinship of both works. He considered both artworks as attempts at creating a "monumental" or "gigantic" art, i.e., an art form that would be innovative and would transcend the borders separating individual arts and artistic genres. Matuszewski also noticed another trait shared by Wagner and Słowacki, that is their way of expressing ideas with the assistance of symbols. He interpreted this form of expression as a clear manifestation of the artist's striving to expand art beyond the borders limited by everyday reality.

The most significant place in the theory of Matuszewski was taken by an attempt at locating Wagner and Mickiewicz within artistic currents flowing through the history of European culture. They became, according to Matuszewski, participants in the "pageant of great spirits." The poet and the composer belonged among the most important contributors to the great heritage of European culture and its evolution toward knowledge and progress. Apparently, these two men were invaluable and noble successors to such great innovators as Leonardo da Vinci or Johann Wolfgang von Goethe. Matuszewski writes:

> Whoever would read and listen intently to Wagner's *Rheingold, Die Valküre, Siegfried and Gotterdämmerung*, this person would immediately feel a certain stylistic kinship between the gigantic Tetralogy of the German reformer of art and the monumental, yet haphazardly moody epic by the Polish romantic. Both in *The Ring of the Nibelungs* and in *King Spirit* the foundation for the work is created by a subjective metaphysical and mystical doctrine, which was to contain the "mystery of the beginning and the end," "the Alpha and Omega" of the world. Both Wagner and Słowacki considered themselves prophets and bards, who influenced human minds and hearts by means of fashioning beautiful artistic forms, in which they captured their internal visions. In the case of both artists, these visions were made more vivid through the use of symbols of a great spiritual-cosmic process. Wagner and Słowacki looked upon the human life as a transient phenomenon behind which the mighty streams of mystical forces were hidden, forces that push the Universe towards higher goals. Therefore, the figures of both poets do not have much in common with everyday life. These are great, Titanic beings; rich in spiritual content, but completely separated from the earth. These artists are embodied dreams and moods, the symbols of powers which…propel forward the heavy "burden" of the real world.[40]

While outlining his vision of the significance of Wagner's art, Matuszewski highlighted associations with the concept of Prometheanism, guided by the imperative of progress; the use of such a rhetorical gesture was typical in Polish neo-romantic literature. This concept gained currency among writers with the background of the positivistic cult of knowledge and among those who believed in the validity of the traditional belief in the role of the artist as a spiritual leader of society.

Another group of writers associated with the neo-romantic period, such a Marian Zdziechowski or Artur Górski, discovered in the oeuvre of Polish romantic poets an ideological attitude transcending, with its scope and moral impact, the idea of Prometheanism. It was the Messianic concept of the progress of civilization, enriched by a religious element and directly linked to a current socio-political reality. A comparison of both concepts (Prometheanism and Messianism) preoccupied Górski; he summarized his views in a monograph on Mickiewicz, published in 1907 with a revealing Wagnerian title of *Monsalvat*. The writer was wonderfully able to capture the difference between both spiritual conceptions by comparing two great personalities of artists who represented them in an exemplary fashion: Wagner as an exemplar of Prometheanism and Mickiewicz of Messianism. Górski interpreted Wagnerian stance as a consequence of a reflective attitude, typical for Germans, i.e., a tendency to enclose oneself in the hermetic circle of "higher spiritual matter." In contrast, Mickiewicz was an example of a creative individual who overcame his alienation and who was capable of connecting the experience of nothingness of contemporaneous world with being active in the same world. Górski writes:

> German philosophy ended on this stage of reflective approach. In contrast, the author of *The Forefathers* went further in the same direction and searched for the foundation of these principles in life. He distinguished intellectual approach from the spiritual, a merely wise man from a sage. He based his work on the hierarchy of spiritual values; he protested against everything that threatened to destroy this hierarchy and suffered profoundly while watching the tightly tied networks of mistakes and crimes committed through the ages and resulting in a horrifying chaos that stole from people their best destinies. German romanticism, while commencing from the same principles . . . was not capable of producing an epoch-changing individuality of vital importance for the time. Its last "knight," Richard Wagner, overwhelmed with contempt for the modern world and filled with a sense of absolute solitude, considered the arts alone as the source of the highest revelation in human life. Furthermore, these arts could come into being solely in the minds of very few individuals. According to this vision of the world, a person may feel free only through an engagement with the arts. Mickiewicz's protest, directed against contemporary civilization had, by its very nature, to go much further, it had to attack the ethical foundation of the existence itself.[41]

Górski's text should be considered as a turning point in the reception of Wagner by the Young Poland movement. It was a symbolic farewell to forms of adoration of the "prophet from Bayreuth" that were initiated by statements by Nietzsche, Shuré, and other early adherents to the "Promethean" approach. The historical moment of this farewell marked a post-revolutionary turning point in Polish literary writings, which, at that time, quite openly and, indeed, rather rudely examined the aesthetic fascinations of artists associated with Young Poland and outlined a new path for the future development of culture which would be both socially and politically engaged. "Action" was the main ideal in this type of culture, an ideal first formulated by Stanisław Brzozowski. The program of such "Action," popularized with a particular zeal by a group of writers whose sympathies were aligned with the ideology of national democracy, was particularly unfriendly towards those manifestations of artistic life which were connected to European fascinations with the previous epoch. An article published in 1912 by the main ideological writer of *Kurier Warszawski*, Bolesław Lutomski, contained accusations cast against the Wagnerian movement, claiming that "with art on its banners and with contempt for the common man, it bypassed the most essential issues and festering wounds of its own society."[42]

The year 1907 is the final cut-off date of the Young Poland's cult of Wagner also in an aesthetic sense. The last of the great Wagnerian premieres produced in Poland—a staging of the *Nüremberg Singers* in Warsaw (1908)—provided Polish music critics with an opportunity to compare and contrast the achievements of the German composer with the oeuvres of other composers who at that time captured the imagination and the hearts of Polish public. These two composers were Richard Strauss whose *Salome*, staged in Warsaw in 1908, gave an excuse for the last universal manifestation of profound interest in music in pre-war Poland, and Claude Debussy, whose greatness found adherents and advocates among the visitors to Parisian performances of *Pelleas et Melisande*. This confrontation was resolved to the benefit of Strauss and Debussy, not Wagner. After 1907, Wagner ceased to be considered the father of new music. This title was taken over by Strauss, Liszt, and, surprisingly, Berlioz. Actually, Berlioz's assumption of this role could give one a pause for thought.[43] A new map of directions in contemporary music was formalized and fixed, reflecting a new historical consciousness, according to which not music drama, but program music (primarily the symphonic poem), constituted the most important embodiment of musical modernism.

Despite the fact that, after 1907, Wagner ceased to be the star of first magnitude in Poland, the interest of music writers in this composer did not entirely disappear. An occasion to deal with Wagner was provided by a celebration of the 25th anniversary of his death, which took place in 1908. Another commemoration, of the 100th anniversary of his birth, was held in 1913. As it was often the case, these anniversaries encouraged scholars to research and write about the person and the music of Wagner. Several decades after Wagnerian ideas entered the domain of Polish reflection about music it was time to critically examine native attempts in the areas of their reception and interpretation. Of these broad historical surveys three deserve to be mentioned: a book *Richard Wagner* by Wacław Tadeusz Dobrzyński;[44] an in-depth study by Zdzisław Jachimecki which provided, for Poland, the foundation of knowledge about Wagner valid until today;[45] and a book by Stefan Kołaczkowski, *Richard Wagner as the Creator and Theoretician of Drama*. These three volumes appeared outside of the chronological scope outlined in my study of the period, but were thoroughly linked with the main ideas and the subject matter of that time.[46]

The first of these three studies brings a polemical reckoning with the whole Polish tradition of writing about Wagner. The author unveils and explains the genesis of the most important prejudices concerning the "decadent" nature of Wagnerian art, while accurately connecting these prejudices to the remnants of positivistic habits kept by writers who used as their models anti-Wagnerian statements by Max Nordau, Leo Tolstoy and others.[47] Instead of following these prejudiced writers, Dobrzyński proposed to view the genesis of Wagnerian art through the lens of the philosophy of Henri Bergson. The central place in reflecting about his concept of the synthesis of all arts in the *Kunstwerk der Futur* belongs to the study of the proportional participation of two opposing factors, intellect and intuition. Both factors contributed greatly to the *Kunstwerk's* realization.

Two later texts by Jachimecki and Kołaczkowski derive their inspiration from an interpretation of Wagner's oeuvre according to a moralistic, Promethean approach, developed by Young Poland writers and still continuing to attract attention of Polish intellectuals. Jachimecki's book casts the composer's figure in a characteristic costume of a "prophet" ("wieszcz"), who "does not see reality, but truthfulness higher than all reality; he sees not the illusion of the world, but its essence."[48] By modeling his approach on that of Matuszewski,[49] Jachimecki brought out the metaphysical aspects of Wagner's creative vision.

Jachimecki identified Wagnerian art with religion and with the divine mission. Simultaneously, he pointed out its humanism, by placing Wagner in the same rank as the greatest geniuses of European culture, such as Leonardo, Michaelangelo, Shakespeare, and Goethe. In Jachimecki's study, a detailed description of Wagner's creative evolution is based on the traditional principle of the unity of life and work, which results in styling the composer's biography upon the heroic-romantic model. Wagner, in Jachimecki's interpretation (to cite a contemporaneous work by Richard Fromme), is "suffering as Tannhauser, fearless as Siegfried, serene like Hans Sachs, and chaste like Parsifal."[50] In a still more distinct way, Jachimecki appealed to the accomplishments of Polish authors of the theory of Prometheanism, whose ideas were inspired by Guyau and Schuré. In Jachimecki's review of the Kraków celebration of the 100th anniversary of Wagner's birth in 1913, we may find the following intensely impassioned appeal, preceded with a longer quotation from Słowacki's *King Spirit*:

> With the thrice-united arts, Wagner wanted to influence humankind. He wanted to raise humanity to a higher level, make it more perfect; he was an apostle of its rebirth. A compassionate heart was an entrance ticket to Wagner's world; yet, without a solid proof of intellectual qualifications nobody could enter and find their bearings within it. Wagner believed in his divine mission; among people he proved the reality of this mission with the wonders of his masterpieces. He is also one of these 'great initiates' who proclaim their religion through their art. In this area, Wagner does not resemble anyone; he is absolutely unique.[51]

The author of the third important study of Wagnerian oeuvre created in the Young Poland period structured his text in a similar vein. Stefan Kołaczkowski belongs with those writers whose inspiration was drawn from Nietzschean ideas, in their activist, vitalist, optimistic versions, characteristic of Polish literature in the final years prior to World War I. (e.g. writings of Wacław Berent and Cezary Jellenta). Kołaczkowski compared Wagner with Wyspiański by emphasizing traits of faith, activity and generosity present in the oeuvre of both masters of drama.

The threads of aesthetic reflection in texts Young Poland writers that I highlighted in this essay reveal that these ideas were strongly grounded in non-aesthetic concepts, especially in social and political issues. This extra-musical background characterized not only Polish, but also all Western discourse about the arts that developed at the turn of the 19th and 20th centuries. At that time, humanistic thought faced the task of reconsidering the past and mapping the path towards the future. The correctness of my approach to this subject, emphasizing the ideological context in the reception of Wagner's oeuvre may be confirmed by a comparison with statements by foreign scholars researching the Wagnerian frenzy which erupted during the same period of 1880-1900 also in other European countries and America.

With insistence, these scholars emphasized the fact that the reception of Wagner's inventions was closely connected to the socio-political context provided by other aspects of culture of a given nation. For instance, Modris Eksteins[52] connected the outburst of the Wagnerian frenzy in France in the 1890s with the French fascination with Bismarck's Germany and its role as the ruler of the world. Similarly, Joseph Horowitz and Burton W. Peretti pointed out connections between American critics' interpretations of Wagner put forward in the same period and social-cultural values accepted by American society. These values were, respectively, religious dimensions of aesthetic discourse in the study by Horowitz, and democracy and its social consequences in Peretti's research.[53]

My study, focused on the synthesis of political and social threads in the reflection about Wagner by Young Poland and its predecessors, necessarily bypassed a series of secondary conceptual threads, which developed from the mainstream. I also omitted a series of famous names connected with these additional strains of thought. A review of the whole Wagnerian controversy in Poland at the turn of the century would require writing a monographic study of considerable size. One day, such a book should be written: the subject itself merits such attention. Wagner's oeuvre was linked to several fascinating episodes in the history of writing about music; reminding our readers about these multifaceted connections provides an opportunity of literally changing the image of Polish musical culture in that period.

Translated by Maja Trochimczyk

ENDNOTES

[1] The article first appeared in Polish, as "Wagner i Młoda Polska," (Wagner and the Young Poland) in *Muzyka* 46, no. 4 (2001): 27-45.

[2] The term "wieszcz" means "prophet" or inspired "bard" and is usually used in reference to three romantic poets, Mickiewicz, Słowacki, and Krasiński.

[3] This view permeates most historical surveys concerning the Young Poland period in Polish music. It is formulated among others by Stefania Łobaczewska ("Twórczość kompozytorska Młodej Polski" in *Z dziejów polskiej kultury muzycznej* (Kraków: PWM, 1966), 533; Józef Michał Chomiński, "Romantyzm- modernizm" in *Muzyka polska-informator* (Krakow: PWM, 1967, p. 120-121; and Teresa Chylińska, "Młoda Polska w muzyce: mit czy rzeczywistość" in *Muzyka polska a modernizm* (Kraków: PWM, 1981), 42-43.

[4] The most important of these performances was the Warsaw staging of *The Valkyrie* in 1903, a concert-stage production (without props or scenery) of *Parsifal* by the Warsaw Philharmonic in 1904, the Lwów premieres of *The Flying Dutchman, The Valkyrie*, and *Siegfried* in 1903. The period of highly publicized Wagnerian performances ends with the Warsaw premiere of *Die Meistersinger* in 1908.

[5] See Jadwiga Waydel-Dmochowska, *Dawna Warszawa* (Warsaw of the Olden Times) (Warsaw, 1958), 183.

[6] In the discussed period the conflicts and tensions between Austria and Prussia increased after Prussia created the North-German Union, from which Austria was excluded. The hostile attitudes between Prussia and Russia were delineated by the military treatise signed by Russia and France in 183. The literary stereotype of the "German enemy" is also discussed in Ewa Skorupa, *Lwowska satyra polityczna* (Lwów political satire) (Kraków, 1992), 87-93. The cited fragment by Zygmunt Jarecki appeared in an article "Narodowość w muzyce" (Nationality in music), issued in *Nowości Muzyczne* (Musical Novelties) no. 10 (1903).

[7] Leon Piniński, *O operze nowoczesnej i znaczeniu Ryszarda Wagnera oraz o 'Parsifalu" Wagnera* (About the modern opera and the significance of Richard Wagner and about "Parsifal" by Wagner) (Lwów, 1883), 3

[8] Stanisław Ciechomski, "Il Pagliacci" (sic!). *Kurier Warszawski* no. 288 (1892).

[9] Jan Kleczyński, "Par-si-fal." *Echo Muzyczne, Teatralne i Artystyczne* no. 4 (1883): 39

[10] Antoni Miller, "Z muzyki. Walkiria." *Głos* no. 10 (1903): 153.

[11] The following musings of the Galicia critic Wiktor Strusiński may illustrate the consequences of this type of approach: "In *Die Meistersinger* Wagner has already shaken off the early antropomorphisms and became an observer . . . We may without doubt call this work his best composition, because musical expression and the dramatic concept create in it a coherent, rational whole. The comedy draws its content from the environment, from the concrete experience of life... Its people are not models of myths and, what is most important, it does not contain any doves symbolizing the evening, nor mysterious swans which could confuse us with misunderstood effects or humor." From Wiktor Strusiński, "O dramatach Ryszarda Wagnera," *Tygodnik Słowa Polskiego* no. 9 (1902): 6.

[12] Maurice Maeterlinck, *Wybór dramatów* (Selected dramas). Translated and introduced by Zenon Przesmycki (Warsaw, 1894; reprinted in Wrocław, 1994), XLIV.
[13] Piniński, op. cit., 57.
[14] In his essay, "Chopin. Impromptu," published in the volume *Na drogach duszy* (On the paths of the soul), Przybyszewski wrote about Chopin-symbolist as the opposition to Wagner-realist: "In contrast to Wagner, who painted in his music the characters of his protagonists, consciously depicted the state of their souls, guided by an ideological, analytical sense adjusted his music to what happened on the stage - Chopin represented his complete subjectivity and represented only "naked" states of his soul, in their most diverse waves, because he contained the whole world within himself; its whole pain and suffering." See *Na drogach duszy* (Kraków, 1900), 99.
[15] Przybyszewski, op. cit.
[16] Zygmunt Noskowski, "Reforma fugi." *Echo Muzyczne, Teatralne, i Artystyczne* no. 399 (1891): 269.
[17] Jan Kleczyński, "Otello." *Kurier Codzienny* no. 274 (1893).
[18] Jan Kleczyński, "Koncert." *Kurier Codzienny* no. 332 (1891).
[19] Wagner's passage to the domain of the "Music of the Past" was announced by Stanisław Ciechomski in the article "Il Pagliacci" cited earlier.
[20] Irena Sławińska noted the existence of this paradox while distinguishing three stages in the reception of Wagner at the turn of the century: the initial period of assimilating his concept of music theatre, the stage of fascination with his philosophy in the early years of the 20th century, and the "late" stage of interest in his music in the final years before the outbreak of the war. See Irena Sławińska, introduction to *Myśl teatralna Młodej Polski* (Warsaw, 1966): 9-10.
[21] See, for instance, Adolf Chybiński, "Śpiewacy—Mistrzowie norymberscy Ryszarda Wagnera." *Sfinks* (April 1908): 270.
[22] This period is delineated by the moment of the debut of the young generation of writers, on the one hand, and by the outbreak of the 1905 revolution, on the other.
[23] Cezary Jellenta (1891-1935) was a well-known literary critic, the editor of social-literary periodicals, *Ateneum* and *Rydwan*. He was educated as a lawyer. Władysław Jabłonowski (1865-1956) was a literary critic and a politician, in the 1920s an eminent politician active in the National-Democracy movement, member of the board of Stronnictwo Narodowe. In the area of literature, he was an expert in Western literature that he promoted in texts published by national-democratic periodicals of the Young Poland period, including *Głos, Przegląd Wszechpolski, Gazeta Warszawska*. Walery Gostomski (1854-?), a graduate of the Rys Polytechnic, in the Young Poland period was a popular journalist specializing in drama (Shakespearean, among others); he collaborated with Poland's most prestigious periodicals, including *Kurier Warszawski*. Antoni Miller (1870-1944), educated as a singer (studied at the Moscow Conservatory), until 1905 was active as a music critic publishing in *Głos, Prawda, Tygodnik Ilustrowany, Niwa Polska*. He later served as a organizer of musical life and theatre director in Vilno; he wrote a valuable study *Muzyka polska i teatr na Litwie* (Polish music and theater in Lithuania), published in 1936. Ignacy Matuszewski (1858-1919), according to Artur Hutnikiewicz, "the most eminent critic of his time, the most representative for the aesthetic consciousness of his generation," was educated as a banker. He graduated from Szkoła Handlowa im. Kronenberga (Kronenberg School of Commerce'). He was well versed in European literature, wrote several valuable monographs dedicated to literary criticism, for instance the study of *Słowacki a nowa sztuka* (Słowacki and the new art), published in 1902. During his mature period he collaborated with the editorial boards of several most popular Warsaw periodicals, serving as the literary editor of *Tygodnik Ilustrowany*. Artur Górski (1870-1959) was a writer and journalist connected to the Cracow *Życie* edited by Ludwik

Szczepański, in which he published as "Quasimodo" a series of articles entitled "Młoda Polska" (since 1898). The whole period was named after his title. He wrote a study about Adam Mickiewicz, entitled *Monsalwat* and promoting a concept of the "moral sense" as the most important spiritual trait of Polish romantics.

[24] Marta Wyka notes these characteristics of the classic interpretation of the Promethean myth in her study entitled "Z problemów młodopolskiego heroizmu" (From the issues of heroism of the Young Poland), in *Światopoglądy młodopolskie* (Kraków, 1996), 100.

[25] Friedrich Nietzsche, "Richard Wagner in Bayreuth," in *Niewczesne rozważania* (Untimely considerations), Polish trans. by Małgorzata Łukasiewicz (Kraków, 1996), 279.

[26] Friedrich Nietzsche, *Untimely Meditations,* trans. R. J. Hollingdale (Cambridge: Cambridge University Press, 1983). Nietzsche's essay "Richard Wagner in Bayreuth" was widely read in Poland in the 1890s, either in the original version, or in a French translation by Maria Baumgartner. The Polish translation by Maria Cumft-Pieńkowska appeared in Warsaw in 1901. The earliest Polish interpreters of Nietzschean thought captured in this essay considered it in a very superficial fashion. An unknown author of the article "Wagnerzyści" (Wagnerians) called Nietzsche a "popularizer who simplifies the issues of the arts.." Published in *Echo Muzyczne, Teatralne, i Artystyczne,* no. 577 (1894): 504. The few Polish reviews of Nietzsche's book were not too enthusiastic. The reviewer of the opinion-making intelligentsia journal *Głos,* Lucjan Konarski, called this book a "heavy-duty and paradoxical discourse" in his article "Z literatury przekładów," (From the Literature of Translations) *Głos,* no. 7 (1903): 104. Only Wacław Berent's reflections (in *Źródła i ujście Nietzscheanizmu* (Sources and Outlet of Nietzscheanism) (Warsaw, 1906), popularized a deepened method of considering Nietzschean writings as the foundation for the modernist transformation of culture.

[27] Nietzsche, op. cit., 260-261.

[28] Nietzsche, op. cit., 273.

[29] Cezary Jellenta, "Prometeiści," in *Wszechpoemat i najnowsze jego dzieje* (The Universal Poem and Its Most Recent History). Cited from Tomasz Lewandowski, *Cezary Jellenta - estetyk i krytyk. Działalność w latach 1880-1914* (Cezary Jellenta - Aesthetics Writer and Critic. Activities in the Years 1880-1914) (Wrocław, 1975), 23.

[30] Zygmunt Noskowski's critical writings about Wagner published in 1890s should be seen in this context; Noskowski was Wagner's main Polish adversary. See his articles "Przyszłość muzyki i muzyka przyszłości" (The future of music and the music of the future), *Wędrowiec,* no. 34 (1892): 539; "Polihymnia," *Tygodnik Mód i Powieści,* no. 43 (1890): 342.

[31] See Władysław Jabłonowski, "Ryszard Wagner: Poeta i myśliciel" (Richard Wagner: Poet and Thinker), *Tygodnik Ilustrowany,* no. 44 (1898): 845.

[32] *Ibidem.*

[33] Walery Gostomski, "Teatr w Bayreuth i jego znaczenie" (The Theater in Bayreuth and its Meaning), *Z przeszłości i teraźniejszości* (Warsaw, 1904), 194-204.

[34] Gostomski, *ibidem,* 291.

[35] Edward Schuré, *Dramat muzyczny. Ryszard Wagner, jego twórczość i ideały* (Music Drama. Richard Wagner, His Oeuvre and Ideals), trans. Emilia Węsławska (Warszawa 1904), 336-337.

[36] See Henryk Markiewicz, "Rodowód i los mitu trzech wieszczów," in Markiewicz, *Prace wybrane,* vol. 2 (Kraków, 1996), p. 58.

[37] Schuré, *op. cit.*

[38] See Czesław Halicz, "Edward Schuré" *Literatura i Sztuka* (Literature and the Arts), no. 13 (1913), an insert in *Nowa Gazeta,* no. 566. An interesting thread in Parisian connections of the Polish reception of Wagner is associated with personal links of several Polish

Wagnerians (Sygietyński, Jabłonowski) with Paris, as well as with the echoes of the visit of Catulle Mendès to Warsaw, Lwów and Kraków in 1904.

[39] Markiewicz, *op. cit.*

[40] Ignacy Matuszewski, "Słowacki i nowa sztuka (modernizm)" (Słowacki and the New Arts (Modernism), in Matuszewski, *Z Pism* (From Writings), vol. 3 (Warszawa, 1965), 202.

[41] Artur Górski, *Monsalwat* (Lwów, Warszawa, n.d.), pp. 60-61.

[42] Bolesław Lutomski, "Sztuka i rzeczywistość (Art and Reality), *Kurier Warszawski*, no. 82 (1912).

[43] Berlioz's new role as one of the founders of modernism is connected to establishing a new hierarchy of aesthetic threads in the music of the second half of the 19th century. This rewriting of history took place after 1900 and resulted in declaring program music, not Wagnerian drama, as the leading in music of the time. Such a hierarchy was put forward by German authors of music history textbooks, including Rudolf Louis. An increased interest in Berlioz was also associated with the French celebrations of 100th anniversary of his birth.

[44] Wacław Tadeusz Dobrzyński, *Ryszard Wagner* (Kiev, 1909).

[45] Zdzisław Jachimecki, *Ryszard Wagner* (Kraków, ca. 1911).

[46] Stefan Kołaczkowski, *Ryszard Wagner jako twórca i teoretyk dramatu* (Richard Wagner as a Creator and Theoretician of Drama), (Warsaw, 1931).

[47] Writings by Max Nordau (*Entartung*) and Leo Tolstoy (*Co to jest sztuka*) expressing a theory of a degeneration of the arts at the turn of the century, inspired, among others, anti-Wagnerian statements by Zygmunt Noskowski. One example of his Wagnerian criticism, based on these ideas is "Sztuka współczesna w świetle badań psychologicznych (Contemporary Arts in the Light of Psychological Research), published in *Kurier Warszawski*, no. 81 (1893).

[48] Jachimecki, *op. cit.*, 254.

[49] Samuel Sandler, in his introduction to the edition of Jachimecki's works cited earlier, pointed out the dependence of Jachimecki's ideas on those put forward by Matuszewski. See Jachimecki, *op. cit.*, vol. 3, p. 54.

[50] Richard Fromme, *Richard Wagner* (Leipzig, 1912), 121.

[51] Zdzisław Jachimecki, "Opera lwowska w Krakowie," *Przegląd Polski*, vol. 189 (1913): 268-269. An allusion to the title of the "cultish" book by Eduard Schuré, dedicated to the creators of great world religions, including Christ, Muhammad, and Buddha.

[52] Modris Eksteins, *Święto wiosny. Wielka wojna i narodziny nowego wieku* (The Rite of Spring: The Great War and the Birth of a New Century), trans. Krystyna Rabińska (Warsaw, 1996), 64.

[53] Joseph Horowitz, *Wagner Nights: An American History* (Berkeley and Los Angeles: University of California Press, 1994); Burton W. Peretti, "Democratic Leitmotives in the American Reception of Wagner," *Nineteenth-Century Music* 13, no. 1 (1989): **28-38**.

A Romantic Interlude IV

Fig. 7: *Three Preludes of Chopin Interpreted by Sigismond Ivanovski.* Drawn by Ivanovski, half-tone plates engraved by H. Davidson. New York: F. C. Gordon, n.d. Plate I: *Molto Allegro*, after Prelude in C-sharp minor, Op. 28, No. 10. Maja Trochimczyk Collection. Ivanovski (or Ivanowski) was a Polish-American artist, active in the first decade of the 20th century. His illustrations, with a fluidity of lines of the Art Nouveau style, appeared in *The Century Illustrated Monthly Magazine* in New York.

ALLEGRO APPASSIONATO

Fig. 8: *Three Preludes of Chopin Interpreted by Sigismond Ivanovski.* Drawn by Ivanovski, half-tone plates engraved by H. Davidson. New York: F. C. Gordon, n.d. Plate II: *Allegro Appassionato*, after Prelude in D minor, Op. 28, No. 24. Maja Trochimczyk Collection.

Fig. 9: *Three Preludes of Chopin Interpreted by Sigismond Ivanowski.* Drawn by Ivanovski, half-tone plates engraved by H. Davidson. New York: F. C. Gordon, n.d. Plate III: *Largo*, after Prelude in E minor, Op. 28, No. 4. Maja Trochimczyk Collection.

Chapter 6

Portraits of Composers and Musicians in 19th Century Polish Music Criticism

Magdalena Dziadek

I. Positivistic Criticism and "Small Romanticism"

Nineteenth-century music criticism in Poland did not extensively deal with the image of a composer or performer nor with his/her relationship with society.[1] This statement seems to be paradoxical because, as is well known, one of the most popular music criticism genres in this period was a portrait of a musician, written on the occasion of an anniversary, jubilee, concert tour, or as an obituary. However, these portraits were focused on biographical facts; and those aspects that dealt with characterizing the activities and personalities of creators and performers of music were strongly limited by social conventions and censorship. Usually, these portraits did not touch upon controversial issues, such as the worldview of their subjects, their attitude to religion nor, for obvious reasons, their views on the government. Popular biographic articles gave little or no information about the actual views, goals, and character traits of the individuals they described. Because of their occasional character and educational function, these portraits were idealizations, deeply rooted within a certain rhetorical tradition. Their authors unwittingly drew upon the interpretative models created in the literature of "small romanticism."[2] Therefore, they were primarily interested in the ideological stance of a composer or artist, as well as in virtues and moral traits. Talent came later, in accordance with the principle that an artist had talent because of being engaged in a profession and not the other way around. At the same time, these critics preserved a romantic way of viewing artists as exceptional creatures, who were superbly gifted by God and elevated high above the commonplace that pervaded the society.

From the portraits and obituaries published at the end of the 19th century an ideal of a creative individual emerges; this ideal is in harmony with the prevailing views of the time about the ideal member of the intelligentsia. Such a person treats his/her work as a vocation or social mission and fulfils this mission even when struggling with unfriendly circumstances, poverty, and the indifference of the society as a whole. A focus on social responsibility resulted in ascribing to the makers of art a role of a "servant" of the society and nation. This focus resulted in highlighting those features which are not usually associated with the artistic profession, and, at times, are even its direct contradiction. The authors of these critical portraits deemed negative such features as: a will to dazzle, vanity, seeking public success, or the will to dominate. In contrast, they singled out for praise such traits as: modesty, focus on work understood as fulfilling a daily duty, as well as the lack of interest in material benefits, or seeking fame.

This image of a creative individual as a "quiet worker of the arts" was adopted by Stanisław Ciechomski when he wrote for *Kurier Warszawski* in the 1890s, publishing numerous portraits of Warsaw musicians. In 1890, he praised Stanisław Barcewicz for his modesty, willingness to self-sacrifice, absence of a will to strive for a personal gain, and finally, what was the most essential, i.e., "placing himself in the background."[3] In 1892, Ciechomski wrote about Władysław Żeleński recognizing "his talent, supported by consistent work habits, not distracted by details; a talent that reaches up to the heights; that does not concern itself with little things and with the benefits of the quotidian, daily life; that is the talent full of masculine power."[4] In 1896, Ciechomski wrote a symptomatic sentence about Piotr Maszyński: "His individuality is always enlivened by the most noble motivation and striving."[5]

It is not possible to ignore the fact that the style of celebratory or obituary profiles of Polish composers and performers of music was strongly linked to a socio-political reality that by itself did not create proper conditions for Polish musicians to dazzle their public or to reach considerable material success. For this reason, a review of the subject of musicians' personal modesty and social virtues would not be complete without statements that describe the actual circumstances in the country, not just express a certain conception of a social role of the artist and musician. Władysław Bogusławski took into account both aspects of the problem when he ended an anniversary portrait of Adam Münchheimer with the following statement: "In a society such as ours, where spiritual life is a never-ending, always distant dawn, that person has merit who, even though slowly and gradually, still continues to try to do something good."[6]

Those authors who came in touch with more recent French critical reflection inspired by ideas stemming from the philosophy of Sainte-Beuve, Taine, and Lemaître, strongly expanded their interests and associated critical methodologies.⁷ Sainte-Beuve was passionate about a particular method of analysis of an oeuvre based on biographical sources, such as letters, memoirs, and documents of social life. Hippolyte Taine's aesthetic theory postulated that artistic individuality resulted from the confluence of biological and social factors. Finally, Lemaître claimed that "man is the measure of things."[8]

In 1880s, from the inspiration with French criticism the biographical trend in Polish literary criticism arose in the writings of such critics as Chlebowski, Chrzanowski, Chmielowski and Bogusławski. The life portrait or a general profile of a writer became an inseparable element in critical studies dedicated to drama, novels or poetry, because this approach allowed the critics to add considerations about the dependence of the content of literary works on the feelings and experiences of their authors. In the 1890s, this method became a standard of sorts. Therefore, it was repeatedly drawn upon by music critics. Juliusz Stattler wrote the following about the purpose of (and ways of applying) the biographical method in music criticism, adding this comment to an anniversary profile of Ignacy Jan Paderewski:

> In order to understand an exceptional phenomenon, one needs to know its causes and the powers that brought it into being; one needs to be able to follow the growth of an emerging spark—how it transforms itself into a powerful fire—and comprehend the causes of dangerous fires. Following this way also results in getting to know people of an exceptional, higher nature. Their past deeds from their youth, the most important facts of their lives, or the unique, characteristic events—all this material may give rise to a certain understanding of the most amazing revelations from their lives, so that it allows one to create a notion about their views and stances taken in life, as well as allows one to have an insight into their souls.[9]

Paderewski was the subject of a great number of biographical sketches not only because of the respect that he enjoyed but also because he was the perfect material for reflection directed towards explaining success as an interaction of social conditions, circumstances of chance and personality traits. Nonetheless, the authors of these texts were the most inspired by the figure of Chopin because of his unquestionable exceptionality as well as the dramatic involvement of his individual life with the life of the nation. Jan Kleczyński provided the best-known examples of positivistic criticism in his biographical interpretations of Chopin's oeuvre. His texts contain a characteristic element as he repeatedly returns to describing the appearance of the composer and attracts the attention of his readers to Chopin's body, behavior, and customs, in order to draw conclusions from this material about his personality, character traits, but also about a particular physiognomy of his oeuvre. The justification of this kind of behavior is, obviously, the fundamental thesis of positivistic philosophy about the unity of sprit and matter, life and work. In the second part of the first series of his lectures *About Performing Chopin's Works* ("O wykonywaniu dzieł Chopina," 1879), Kleczyński thus considered the genesis of the composer's idealism, by starting from an outline of a romantic, spiritual image of the composer:

> Whoever only once in a lifetime has seen the portrait of Chopin by Ary Scheffer, whoever looked intently at this idealized, frail, too frail a figure, marked by such superiority, nobility and charm, to that person one side of Chopin's muse will become understandable at once. That person will be able to comprehend that this figure lives in an ethereal sphere, that social grace and elegance are not only among his needs, but—as it were—they are his very nature. That person will also understand that when encountering the mundane world many things that are tolerable for others, seemed to be too rough for this soul. However, if we were to bypass describing his customs, preferences, manners of behaving (for which Liszt called him "prince") we will encounter in aesthetic images of Chopin certain features that strongly differentiate him from all contemporary and many later composers. The typical pianistic "touch" was in his art more quiet, the shading more gentle, the use of power less frequent. He strongly avoided whatever is brilliant and dazzling and effective; while searching for a more noble aura filled with poetic charm, inaccessible to crowds.[10]

In the 1890s, similar descriptions were practically a constant element in reviews of concerts by virtuosi and of opera spectacles. In the case of opera, paying exaggerated attention to the appearance of the actors may seem to be natural in a merit-based, critical appraisal of performance quality, complete with the physical descriptions of the actors and singers, their costumes, ways of performing and the scenery. Actually, the 19th-century critics of opera performances were concerned with the appearance of singers-actors for its own sake. This intense interest should be seen in the aesthetic-sociological categories of the "cult of stars."[11] At that time, opera singers themselves as well as stage performers considered their appearance and behavior as elements of artistic creations. They had an unusual concern for expensive clothes (increasingly adapted to the style of the performed repertoire), fancy hairstyles, and well-practiced stage behavior and gestures. These aspects of operatic performance are well documented in many polemical texts, written by individuals critical toward the cult of stars.

The end of the 19th century is the time when such long-haired performers appeared who even used artificial hair and wigs, who manicured their nails, who tried (as, for instance, Vsievolod Boujukli) to influence the audiences by unconventional behavior, which was supposed to reveal an exceptional individuality and enormous temperament. Such behavior, encompassing planned late appearances at concerts was designed to increase the curiosity of the public. This cult of the opera star reverberated in an increased interest of music critics in the figure of the artist. At times, this interest was only a proof that the reviewer was caught up in the attractiveness of a well-acted stage masquerade or that he simply succumbed to the magic of the stage, its dimmed lights and enchanting decorations.

After seeing the photographs of singer Gemma Bellincioni we may have no doubt that "succumbing to the magic of the stage" explains the enthusiasm of a reviewer of her Lvov performances in 1904. Mieczysław Reyzner, using an expressive *nom-de-plume* of Parisette de Leopol, wrote in *Gazeta Lwowska* about the enchantment felt in the presence of the divine Gemma:

> Again, a light shone on our stage and again it dazzled everyone with its brilliance. Strange is her beauty, all in expression, in the brilliance of her very deep irises, in the smile both charming and revealing beautiful teeth, in the outlines of harmoniously and gracefully built body, in the serpentine motions filled with rare distinction and emphasizing every word, each note of her intonation by a proper expression… What a treasure of motives of motion and line for a painter or a sculptor… and being all elegant you can see what a true artist she is—even in the way of dressing. (A detailed description of her clothes follows—M.D.) [12]

Critics sensitive to the personal charms of female performers included Stanisław Niewiadomski, Aleksander Poliński, and Stanisław Meliński, the author of many remarks similar to this one: "unusual personal charm, this undefinable, unusual, and overpowering 'charme personnel' is the main secret of the stage success of Sigrid Arnoldson."[13] It is worth to research the preferences of critics especially in the area of literary style of the description of the performers. They frequently rely on the vocabulary of "heroic" descriptions: the virtuosi are depicted as titans or victors, in other words, as individuals possessive of a strong, magnetic personality. Aleksander Poliński thus described the figure of Anton Rubinstein: "Who does not know this titanic figure, with facial features strongly resembling those of Beethoven, with eyes that cast lightning, with majestic gestures that bespeak both of a physical strength and spiritual energy?"[14]

At the turn of the century, the traditional image of the "lion of the stage" was competing with the image of a "magician"—a magnetizer, an illusionist. These descriptions were usually used by enemies of virtuosity to debunk the false foundation of virtuosic art, but at times also appeared in a positive semantic field. Reviewers sensitive to linguistic fashions liked to use these expressions, which may be associated with the *fin-de-siècle* fascination with the spiritual and the occult. They also indicate an interest in contemporaneous inventions in the domain of physics; the term "magnetism" was accompanied by a range of related terminology such as "electricity," "ultraviolet," or "x-rays." These expressions appeared in music criticism in the context of metaphorical description of the "mysterious impact" of musicians' performances on the audiences.

Fig. 1: Postcard of the young Paderewski with his golden-red hair.
Published by BKWP, probably in Poland, n.d., ca 1890.
Maja Trochimczyk Collection.

In the portraits of virtuosi such traits were associated with characteristics typical of an elevated image of an artist-as-social-activist, filled with moral virtues and such desirable traits as: nobility, goodness, sacrificial spirit, modestly, without excess. In this way Jan Kleczyński portrayed Ignacy Paderewski. He frequently emphasized his belief that the public image of "the lion of the stage" concealed a man of a great heart and noble character, a man "possessed of a healthy, internally harmonized psyche." In 1894, Kleczyński wrote in Paderewsk's portrait that:

> Paderewski is of medium height, with regular facial features, expressing wittiness and goodness. His enormous golden hair impressively adorns his head and in the eyes of his admirers constitutes a kind of a halo. His nose is shapely, mouth narrow, the chin thinly sharpened, filling in the frame of physiognomy that is extraordinarily nice and attractive.[15]

Critics often used the effect of contrast, by describing a metamorphosis that a modest, unattractive "worker of the arts" undergoes on the stage. This effect allowed the authors to connect the ideology of citizens' virtues of the artist with a romantic approach to his exceptionality. This is the statement of Antoni Dobrowolski, a specialist in musicians' portraits, who uses this effect in the description of a performance by Aleksander Michałowski:

> He is known by the whole Warsaw, and the most he is known and highly appreciated by our music public, which applauds him with enthusiasm wherever he appears on the stage. He enters the stage slowly, moving forwards as if uncertain and embarrassed He is shortsighted by nature and as a result of his work, by reading too much music. But when he sits at the piano and when he let his artistic fantasy reign—his eye looks into a far distant space and sees the most distant horizons of art.[16]

The description of the appearance of the musician often revealed the aesthetic and ideological views of the critic. By means of properly selected visual characteristics, proponents of the romantic approach indicated that the soul of the musician or composer was moved by powerful, intense feelings. In contrast, the proponents of the "work at the foundations" worldview, presented musicians and composers as humble "workers of the arts." The third group, of critics fascinated with the idea of decadence found in the individuals they profiled various traits that emphasized their "morbidity." Several authors, strongly depending on the language fashion of the *fin-de-siècle* period, endowed Paderewski with decadent features. In 1901, Marrene-Morzkowska wrote:

> Do you know a face that is tired, subtle, a face that was sculpted by life with such diverse traits? Life carved in this face un-erasable traces of work, feelings, thoughts and first of all, suffering? What caused it? Perhaps losses inseparable from life? Perhaps the worries of ambition, perhaps worries of the heart? Perhaps the first and the second but first and foremost, first because there is something austere and at the same time anxious in this suffering face. One could gaze for a long time at him and read a distinct trajectory of the past in this network of moving nerves.[17]

Finally, the adherents of the neo-romantic program of "action" assigned to the Polish musicians traits selected to attest to their physical and psychic power that stemmed from belonging to a healthy, vigorous "race." This characteristic approach may be illustrated by a commentary published in *Kurier Poznański* about the appearance of a young violinist, Artur Argiewicz:

> We gazed at the young Argiewicz not only with worship of his talent but also with pleasure about his physical condition. The boy is built well, fed well, has full and rosy cheeks, and with the Slavic fringe he looks better than with those extensive hairdos that are favored by some adult artists—i.e., hair that may be both real and assumed.[18]

Some performers were aware of the need for cultivating a "Polish" appearance. This need was addressed by young virtuosi who performed in national costume; for instance in 1902, a 9-year-old pianist Mieczysław Horszowski debuted on the stage of the Warsaw Philharmonic wearing a Cracovian costume.

II. Romantic Images and Weltschmerz

While the "small-romantic" approach created the figure of an artist-citizen, other music critics drew upon a romantic image of an artist as an exceptional individual—someone sensitive, with an unusually developed spiritual side, placing him/her high above the average. This image appeared most often in the analysis of the personality of Chopin. In contrast, Moniuszko was stubbornly depicted by critics in the light of the earlier described "mundane" image. Chopin's portraits existed in two versions: the "feminine" and the "masculine." I consider these descriptions as indicative of the discussions about Chopin's personality which commenced after his death and ended with the emergence of two oppositional images—that of an "ultra-sensitive person" and the "bard."

As Irena Poniatowska reminds us, the image of Chopin as a "ultra-sensitive person" filled with *Weltschmerz* was popularized in European musical thought in the second half of the 19th century. It was Franz Liszt who introduced to his famous biography of Chopin the interrelated concepts of sorrow ("żal") and morbidity, assigning to the composer traits of physical weakness and sensitivity rooted in a feminine way of feeling.[19] This interpretation, considered valid until the threshold of the 20th century was preferred by authors well versed in German-language literature.

Fig. 2: *Chopin's Funeral March from Piano Sonata, Op. 35*.
Postcard published in Warsaw: Nakładem Braci Rzepkowicz, and mailed in February 1911. Maja Trochimczyk Collection.

For instance, Jan Kleczyński in his lectures *O wykonywaniu dzieł Chopina* (1879) alluded to this concept by using the category of *Weltschmerz* in reference to Chopin; his was the first documented usage of this term in this context. Nonetheless, Kleczyński was critical of such a "morbid" interpretation of Chopin's personality. In contrast, Bronisław Chlebowski published a portrait of Chopin in 1891 in *Ateneum* that fully embraced this vision of the composer as a "singer of nervous and feminine souls:"[20]

> In the majority of Chopin's works the attitude of feeling to the stimuli which causes the feeling testifies to a purely feminine nature of his emotive states... Feminine emotive quality is characterized either by entire reversed relationship between the objective value of objects and their subjective impression, or an inclination to express the same delight for the most mundane details of life and the most serious matters. When knowing Chopin, we have all the right to think that in many of his works there is a reflection of this feminine emotive states—melancholy complaints against inconveniences of life, seductive coquettish fainting, outbursts of nervous irritation... Under the influence of both physical and psychic factors, the sensitivity of feeling is transformed in Chopin in the last years of his life into a morbid ultra-sensitivity, as a result of which in the trembling of emotive waves and their lines will appear feverish accelerations, strong depressions, fainting, expressed in lack of clarity, hesitant flow and weirdness of form.[21]

The same image was used by such eminent critics as Zygmunt Noskowski and Czesław Jankowski. On the occasion of the 50th anniversary of Chopin's death, Noskowski thus summarized his oeuvre in an article published in the daily paper, *Kurier Poranny*:

> In general the majority of Chopin's works is saturated with the sorrowful tone ("żałosna nuta"). This was a consequence of personal suffering, that fate did not spare him and the musician, possessive off a disposition that was sensitive and thoroughly subjective, expressed all of his feelings in sound... The woks of Chopin may be compared to our autumn, in which the dying nature expresses its beauty by faint rays of sunlight. Everything there is permeated with longing: leaves falling off the trees like tears from eyes, the landscape veiled with a delicate fog, the key of cranes in formation flying away to warmer countries, the bluish little clouds in the sky - these images come to mind with one enormous feeling of sorrow ("żałość") that Chopin talked about with a certain predilection repeating the word itself several times. In this factor is hidden the distinction of

ideas of the great musician, the novelty of the direction and unknown up to then in art—mood.[22]

Nearly the same belief was expressed by Czeslaw Jankowski on the occasion of the Chopin jubilee in 1910:

> All of Chopin's music is as if wrapped—the thorns and flowers— into veils of melancholy and sorrow ("smutek"). The burning power of feelings, the passionate outbursts shine brightly only through this fog or burn in it as light in lamps covered by black crepe.[23]

Of all the critics who used the category of Chopin's "żal" (sorrow) only Antoni Sygietyński attempted to separate its subjective and objective context. He explained that the word "sorrow" should only be considered as a key to Chopin's "psychological puzzle" without being used to explain the expressive character of his music.[24]

Fig 3: *Е. Цичкиевичъ, Ноктюрнъ Шопэна. (E. Cickiewicz, Chopin's Nocturne).* Postcard published in Russia, ca. 1900. Maja Trochimczyk Collection.

The expressive characteristics of "autumn" melancholy so thoroughly predominated in popular descriptions of Chopin's works that at a certain moment it started to be considered as their primary trait in general. Furthermore, this characteristic impacted the works of Chopin's followers and their interpretation. The author of an unnamed review of a concert given by Ignacy Paderewski, (published in *Nowa Reforma* in 1889) outlined a peculiar theory of the genesis of contemporaneous Polish decadence which the reviewer detected in the oeuvre of Paderewski; he located the source of this decadence in the music of Chopin:

> The performer's own compositions were usually interesting, with poetic flights of fancy, which were magnified in all their plasticity by the magnificent interpretation. *Legende* is the spoilt child of our times, in which we may feel the reflection of currents of contemporary validity. In this work, characterized by a youthful boldness, a certain sorrowful, longing thought is nurtured, and the creator is trying to shake off this thought by sudden modulatory passages, thus entangling himself unwillingly with dissonance, which once attached to him do not leave him for a long time, because they cannot find a way out a solution and they fall ever deeper and deeper into hopelessness and aimlessness. This strange pessimism of feeling was sown by Chopin in his last works, and of our composers Zarębski took it to the extremes."[25]

Of the countless analyses of Chopin's purported "feminine" way of feeling, the greatest popularity was gained by those which were written by the representatives of a younger generation. These essays transcended the level of conventional and occasional writings by introducing scholarly arguments and new ideological elements. Of these, the most famous was the study by Przybyszewski, *Z psychologii jednostki twórczej* (From the psychology of a creative individual).[26] The writer thus introduced a biological and deterministic justification of Chopin's *Weltschmerz*:

> The morbid culture, saturating and permeating all relationships, i which he lived, the landscape surroundings and the most important of its impressions gave birth in him gradually to this longing which was fixed in his brain as a sediment... Chopin is a creation of a crossing of two individuals the belonging of whom to two different races and different cultures was for him in advance for his essence a predetermined meaning. Already in this duality was hidden the kernel which in time became a enormous center of disharmony.[27]

Few authors attempted to critically approach the concept of Chopin's *Weltschmerz*. It was adopted by faith as a factor of his personality. Even more often in was used rhetorically. Marian Seyda associated the dissemination of the image of Chopin as an ultra-sensitive individual with the dominance of his sorrowful, melancholy works in the repertoire of pianists:

In wider circles, people usually view Chopin's feelings and musical thoughts one-sidedly, that is, only through the sorrowful tone that cries and weeps, hides and embraces ("żałosna nuta"). This is explained by technically more accessible character of certain polonaises and nocturnes and certain mazurkas and waltzes which are close to those sorrowful ideals in spirit and color. But beyond these, undoubtedly very typical compositions sharing a basic sentimental tone, there exists a whole series of works which move with the freedom of life, which overflow with vivacity and at times frenzied and boisterous strength of masculinity, especially in polonaises and sonatas, scherzos and etudes.[28]

III. Portraits of National Bards

The image of Chopin as a ultrasensitive person was attractive to writers who succumbed to the "steamy, suffocating breath of pessimism blowing above this generation."[29] Their most insistent opponents were the representatives of the conservative thread in music criticism, sympathizing with the neo-romantic literary ideals and primarily attached to a traditional aesthetics. This approach centered on the Platonic connection of beauty, goodness and truth, and postulated an interpretation of artworks in relation to ethical categories and to elements of a Christian worldview. For these writers, the synonym of value was spiritual health and the preferred content of the message of the arts, articulated by inspired artists, was the raising of man to a higher level as a subject of God's saving action. In the conservative circles, the "decadent" philosophy of art marked by pessimism and "nervousness" was considered to be socially harmful. It was associated with the attitude that was negative and decadent, with a contempt for the world and culture and even with the negation of Christian values. From this point of view, conservative critics fought against the widespread thesis about the morbidity of Chopin's spirit and of the lack of "masculinity" in his personality. These writers found support in the lectures of Kleczyński who sought to prove that the world of Chopin's feelings transcended the vicious circle of melancholy because it embraced the categories of calm, joyous feelings, and even reached the level of crude humor.[30] Stanisław Tarnowski based his argument on similar premises when he sought to demonstrate an essential health of Chopin's psyche:

> The nature rarely complicated even in the age of complicated natures… the background or this soul was a certain consistent sorrow, melancholy that at times shifted into paroxysms of despair. But besides sadness and

longing, beside feminine gentleness of the nerves, there was also a childish free joy and moments of such humor, such fantasy and boisterousness that this brother of Słowacki and Musset appears sometimes to be a contemporary and companion of Mr. Pasek.[31]

Composer and critic Władysław Żeleński seconded this defense of Chopin's emotional health in the following words:

> The master, despite his distinction, despite the fact that the life that he led could not have protected him from a certain morbid melancholy, was able to see truth clearly and express it in a healthy manner. Whoever wants to comprehend Chopin...has to first learn the more healthy classical music.[32]

The trait of spiritual health was also sought by writers who identified themselves with neo-romanticism and were not approaching art solely from the point of view of Christian values. They insisted on the importance of health in the context of viewing composers as artist-bards ("wieszcz")—a characteristic concept in Polish neo-romantic movement. The bard was a creative individual who had a social mission to fulfill and who could become the leader of the nation.[33] The image of the bard was in diametrically opposed to the image of a "super-sensitive person" suffering from Weltschmerz, At the same time, the concept of the "bard" was a crucial element in the ideological program of writers adhering to a national orientation. They bestowed the title of a bard upon those artists who played a particularly important role in the political and social life of the country.

During the second half of the 19th century and especially in the 1890s, music critics assigned the distinguished title of bard to three composers: Chopin, Paderewski and Wagner. All three represented the type of an artist who was socially active, who wished to have an impact on the fate of society and who would, because of their dedication to their cause, be prepared to experience serious psychological or other consequences stemming from their artistic sacrifices. At times, the notion of the bard became a variant of the image of artist-victim, especially where it was interwoven with the messianic myth, resurrected by neo-romanticism.

In general, in this approach the emphasis was placed on activism, on the composers' ideological stance, and on the connection of art and life, resulting in transformation of social reality by artistically-and-spiritually inspired individuals. The concept of a musical bard was created by Stanisław Tarnowski in the text about Chopin published in 1892 (it originated two decades earlier: the published text was a transcript of a lecture given in Kraków in 1871). The scholar represented Chopin as the "fourth great poet of partitioned Poland."[34] He indicated the kinship of Chopin's creative ideas with those of romantic poets: Adam Mickiewicz (1798-1855), Juliusz Słowacki (1809-1849), and Zygmunt Krasiński (1812-1959). Tarnowski posited that Chopin belonged to and was an important member of the generation of Poland's most famous romantic writers. He studied the genealogy of Chopin's despair as an "illness of the generation" by comparing the composer to his contemporary, a French writer, Alfred de Musset (1810-1857). Tarnowski showed that particular form of despair experienced by this generation of Polish poets was connected with the tragic national experience of partitions, loss of independence, and failed uprisings. In Tarnowski's opinion, this generational experience ennobled Polish pessimism, filling it with mystical features:

> How much more justified were those of the Poles in whom the sorrow was transformed into morbid melancholy and the hope in mysticism. The more tender and greater nature predisposed them easily to this and the circumstances of all the most sorrowful, the most distant from what should be, helped the inclination and developed the organisms already too tender and sensitive: beautiful and noble; they were destined for their fate, so that they would never be in constant and complete balance.[35]

Tarnowski ended his consideration of the genealogy of despair with a characteristic remark about its Polish variant as being never fully complete, nor finite, because at the bottom of it there was a "love of goodness and consistent faith in goodness."[36]

The image of Chopin as a bard presented in Tarnowski's work remained current until the end of the 19th century. In this vision, Chopin became a bard who, while creating his art in exile in a foreign country, fulfilled the mission of an ambassador of the native culture and reminded the world about the national tragedy of the loss of independence. After the turn of the century, during the period when writers and artists associated with the *Młoda Polska* (Young Poland) movement took the central place on the national stage, the prophetic image of Chopin was overshadowed by another, that of Chopin as an European, i.e., as a composer whose oeuvre had a universal character and significance.

This vision was articulated by: Zdzisław Jachimecki in the anniversary sketch from *Biblioteka Warszawska* (1910), Adolf Chybiński in the article "Chopin, Moniuszko i ich stanowisko w muzyce polskiej" published in *Sfinks* in 1908, and Henryk Opieński in his monograph *Chopin* (1910). Similar ideas appeared independently in the writings of some critics from the older generation. One adherent to the thesis of the universality of Chopin's oeuvre was Franciszek Bylicki. In 1910, he questioned Tarnowski's theory which was emphasizing the connection of the message in Chopin's music with patriotic experiences. In contrast, Bylicki proposed an understanding of Chopin's music as being Polish "above time", i.e., with its most basic value resting in its universal greatness. For Bylicki, Chopin was the "summit of raising music to the great dignity and meaning in universal culture."[37] The image of a "universalist" Chopin was a part of a cosmopolitan aesthetic program proposed by the Young Poland. But its ascendency was not final; the vision of Chopin as a bard returned at the end of the period in the statements of those writers who sympathized with the nationalist ideology of National Democrats ("Narodowa Demokracja," or Endecja).

The second embodiment of artist-bard was Ignacy Jan Paderewski. At the turn of the century, this pianist-composer truly fulfilled the role of the ambassador of Polish culture in the world. His Polish concerts in 1891, 1901, and 1904, were welcomed by the press in the three partitions of the country as events of great patriotic signification and profound ideological meaning. These events mobilized society and inspired interest in the national cause by stimulating pride in foreign accomplishments of a fellow Pole. Reviewers of Warsaw performances of Paderewski in 1899 uniformly emphasized their unique character, by noticing in these concerts not only an artistic event, but also a patriotic manifestation. This was not only due to the fact that musician designated the income from these concerts to charity. At the turn of the century, Paderewski enjoyed in Poland an opinion of a truly charismatic artist.

Leon Chojecki wrote: "The artist possesses a charisma that influenced the public, which was overwhelmed with adoration of the master poeticising on the piano."[38] Other reviewers of Paderewski's performances tried to capture the charismatic traits of his personality. Therefore, a characteristic aspect of reviews of his concerts was the concentration on the spiritual dimension of his playing, which was translated into values beyond aesthetics, i.e., in a context that was first and foremost ideological and moral. This is what Marina Gawalewicz did, while writing a Paderewski portrait printed in the weekly *Tygodnik Polski* on the eve of the first concerts in January 1891:

> Talent is light. Individuality is warmth. Only united together they create the sun in the firmament of art, in its rays human souls open like flowers. Beyond a great artist is a unique man; unique as a mind, heart, and character. In Paderewski, knowing his moral value, his intellectual

superiority, his aesthetic nature, we can understand why his art is such an exceptional phenomenon.[39]

A characteristic motive in the reviews of Paderewski's concerts is a focus on his strength and health, expressed in his overwhelmingly abundant vitality. In approaching this subject, many critics did not hesitate before calling his nature "Sarmatian." Thus, they followed the principle of emphasizing physical and psychological health of the artist as an eminent representative of a healthy nation. Władysław Żeleński wrote:

> It would seem while listening that he encompasses in himself the soul of an arch master which blossoms in him, pulsates with eternal life. To Chopin's charm, to his thoughtfulness, to those subtleties of a super sensitive spirit, to his funereal note ("żałobna nuta żalu") of infinite sorrow, his (Paderewski's) music adds the note of the vivid, boisterous fantasy, resounding broadly within a Slavic nature—young, strong and healthy.[40]

Fig 4: Paderewski as a national bard, evoking ancient Polish kings and heroes with his music. Postcard "I.J. Paderewski – Improwizacya." Kraków: Wydawnictwo Salonu Malarzy Polskich, n.d. (late 19th c.) Maja Trochimczyk Collection.

The way of perceiving Paderewski's artistic activities as a patriotic mission and himself as a national leader-bard appeared attractive also to younger authors who sided with the national democratic political program. These included writer-composer Henryk Opieński who had a personal reason to worship the master who had supported him in Paris. In periodicals with which he collaborated, Opieński presented the oeuvre of Paderewski as a continuation of Chopin's work.[41] He used all of his talents for publicity in reviews of Paderewski's concerts given at the Warsaw Philharmonic in 1904 and 1913. In these reviews, the term "wieszcz" (bard) is used explicitly in reference to the musician portrayed as a national hero, with the presence of traditional tropes and formulas indicating the connection between artistry and virtue. Opieński wrote the following in *Kurier Poranny*:

> The powers of the bard of tones are exhibited by Paderewski—these powers are active and free—the powers of a sage and an activist are revealed so strongly, as in very few of the chosen ones. Paderewski considers what he acquires in material possessions only as a means for fulfilling great—beautiful and good—deeds (everyone knows it for whom he has been great, beautiful and good) and therefore he gives countless proofs and gives them continually and he dreams about creating still more great and beautiful things.[42]

Opieński developed the concept of a "musician-bard" to a greater extent in another review published in *Słowo*. This review is filled with echoes of neo-messianic expressions about the priesthood of the arts, predestination, and great deeds, with a capital "D:"

> There are in art, not only in creative art but also in that of a performer - aspects of the deed, the energy of which is non-transitory and indestructible, similar to the energy of motion in nature which undergoes through different states. If in the universe the work of the nature does not dissipate, how could the work of the spirit die and disappear? Each sincere, true prayer is this work of the spirit, this Deed. Feeding souls that thirst for a breath of beauty, lifting these souls up even for a moment into the domain of other worlds, other feelings—this also is the spiritual Deed.
>
> However, in order to nourish others with one's spirit, for this task both grace and work are needed. Grace is sometimes given: this is genius or talent; work has to be acquired by the effort of the will, by endurance. This is the only, greatest reward for the work of a true and great artist that with his spirit he can nourish others, and this feat gives him the title of the bard and places him at the heights of priesthood.[43]

Once again, Opieński approached creating an image of Paderewski in 1911, in a small book *Ignacy Jan Paderewski. Zarys charakterystyki*, written in cooperation with Stanisław Rossowski.[44] The book contains a characteristic description of the physical appearance of the musician:

> In an amazing way, two usually contradictory elements have been brought here to a common denominator: a high degree of spirituality with the amazing riches of the physical development, unusual sensitivity with the truly masculine energy.[45]

Similarly, the theme of the creative oeuvre of Paderewski being a continuation of the work of Chopin makes another appearance:

> He was the only Polish composer—from the post-Chopin era—who in his musical individuality has proven himself to be the true successor to the great genius... Paderewski modeled his works on Chopin... and this was solely the accomplishment of his personal intuition.[46]

The image of Paderewski as a bard was disseminated, in addition to Opieński, by other critics belonging to the political orientation of national democracy. For instance, a similar homage was paid to Paderewski after his Lwów concerts in 1913 by Mieczysław Pawlikowski who compared the pianist-composer to Sienkiewicz. Pawlikowski emphasized the similarity of the social role played by both creative individuals, a role focused on disseminating elevated national and ethical values:

> The concert halls of the Old and the New Worlds worship in him a genius virtuoso—but the attitude of these great centers to Paderewski does not exhaust itself with applause and the enthusiasms of nameless masses, with the wreaths and delights. What remains is the profound respect that is not outwardly as obvious, a respect felt for Paderewski by all who may consider themselves to belong to the social summit of the world . . . - the elites of the spirit and will of societies. These people encounter in our musician and pianist a man who is equal to them at least in respect to the mental horizon, a man carrying to them through his exceptional individuality, news about the spiritual scope of a nation from which he emerged and which does not have an opportunity for historical enunciations, a man associating in himself the case of the genius with the foundation of a high spiritual culture.
>
> Through the person of Paderewski as well as through the works of Chopin—perhaps only through these two phenomena the civilized world has an occasion even today of comprehending that there could be no discussion about the ethnic decadence in Poland, if the awareness of this country is crystallized in individualities with such masculinity conquering the challenges of the arts, if through their arts and their personalities in general flows such an amount of energy's creative juices—all of this explains the significance of Paderewski for our society.[47]

The highly charged, patriotic atmosphere surrounding Paderewski's Lwów performances may be best expressed in the following statement of Edmund Walter:

> In Paderewski you can feel not only a genius creator and performer, but simply a great man, great under every respect; you can feel that this is one of those higher minds that rule over their surroundings and become the milieu in which everything becomes focused. For us, Poles, he is for that a hundred times more precious; his spiritual heritage should, therefore, be—to us—holy.[48]

At the turn of the century, besides Chopin and Paderewski also Wagner was presented in the costume of the bard ("wieszcz"). The term "bard" appeared in reference to Wagner for the first time in 1901 in a review of Nietzsche's study written by Otto Mieczysław Żukowski.[49] This term became further popularized a year later in Ignacy Matuszewski's study, *Słowacki i nowa sztuka (modernizm)*.[50] Matuszewski dedicated the fourth chapter of this book to the subject of the ideological kinship between Wagner's Tetralogy and *King Spirit* ("Król Duch") by Słowacki, pointing out the presence of a common thread of mysticism.

In the final years of the 19th century, Władysław Jabłonowski and Cezary Jellenta published articles casting Wagner as a Prometheus, offering to humankind both self-awareness and the impulse of progress.[51] Jabłonowski interpreted this progress by applying Mickiewicz's formula from the poem *Ode to Youth*, "moving the sphere of the world from its foundations." This vision has an obvious connection to the neo-romantic ideology, enforcing an activist program which was to be the counterbalance for ideological disorientation, utilitarian approaches and the atrophy of will characterizing a decadent society.

Such overheated rhetoric was common in this period. One of the most ardent adherents of Wagner, Zdzisław Jachimecki compared both Wagner and Słowacki to humanity's Messiahs. In his 1911 monograph, Jachimecki put forward a mystical, prophetic interpretation of the category of "bard" as applied to Wagner:

> The 'bard' sees not reality, but a higher than all reality "true being." He sees not an illusion of the world, but its essence.[52]

I further discuss the cult of Wagner by neo-romantic critics associated with the Young Poland movement in another article.[53] Here, let it suffice to say that the Polish composers' fascination with Wagner had a generational character and was founded on Wagner's own literary works, as well as interpretations of his oeuvre by such Western writers as Nietzsche, Schuré, Lichtenberger, or Fromme.

Translated by Maja Trochimczyk

ENDNOTES

[1] This chapter is a translation of a section from Magdalena Dziadek's monograph, *Polska krytyka muzyczna w latach 1890-1914* (Polish music criticism in the years 1890-1914), vol. 1, (Katowice and Cieszyn, 2002).
[2] See Czesław Miłosz, *History of Polish Literature*, 2nd ed. (University of California Press, 1983).
[3] Stanisław Ciechomski, "Stanisław Barcewicz," *Kurier Warszawski* no. 344 (1890).
[4] Stanisław Ciechomski, "Władysław Żeleński," *Kurier Warszawski*, no. 67 (1892).
[5] Ciechomski, "Z muzyki (Jublieusz Piotra Maszyńskiego)," *Kurier Warszawski*, no. 872 (1896).
[6] Władysław Bogusławski, "Z Krainy tonów," *Tygodnik Ilustrowany* no. 20 (1890).
[7] Editor's note: Charles Augustin Sainte-Beuve (1804-1869) was a French literary critic and historian. Hippolyte Taine (1828-1893) was a French historian of culture, chief proponent of naturalism and social positivism. François Élie Jules Lemaître (1853-1914) was a French critic and playwright.
[8] See Edward Przewoski, *Krytyka literacka we Francyi*, (Lwów-Warszawa, 1899).
[9] J(uliusz) S(tattler), "ignacy Paderewski," *Kurier Codzienny*, no. 14 (1899).
[10] Jan Kleczyński, "*O wykonywaniu dzieł Chopina* (Kraków: PWM, 1960): 40.
[11] See Anna Wypych Gawrońska who lists the interests of Lwów critics in the presentation of opera artists as well as their costumes and makeup, by interpreting them as elements of the workshop of opera critics that has to take into acocutn the visual aspect of stage performances. See Anna Wypych Gawrońska, *Lwowski teatr operowy i operetkowy w latach 1871-1918*, (Kraków: PWM, 1999), p. 221.
[12] Parisette de Le'opol (Mieczyslaw Reyzner), "Gemma Bellincioni," *Gazeta Lwowska*, no. 15 (1904).
[13] Stanisław Meliński, "Z muzyki," *Kurier Lwowski*, no. 201 (1908).
[14] Aleksander Poliński, "Anton Rubinstein," *Tygodnik Ilustrowany*, no. 257 (1894): 341.
[15] Jan Kleczyński, "Ignacy Jan Paderewski," *Bluszcz*, no. 1 (1894): 2.
[16] A(dam) D(obrowolski), "Migawka," *Kurier Warszawski*, no. 55 (1907).
[17] Waleria Marrené-Morzkowska, "Z literatury, sztuki i życia," *Słowo Polskie*, no. 538 (1901).
[18] "Kronika miejscowa, prowincjonalna i zagraniczna. Koncert Argiewicza." *Kurier Poznański*, no. 35 (1894).
[19] Irena Poniatowska, *Histora i interpretacja muzyki. Z badań nad muzyką od XVIII do XIX wieku* (Kraków: Musica Jagellonica, 1993), 123-124.
[20] Bronisław Chlebowski, "Fryderyk Chopin," *Ateneum*, vol. 3 (1891): 21.
[21] Bronisław Chlebowski, "Fryderyk Chopin," *Ateneum*, vol. 3 (1891): 22.
[22] Zygmunt Noskowski, "50-ta rocznica skonu Chopina" *Kurier Poranny* no. 288 (1899). English version in Maja Trochimczyk, ed. *After Chopin: Essays in Polish Music* (Los Angeles, Polish Music Center, 2000).

[23] Czesław Jankowski, "Muzyka Chopina," *Słowo*, no. 84 (1910).
[24] Antoni Sygietyński, "Fryderyk Chopin (w 50 rocznice zgonu)," *Gazeta Polska*, no. 237 (1899).
[25] D(roszowski Jan?), "Drugi koncert Paderewskiego," *Nowa Reforma*, no. 238 (1889).
[26] Stanisław Przybyszewski, "Z psychologii jednostki twórczej. Chopin i Nietzsche." Transl. Stanisław Helsztyński, in *Przybyszewski, Wybór pism*, (Wrocław-Warszawa-Kraków: Ossolineum, 1960).
[27] Przybyszewski, *op. cit.*, 13.
[28] Marian Seyda, "Śliwinskiego koncert Chopinowski," *Kurier Poznański*, no. 26 (1910).
[29] Expression cited from the text by Teodor Jeske Choiński, "Dekadentyzm w literaturze," *Wędrowiec*, no. 39 (1899), 764.
[30] Jan Kleczyński, "O wykonywaniu dzieł Chopina," *op. cit.*, 31-34.
[31] Stanisław Tarnowski, *Chopin i Grottger. Dwa Szkice* (Kraków, 1892), pp. 10-11.
[32] Władysław Żeleński, "Fryderyk Chopin, " *Echo Muzyczne, Teatralne i Artystyczne* no. 41/837 (1899): 479.
[33] Henryk Markiewicz, "Rodowód i losy mitu trzech wieszczów," in Markiewicz, *Prace Wybrane* vol. 2, *Z historii literatury polskiej*. (Krakow 1996), 21.
[34] Tarnowski, "Chopin i Grottger," 7.
[35] *Ibidem*, 10.
[36] *Ibidem*, 10.
[37] Franciszek Bylicki, "O setnej rocznicy urodzenia Chopina," (On the hundredth anniversary of Chopin's birth), *Czas*, no. 84 (1910).
[38] L)eon) Ch(ojecki), "Przegląd Muzyczny," *Nowości Muzyczne*, no. 3 (1911).
[39] Quis (Marina Gawalewicz)" Paderewski,," *Tygodnik Polski*, no. 3 (1899): 41.
[40] Władysław Żeleński, "Ignacy Jan Paderewski," *Echo Muzyczne, Teatralne i Artystyczne*, no. 1/797 (1899): 4.
[41] Henryk Opieński, "Ignacy Jan Paderewski. 12 Pieśni do słów Catulla Mendèsa," *Słowo*, no. 320 (1906).
[42] Opieński, "Ignacy Jan Padrerewski," *Kurier Poranny*, no. 8 (1904).
[43] Opieński, "Przegląd Muzyczny," *Słowo*, no. 9 (1904): 3.
[44] Stanisław Rossowski, Henryk Opieński, *Ignacy Jan Paderewski. Zarys charakterystyki*. (Lwów-Warszawa, 1911).
[45] *Ibidem*, 12.
[46] *Ibidem*, 42.
[47] Mieczysla Pawlikowski, "Koncerty Paderewskiego," *Museion*, vol. 3 (1913), 59-60.
[48] Edmund Walter, "Z muzyki," *Gazeta Lwowska*, no. 60 (1913).
[49] (Otto) M(ieczysław) Żukowski, "Nowości wydawnicze. Fryderyk Nietzsche, *Ryszard Wagner w Bayreuth*," Review in *Wiadomości Artystyczne*, nos. 1-2 (1901), 16.
[50] Ignacy Matuszewski, "Słowacki i nowa sztuka (modernizm)" in Matuszewski, *Z pism* (From writings), vol. 3 (Warszawa, 1965), 202.
[51] Władysław Jabłonowski, "Ryszard Wagner (poeta i myśliciel)" (Richard Wagner, a poet and thinker), *Tygodnik Ilustrowany*, no. 44 (1898), 845; Cezary Jellenta, "Prometeiści," cited from Tomasz Lewandowski, *Cezary Jellenta Estetyk i Krytyk. Działalność w latach 1880-1914*. (Wrocław, 1975), 23.
[52] Zdzisław Jachimecki, *Ryszard Wagner* (Kraków, 1911), 254.
[53] See Magdalena Dziadek, "Wagner i Młoda Polska," *Muzyka*, no. 4 (2001) and the article's translation in Chapter 5 of the present volume.

A Romantic Interlude V

Fig. 10: A Polish postcard of a village couple in Cracovian costumes (from the Małopolska region), with a krakowiak couplet: "From Kraków I ride, / The road is full of rocks, / Lassie, give me your mouth, / And be afraid of God." Kraków, ca. 1890. Maja Trochimczyk Collection. No. 628 in the section of krakowiaks in Wacław Zaleski, *Pieśni polskie i ruskie ludu galicyjskiego z muzyką instrumentalną Karola Lipińskiego* (Polish and Russian Songs of Galician People with Instrumental Music by Karol Lipiński), Lwów: Nakładem Franciszka Pillera, 1833.

Fig. 11: A Polish postcard of a village couple in Cracovian costumes (from the Małopolska region), with a krakowiak couplet: "Whoever does not know love / is very happy indeed, / the night is free for sleeping / and the day is free of longing!" Published in Kraków, Poland, ca. 1890. Maja Trochimczyk Collection.

Fig. 12: A Polish postcard of a village couple in Cracovian costumes (from the Małopolska region), with a krakowiak couplet: "The mountain of Krak is ablaze with sunlight / At my Kasinka's a string of beads shines, / the beads are pretty, the sunlight is bright, / but the nicest of all is Kasia's own heart." Published in Kraków, Poland, ca. 1890. Maja Trochimczyk Collection.

Fig. 13: A Polish postcard of a village couple in Cracovian costumes (from the Małopolska region), with a krakowiak couplet: "A flower is a true proof of love / and we will always live in happiness!" Published in Kraków, Poland, ca. 1890. Maja Trochimczyk Collection.

Chapter 7

Searching for Poland's Soul: Paderewski and Szymanowski in the Tatras

Maja Trochimczyk

I. Paderewski's Image and Reception

Sixty years after the death of Ignacy Jan Paderewski, the position of this "modern immortal" in the annals of music history is by no means secure.[1] If we take our cues from *The New Grove Dictionary of Music and Musicians*, our conclusion will be inevitable: Paderewski was a minor composer who offered a negligible contribution to the art of composing and a remarkable, if controversial, contribution to the art of piano performance.[2] If, instead, we believed his students, friends, and biographers in Poland, Paderewski would appear to be an extraordinary individual whose mastery earned him a unique place in music history.[3]

Books about Paderewski published before 1945 include several biographies, or rather hagiographies, written to spread the cult of the pianist-statesman. Henry Finck wrote a profile to introduce the pianist to his American audiences (*Paderewski and His Art*, 1895); it was supported by the sponsors of Paderewski's tours, piano-maker Steinway and followed by a biography by Baughan (1908).[4] Charles Phillips published an extensive "song of praise" of Paderewski and his political, not just musical accomplishments (New York, 1933; Phillips also wrote a poem for Paderewski).[5] In 1938, Paderewski himself issued the first volume of his memoirs, written with Mary Lawton and covering the years to 1914.[6] Ron Landau published a sensational account of the pianist's life in 1934; it was designated for the general public and was highly disliked by the composer. Józef Orłowski gathered materials about Paderewski in America, focusing on his patriotic mission and relationship to Polonia in a two-volume album issued in 1940.[7] In 1943, a brief, laudatory biography by Antoni Gronowicz appeared in England.[8]

After World War II, the interest in Paderewski has waned. In 1947 Simone Giron started her challenges to the handling of Paderewski's estate by his secretary and the executor of his will, Sylwin Strakacz and his associates.[9] Strakacz's wife wrote about Paderewski in her memoirs published in 1949.[10] Some work appeared in the 1950s and 1960s,[11] but the most recent English language book is an extensive biography by English writer and journalist of Polish descent, Adam Zamoyski (1982).[12] In California, the online peer-reviewed *Polish Music Journal* dedicated two issues to Paderewski on the occasion of the 60th anniversary of his death in 2001.[13]

English-language texts continue to be few and far between: according to the RILM database, there have been 172 articles mentioning Paderewski ("keyword"), including 28 texts in English and 83 in Polish. After narrowing the search to publications dealing exclusively with Paderewski ("subject"), I found 130 texts about him, including 21 in English and 77 in Polish. That is not an extensive bibliography, compared with 1,371 entries about Richard Strauss, 632 entries about Max Reger, 267 entries about Edward Elgar, or 260 entries about Sergey Rachmaninoff. The dissertations most frequently deal with his political role in the rebirth of independent Poland after World War II.[14]

Polish publications also started from the hagiography model. Henryk Opieński issued a monograph on Paderewski in 1928 (Gebethner and Wolff), it was published in French in the same year; revised in 1948 and retranslated into Polish in 1960. Wieńczysław Brzostowski prepared a monographic issue of a Poznań periodical dedicated to Paderewski in 1935, on the occasion of unveiling of a monument of President Woodrow Wilson that was generously funded by the composer-statesman, the President's personal friend.[15]

Polish scholars involved in archival research provided a solid framework for future studies. Andrzej Piber's research benefited from his earlier work as one of the cataloguers of the Paderewski Archives at the Archiwum Akt Nowych in Warsaw, Poland.[16] His research, however, focused on the biography and reception, and not the analysis of Paderewski's compositions. Scholarly interest increased after the establishment of the Paderewski Studies Center at the Jagiellonian University in Kraków in 1974. Małgorzata Perkowska, the director of the Center, discovered numerous forgotten works by Paderewski during her archival research, wrote a catalog of his compositions (with Włodzimierz Pigła, 1988); authored a detailed diary of his concert activities with a full account of his repertoire and public appearances of any kind; and edited the memoirs and letters from Paderewski's secretary and his wife, Sylwan and Aniela Strakacz (1994).[17] Polish-American historians, like Mieczysław

Biskupski, undertook studies of interest to the diaspora, especially Paderewski's politics and his role as a leader of Polonia.[18]

After the change of government in 1989 and the return of Paderewski's body to Poland in 1992 (he was buried at the St. John the Baptist Cathedral in Warsaw) a spate of popular biographies and research projects appeared. Two scholars, Marian Marek Drozdowski and Henryk Przybylski, focused on Paderewski's political career and achievements, often overshadowed by those of his archrival, Józef Piłsudski.[19] During a conference dedicated to Paderewski at Jagiellonian University in 1991, several papers presented new approaches to aspects of Paderewski's life and music seen in contemporaneous context, not necessarily Polish (e.g. Woźna-Stankiewicz's study of Paderewski's songs to texts by Catulle Mendès).[20] The conference proceedings, edited by Wojciech Marchwica and Andrzej Sitarz, have been issued the same year. Another Paderewski anthology, edited by Jerzy Jasieński appeared in 1996.[21]

Who was Paderewski, then? A pianist, composer, or politician? In the first option, prevailing among Western scholars, Paderewski is viewed primarily as a performer.[22] Too often the Polish musician changes into his own caricature and is seen merely as a "music-making-machine"—as portrayed, for instance, in the image issued on the occasion of Chicago's World Fair in 1893 (see Fig. 1).[23]

In this image, entitled, "A Peaceful Solution," a young virtuoso with a wild mane of hair uses his multiple arms to reach each of the keyboards that surround him to play all the pianos simultaneously—thus ending the wars for sponsorship that pitted Steinway against Weber and others. The comment underscores Paderewski's business acumen and pianistic bravado; yet he is diminished to the level of a circus curiosity, not a true artist. As a digression, let us recall that the World Fair was also a site of the success of a symphonic overture, *Rusałka* by a Polish composer Ludmiła Jeske–Choińska, née Mikorska (1849-1898).[24]

Paderewski entered the realm of serious composition primarily through writing large scale works, including the Piano Concerto in A minor Op. 17 (1882-1889), the critically acclaimed, though controversial opera *Manru* (1893-1901), and the programmatic Symphony in B minor "Polonia" (1903-1909) that ambitiously sought to portray the entire history of the nation. His large-scale compositions failed to remain in the world repertoire, though they recently have begun to enjoy a renaissance in his home country.[25] A full reevaluation of his contribution to the history of Polish music still remains to be written.

Negative critical responses may have influenced Paderewski's decision to stop composing entirely; this choice was partly motivated by what he deemed a political and moral necessity at the outbreak of World

War I. At that time, Paderewski chose "action" on behalf of restoring a fully independent Poland over "production" of musical artifacts as a primary means of expressing his values. His ethical and political commitment to the national cause trumped his interest in creating new music. In 1917, he created his last work: a patriotic anthem for the Polish Army in America, *Hej, Orle Biały!*[26]

Fig. 1: Paderewski caricature from 1895. "A Peaceful Solution: At the Next World's Fair Paderewski Will Play on All the Pianos at Once," caricature on the cover of *World Fair Puck*, published in Chicago, 15 May 1893. New York Public Library, Performing Arts Division, Research Collection. Used by permission.

During World War I, instead of composing or giving traditional recitals, Paderewski embarked on a one-man campaign to help Polish victims of the war and to rebuild the country. His pleas to save "Poland's starving millions" by donating to the Polish Victims' Relief Fund appeared in his concert programs and in music journals. Paderewski's appeals for financial assistance to Poles stricken by the war were addressed to the compassionate side of his listeners, to their feelings of pity, especially for the suffering women and children.[27] A program of his recital for the Polish

Victims' Relief Fund held at the Symphony Hall in Boston on 10 October 1915 included the following inscription:

> The Daughters of Poland
> Walk in Sorrow, Mourning for their Children,
> their Husbands, their Lovers.
>
> Desolation
> has fallen upon the Land of their Home.
> Let your heart Feel their Grief.
> Let your Pity sustain them.[28]

Paderewski's appeals also mentioned workers, peasants, Jewish shopkeepers—representatives of the whole populace of the Polish countryside. In the Boston appeal, he wrote:

> Nobody knows better than I do the kindness and generosity of the American people. Ardent and prompt, warm-hearted, free-handed, they always respond with the enthusiasm of youth to everything that is true, sincere. Is there anything more true than human pain? Is there anything more sincere than the cry for help from those who suffer? In the name of charity, in the name of common humanity, I, therefore, appeal to the great American people.[29]

His patriotic speeches were short and delivered with a great passion, moving his listeners to tears. They were all variations on the same theme; repeated until the desired effect was achieved. In this period, his public image changed: he was now an elder statesman, stern and noble, inspiring thousands with his charisma (Fig 2: Paderewski's 1915 image, as reproduced in 1940 on the cover of Orłowski's book). The selection of music for Paderewski's patriotic lecture-recitals—mostly, or exclusively by Chopin—also contributed to the overall somber, dramatic and poignant effect. At the concert in Boston, mentioned above, the Piano Sonata in B-flat minor, Op. 35, with its famous Funeral March, was framed by a Ballade and a Nocturne. The program ended with two musical signs of Polishness: a nostalgic Mazurka and a heroic Polonaise (in A-flat major Op. 53). Typically, numerous encores followed.

What if Paderewski continued to compose operas instead of switching to patriotic symphonies and songs? What if there had been no World War I? What if Poland, when Paderewski's international career began, had already been an independent and strong country? Would he still have been so inclined to sacrifice his musical achievements for the sake of serving the cause of Poland's sovereignty? The game of "what-if" is futile enough. Yet, Paderewski's public image has been colored by his politics to a greater extent than by his music; both areas of his activities are forever intertwined. How "Polish" was Paderewski's music, then? And why did it matter?

Fig. 2: Paderewski as a patriotic orator (image by Henrietta Beckert from the cover of Orłowski's book of 1940, based on a 1915 photo).

II. Defining a Polish "National Style"

In an essay about the "The Dilemma of Twentieth-Century Polish Music: National Style or Universal Values,"[30] Zofia Helman ignored Paderewski's role in establishing the "national" late romantic style in Polish music, thus following in the footsteps of her eminent predecessors, like Adolf Chybiński, or Zbigniew Jachimecki. Helman summarized the relationship of music to nation-building with the following observation:

> Within the mutual interactions between national and universal factors in the historical process of creating music, national idioms must be considered as "sub-styles" which are determined by the similarity of

tradition and the conscious choices of some composers in particular cultures. Whether the composer's choices remain on the margins of universal music or enrich it with new aspects depends on individual talent, in the individual approach to composition, and on the mastery of artistic vision.

And, we could add, on the art of persuasion of the musical milieu, the art of creating and disseminating a particular approach that is recognized as valuable and enriching the national and universal heritage of music. If the image focused on one aspect of a musician's achievements at the expense of others, his or her contribution and significance were easily forgotten. Such was the case of Paderewski.

The issue of expressing "national identity" in music preoccupied scholars for generations; its most recent manifestation in the area of Polish music are conferences dedicated to "National Topos in Polish Music," held annually since 2006 in Warsaw.[31] To reduce the topics to the basics, composers could express their nationality in music by means of using certain a) texts; b) subjects, i.e. titles and programs drawn from a nation's history, literature or myths, especially prominent in opera; c) genres, e.g. folk, or national dances such as mazurka, polonaise; d) quotations from well-known national music (e.g. from Chopin, folklore, or national anthems); e) stylization of national melodic and rhythmic elements, esp. from well-known national or regional folk songs and dances.[32] The national spirit could be also hinted upon by f) portraying its most prominent general characteristics (first, defining what they were, e.g., "heroism" or "sorrow"), and, of course also, g) a combination of some, or all of the above.

Musical Expressions of National Identity

a) the use of Polish texts;
b) the use of Polish subjects, from history or literature;
c) the use of Polish genres, especially national dances, such as mazurka or polonaise;
d) the use of quotations with national signification (e.g. Chopin's music, folk melodies, or national anthems);
e) the use of melodic and rhythmic elements, esp. from Polish dances or various regions of the country, in particular the areas of Mazowsze, Małopolska and Podhale;
f) the use of general characteristics of the "national spirit" (including such common themes as "heroism" or "sorrow");
g) the use of various elements in combination.

According to recent research by Magdalena Dziadek, the constructions of the national style based on national spiritual and emotional characteristics preceded that based on folklore quotations and could be invoked in assigning "national" character to "non-national-themed" works regardless of the absence of such obvious characteristics as national genres, titles, themes, quotations, and subjects or programs.[33] At the end of the 19th century, the Polish national characteristics typically included being: a) vivacious and boisterous (expressed in uplifting melodies and fast tempi of many krakowiaks, mazurkas, and obereks); b) noble and heroic (this trait was mostly found in the polonaise); c) spontaneous and filled with fantasy (or inconsistent, hence *tempo rubato*); d) for those neo-romantics who focused on the decadence of the turn-of-the-century period, being nostalgic and sorrowful (this trait of *żal/sorrow* was found in slow dances, especially mazurkas and kujawiaks); and finally, e) generous, kind and, even, polite (so much so that in one early 20th century American genealogy of the word "polite" its root was supposed to have been derived from "Pole").

Since Chopin's oeuvre defined musical Polishness for generations, and since he was raised in and associated with the central region of Mazowsze, surrounding current capital of the country, Warszawa, the association of national style with this region was and is the strongest. Mazowsze and its musical traditions has played a prominent role in definitions of national Polishness also because it was the birthplace of "mazurka"—a dance that has served as the nation's anthem since the country's rebirth (actually, since 1926).[34] In addition this was the favorite Polish dance of many composers, including Maria Szymanowska, Chopin, Karol Szymanowski, Roman Maciejewski and Aleksander Tansman.[35]

The second candidate to the position of a general signifier of "Polishness" in music was the folklore of the southern-central region of Małopolska, centered on Kraków, Poland's historical capital of the Piast and Jagiellonian dynasties.[36] The area's costumes and the dance *krakowiak* (Cracovienne) are considered signs of national identity until today; they are used in this function by Polonian folk dance groups around the world.[37] Chopin (*Krakowiak - Grand rondeau de concert* for piano and orchestra, Op. 14, 1828) and Paderewski composed the most famous examples of artistic stylizations of this genre. Paderewski's fondness of the krakowiak may be seen in its appearances in *Dances polonaises*, Op. 5, 1882 (two pieces); as No. 1 in *Danses polonaises*, Op. 9; as *Cracovienne fantastique* in B major, No. 6 in *Humoresques de concert*, Op. 14 of 1886; and in *Fantaisie polonaise sur des thèmes originaux* in G-sharp minor, Op. 19, 1891-93.

A somewhat weaker association of the general national quality with the music and culture of the Podhale area in the foothills of the Tatra Mountains in the southern part of the country stemmed from the clearly "regional" character of the area, with distinct dialects, costumes, music and traditions. Nonetheless, the region inspired an early venture into Polish musical theater in *Cud mniemany, czyli Krakowiacy i Górale*, by Jan Stefani to a libretto by Wojciech Bogusławski, composed in 1794.[38] An important national opera by Stanisław Moniuszko, *Halka* (1846-1858), did not include much in the way of stylized Podhalean folklore, even though its heroine was a *Górale* girl, seduced and abandoned by a Polish nobleman.

Tatra-themed music composed by late romantic symphonists, Władysław Żeleński (overture *W Tatrach*, 1872), and Zygmunt Noskowski (overture *Morskie Oko*, 1875), portrayed subjective emotional responses to sublime mountain soundscapes and landscapes, not the authentic folklore of the region's inhabitants. The more "authentic" (the term is controversial, hence the quotation marks) association came to the fore in the oeuvre of Paderewski and was later highlighted by Karol Szymanowski (1882-1937), who, as I demonstrate in this article, followed in Paderewski's footsteps, whose passion for all things Polish knew no bounds.

Fig. 3: A 1901 postcard of Morskie Oko seen from the trail to Czarny Staw, in Tatra Mountains. Zakopane: Wyd. Księgarni. Zwolińskiego. Maja Trochimczyk Collection.

III. Paderewski in Tatra Mountains

An inspiration for Paderewski's ethnographic endeavors and folksong collecting came from Dr. Tytus Chałubiński (1820-1889), a tireless promoter of the Tatra Mountains and the culture of its inhabitants, Polish highlanders, or *Górale*. This discoverer of the unique culture of Podhale was the moving force in "marketing" Tatra Mountains as a tourist destination and the *Górale* culture as a pure example of an unbridled Polish spirit and untainted folklore, created and preserved in isolation.[39] Ethnomusicologist's Timothy Cooley's ground-breaking work *Making Music in Polish Tatras* (2005) showed that these images of purity and isolation were nothing more than myths.[40] In an earlier article, Cooley wrote:

> Ethnographers tell two contrasting stories about Górale: one stresses purity, independence and distinctiveness associated with the myth of mountain isolation; another recognizes ancient connections with Górale to culture groups along the Carpathians and extending down into the Balkans.[41]

As Cooley has convincingly demonstrated in his book, based on his doctoral dissertation, the supposedly "pure" and unadulterated Podhalean folklore was actually created with significant input from and guidance by outsiders, i.e., Chałubiński and his circle. In this version of the highlanders' music, connections to the repertoire of Polish lowlands and the Balkans were downplayed, the imported dances ignored or removed.

Since their first meeting in 1883, Chałubiński tried to interest Paderewski in collecting Podhalean folklore; the young pianist-composer became his first and the most important musical follower.[42] Chałubiński encouraged the pianist to collect folk melodies to quote and stylize them in his music. They traveled together into the Tatra Mountains with *Górale* musicians: the famous string group, *kapela*, of Bartek Obrochta.

In the summer of 1883, Paderewski took a trip through the Tatras and Podhale with pianist and composer Jan Kleczyński (1837-1895), notating all the melodies of songs and dances of *Górale* that they encountered. Both wrote down about 70 tunes; Paderewski chose what he considered "the most characteristic" and created pieces to be included in the piano cycle *Album tatrzanskie/Tatra Album,* op. 12. The first of his compositions from this set of ten was published in October 1883 in *Echo muzyczne i teatralne.* The pianist performed them in 1883 in Zakopane; Chałubiński was delighted by this performance, witnessed also by actress Helena Modrzejewska, one of the young pianist's mentors.[43]

The young pianist returned to the Tatras in the summer of 1884, again traveling with Chałubiński. On 18 August 1884, Paderewski, Chałubiński, and Kleczyński left together with folk musicians, fiddler Bartek Obrochta and Kuba Gut, bassist, to collect new melodies. The Podhalean performers invited other *Górale* musicians to play for the visitors;

thus, Paderewski and Kleczyński listened to and transcribed performances not only by the legendary fiddler, Bartek Obrochta, who was then at his prime. They also heard a number of other musicians that Obrochta introduced them to. Since Kleczyński lost his notebooks during the trip, his subsequent publications of *Górale* melodies in 1883 to 1888 were based on Paderewski's transcriptions.[44]

Paderewski arranged selected Tatra melodies in his pioneering work of "Podhalean style," the *Album Tatrzanskie / Tatra Album*, Op. 12 (1883-1884).[45] The Polish version of *Album tatrzańskie* Op. 12 includes four movements, three composed in 1883 and the fourth one in 1884. The German version of 1884 was expanded by two additional movements.[46] Let us note the composition's dates: about 20 years before Bartok's "pioneering" folklore-based music and about 40 years before Szymanowski's first forays into the Podhalean domain.

Fig 4: Fragment from Paderewski, *Tatra Album*, Op. 12, No. 4, based on a *Górale* song, "Hej, idem w las" (Hey, I'm going to the woods), later used by Szymanowski.

In Paderewski's *Album*, No. 1 is based on "W murowanej piwnicy" (In the basement). The folk model for the first dance is called the "zbójnicki" (of highland robbers) and consists of figures danced by a group of men armed with "ciupaga," a highlander's axe. No. 2 uses a less-known tune, "Dziewczyno kocham cię," (Girl, I love you); No. 3 is based on the popular "Za górami, za lasami," (Beyond mountains, beyond forests); and No. 4 on the even better known song of a boisterous young *Góral,* "Hej, idę w las" (Hey, I'm going to the forest). The latter tune later appeared in Szymanowski's song cycle *Słopiewnie* of 1921 and returned in a prominent role in his ballet, *Harnasie* (1921-1933).

In musical terms, the proper context for Paderewski's *Tatra Album* is provided by stylized *Slavonian Dances* by Antonin Dvorak, not the later Bartokian-style bold harmonic experiments based on more authentic and detailed transcriptions of folk music. Yet, Paderewski's use of real folklore, heard and notated in the field, was a complete novelty during that time. Paderewski's pioneering position in the movement of folklorism may be recognized when noting that Ralph Vaughan Williams, Percy Granger, and Bela Bartók began collecting folksong twenty years later, in 1903 and 1905 respectively. The Polish composer's interest in the folklore of the Tatra Mountains continued and was expressed in his only opera, *Manru,* of 1894-1901.

IV. Manru, Polish Villagers and the Gypsies

Paderewski's opera, a tragic love-story of a Polish-Gypsy couple, was written to a libretto by a Jewish writer, political activist, sculptor, and scholar, Alfred Nossig (1864-1943). The basis for the libretto was a Polish novel about ethnic hatred and identity conflicts between ethnic Poles and Romas, *Chata za wsią* (Hut beyond the village) by Jan Kraszewski, first published in 1854-1855.[47] This was an unusual collaboration of two men whose later years took widely divergent paths, both marked by national politics. Paderewski's years as the Prime Minister of Poland were preceded and followed by an illustrious musical career; his life ended in 1941 with a worldwide recognition of his greatness. Let us consider the life of Alfred Nossig, who did not fare so well.

This prolific writer, social scientist, sculptor and Zionist theoretician was born in 1864 at Lemberg/Lwów, Galicia. He studied law, philosophy, and natural science at the universities of Lemberg and Zurich (Ph.D.), and medicine for several years at the University of Vienna. He began his literary career with some poetical works in Polish, including *Tragedia Myśli* (The Tragedy of Thought), a drama (1884); *Król Syjonu* (The King of Zion), a drama produced at the National Theater at Lemberg, 1887; and *Jan Prorok* (John the Prophet), an epic poem (1892). Fluent in German, he published dramas *God's Love* (Göttliche Liebe) in 1901; *Die Hochstapler* 1902; and the libretto to Paderewski's opera *Manru.* Nossig's scholarly works were written in German and chiefly sociological, dealing with issues of social hygiene, socialism, world peace, agrarian question and other issues.

He also wrote books about Paderewski, philosophy (criticizing Spinoza), the art of the Austro-Hungarian empire, and essays about aesthetics and various aspects of drama.[48] His work as a sculptor was exhibited at Paris (1899) and Berlin (1900), and attracted much attention.

The majority of his writings dealt with social and political issues of Polish Jewry. As a Zionist theoretician, Nossig has devoted especial attention to the Jewish question. He published six books on this topic between 1887 and 1904, advocating the return of Jews to Palestine. In 1887 he proposed the creation of a Jewish state in Palestine and advocated Jewish emigration as the only option guaranteeing the survival of Jewish culture. In the 1920s, he became a spokesperson for another far-reaching, prophetic idea: the federation of European states. Inspired by this futuristic plan, representatives of twenty-six countries participated in a 1926 conference in Geneva devoted to this cause. Nonetheless, Nossig's misguided beliefs that all Jews should return to Palestine and that the Nazis would help accomplish that goal led to his collaboration with the Nazi government that ended when he was shot by Jewish resistance fighters in 1943.[49] Apparently, the elderly Zionist came to believe that the Nazis would help him realize his life-long dream: resettlement of Jews to Palestine.[50]

Nossig approached Paderewski with the idea of writing an opera libretto for the pianist-composer and continued pressing for this project for several years before Paderewski agreed. *Manru* contained ideas about racial and national identity that Paderewski and Nossig shared at the time of the work's creation and that had a bearing on their artistic ideologies. However, it was not the first project that Nossig presented for Paderewski's approval. He contacted the composer in September 1889 with an idea for a different Gypsy-themed opera, *Manolo*. It was clearly similar to *Aleko (The Gypsies)*, an opera by Sergei Rachmaninoff based on a poem by Pushkin and composed in 1892.[51] Paderewski did not like Nossig's first libretto, but accepted his second choice using Kraszewski's novel, *Chata za wsią*. The libretto was ready in 1893 and a year later Paderewski started composing the opera *Manru*; it took him eight years to finish.

Manru's world premiere took place at the Royal Opera in Dresden on 29 May 1901, amidst immense interest of international music circles. The spectacle was considered a success for Paderewski the composer and a failure for Nossig the librettist. Similar evaluations were repeated after each subsequent premiere of *Manru*.[52] The Polish premiere of the opera took place a week after its opening in Dresden, on 8 June 1901 at the City Theater in Lwów. After that performance, Stanislaw Radzikowski wrote to Stanislaw Witkiewicz (Witkacy): "this is a wonderful work, makes a huge impression, the music is lovely and one could say that finally we have a Tatra opera! Strążyska and the wall of Giewont, then Morskie Oko, the dances set very well, not losing any of their character, górale dressed very well..."⁵³ *Manru* was also staged in Prague, Cologne, and, on 14 February 1902, at the Metropolitan Opera in New York. Prior to that, in 1901, Schirmer published a piano-vocal score for the opera with English translation of the German libretto by music critic Henry Krehbiel.

In the 1901-02 season, the Metropolitan Opera Theater presented 21 operas, including five music dramas by Wagner, three operas by Verdi, and two operas by Gounod. These operas had constituted the "core repertoire" of the Met since its creation. The company also produced two operas by Donizetti, Puccini's *Tosca*, Leoncavallo's *Pagliaci*, Mascagni's *Cavaleria rusticana*, Bizet's *Carmen*, and Mozart's *The Magic Flute*. *Manru* was scheduled for 14 February 1902, Valentine's Day, and the opera had a contractually guaranteed run of 10 performances in New York, Baltimore, Boston, Philadelphia and Pittsburgh.⁵⁴ The American premiere was a resounding success and was described as "the most significant for the public of the Metropolitan Opera in the past decade" (*Telegram*, New York, 15 February 1902). In Boston's *Sunday Herald*, the music critic Howard Tickner stated that, "while considering the whole, Manru is an excellent, powerful, and outstanding dramatic composition, and its staging calls for artists that are not only able to sing with emotion, but also are able to act with a great intensity."

Fig. 5: Scene from *Manru* at the Metropolitan Opera Theater in New York, 1902. From Emily Grant von Tetzel, "At the Opera," *The Theatre* vol. 11, no. 13, March 1902. Maja Trochimczyk Collection.

Prior to the New York premiere, Paderewski gave a press conference (January 30, 1902) where he stated:

> I believe that the novelty of *Manru* lies in this: that, in contrast to a usual romantic story, its theme is developed against the background of the conflict of two races, Slavs and Gypsies. Needless to add that this theme is thoroughly musical. Manru, the hero of this drama, abandons his wife not because he falls in love with another woman, but because of music, that he unexpectedly remembers, reminded by his favorite gypsy melody. . . . Madame Sembrich will sing the main female part and also at my request; she is Slavic herself and will be able to empathize with Ulana, the heroine that she will portray.[55]

The introduction to the printed piano-vocal score included an excerpt from a book of a Mr. Leland on the Gypsies, the Romany with the following characterization of that "race:"

> Now, as you wander along, it may be that in the wood and by some grassy nook you will hear voices, and see the gleam of a red garment, and then find a man of the roads with a dusky wife and child. You speak one word, "Sarishan!" and you are introduced. These people are like birds and bees, they belong to out of doors and nature. If you can chirp or buzz a little in their language and know their ways you will find out, as you sit in the forest, why he who loves green bushes and mossy rocks is glad to fly from cities, and likes to be free of the joyous citizenship of the roads, and everywhere at home in such boon company.[56]

The score also contains an unsigned summary of the opera penned by music critic Egbert Swayne, who also included it in a preview of the premiere in the journal *Music*:

> The story at the base of *Manru* is romantic in character and scene and tragical in outcome. In a general way it illustrates that irrepressible desire on the part of the Gypsy to wander, which Mr. Leland has characterized in his books on the Romanys; also, in an allegorical way, the contest supposed to exist between the artistic and domestic natures. The plot was borrowed from a Polish romance. Manru has won the love of a fair Galician maiden, Ulana, and married her Gypsy fashion. After a space she returns to her native village, among the Tatra mountains, to seek her mother's forgiveness and help. She receives instead the contempt of the villagers and a mother's curse. Her former friends taunt her with a song which tells of the inconstancy of all Gypsies under the influence of the full moon. Having already observed signs of uneasiness in her husband, Ulana seeks the help of Urok, a dwarf, who has the reputation of being a sorcerer, and who loves her. From him she obtains a magic draught, and

by its aid wins Manru back to her side for a time. Alone among the mountains, however, the baleful influence of the moon, the charm of Gypsy music, and the fascinations of a Gypsy maiden, break down his better resolutions and he rejoins his black-blooded companions. Oros, the Gypsy chief, himself in love with the maiden Aza, opposes Manru's rehabilitation in the band, but through the influence of Jagu, a Gypsy fiddler, he is overruled, and Manru is made chief in Oros's stead. Oros takes his revenge by hurling his successful rival down a precipice, a moment after a distraught Ulana has drowned herself in a mountain lake.[57]

Almost identical was a summary of the opera by Emily Grant von Tetzel in "At the Opera" report published in *The Theatre* in March 1902 (two illustrations used here come from this volume). Grant von Tetzel pointed out that "the argument of the libretto is of itself exceedingly simple, but as Paderewski has scored to it, it becomes almost as psychological as one of Richard Strauss's tone poems."[58] This similarity of Paderewski to Strauss is important, as *Manru* became a predecessor and one of the inspirations and models for Strauss's *Salome*.

There are two powerful conflicts permeating the opera and ending with double tragedy: the story of ethnic hatred and rejection between the Polish peasants and the Gypsies (who, as will be shown, are described in negative language usually referring to Jews), and the story of a failed cross-cultural marriage, replete with a "monster-in-law" mother of the heroine, domestic violence, love triangle, and irreconcilable differences, known in current American divorce epidemic. The two dramas intersect in the intimate story of Ulana and Manru who are unable to forge a new life together away from their respective ethnic communities and who are rejected by both as "renegades" and "traitors" to their own "blood."

The interactions of the two arches of the national/romantic story and its dark underpinnings troubled the composer, so Paderewski and Nossig continued to revise the libretto during the compositional process. According to reports in Polish and American press, the composer rewrote some parts three times and other up to ten times. The score of the opera (held on display in the Nationality Classrooms at the Cathedral of Learning in Pittsburgh) was written in pencil. It bears traces of numerous corrections and changes; in some places the notes were erased so intensely that the staves were removed with them.

The whole dramatic structure was changed from initial layout in two acts into three acts, with the addition of the character of Ulana's mother, who by cursing and rejecting her daughter increased the ethnic tension. Another addition was the Gypsy violin, inserting solo fragments of great beauty to the music in the third Act. Perhaps this expansion to clarify the ethnic characterization and conflict is the reason why the characters do not change much over the course of the story. The "racially-based" drama set out in Act I plays itself out in Act III; in between we only find out more about the characters' past history and motivation. They do not change. There are no surprising twists of plot, just explanations. This lack of dramatic surprises and the predictability of the final tragedy are among the work's primary weaknesses. Another flaw is the language, laden with overwrought cliché expressions. Nonetheless, it is worthwhile to review the opera in its entirety, indicating its most significant aspects.

Fig 6: Marcella Sembrich as Ulana in Paderewski's *Manru* at the Metropolitan Opera in New York, 1902.

The opera begins when the hero's wife, Ulana returns to her village, where a harvest festival is in progress. The Polish village is musically characterized by lively *krakowiak* rhythms and pretty melodies in a major mode, setting up generally a joyous atmosphere. Musically and dramatically, the first scene closely resembles the opening of Tchaikovsky's *Eugene Onegin* (1877-1878). It is surprising that the name of this and other Russian composers does not appear in Polish musicological studies of the opera by

Alexandra Konieczna and Andrzej Piber.[59] Russians, as far as traditional Polish music history writing is concerned, do not exist and have had no impact whatsoever on its development. Americans are able to see the parallels clearly (the similarity of *Manru* to *Aleko* was suggested to me by Steven Huebner, a specialist in 19th century opera), but Polish scholars are unwilling to acknowledge or search for them, and focus instead on the Western influences from Wagner or Verdi.

Ulana complains about Manru's marital unhappiness and tendency to stray: "When the full moon floods the night, errant grows the Gypsy weight. Burns his soul with longing wild, forsakes he wife and child!" These words become a self-fulfilling prophecy as the opera progresses. She feels that "his love grown cool, blind impulse his only rule" and if a Gypsy band comes by, they'll bewitch her husband, "o'er him they'll cast their spells infernal, and turn his heart by means unclean." The unhappy wife wants to return to her home village, but her mother Hedwig rejects her, since that return means the coming of the dreaded son-in-law, "a pagan, a vagabond." Ulana herself is mocked as a "gay Gitana" by the girls of her village.

The villagers dance in a peasant festival that is set as a courtship ritual in unity with the life-giving earth (Act I, Scene 8): "Join the gladsome dance! Let us dance and sing … Let the glad earth shake with our dancing." The ritual soon turns violent, with men chasing and capturing young women whom they force to dance in a circle of the village's youth. Ulana, caught in the whirlwind, is captured and forced to stay; Manru arrives to protect her and is chased away by the villagers: "Him we'll chase! Away, thou lout!…The hut of the Gypsy burn to the ground!" The echo of Russian pogroms is chilling. Ulana's hateful mother is no help: "Touch not the lepers! Back from the pestilent, poisonous pair!" Dramatically, the piece would have been better without her, but the intensity of ethnic hatred was essential to polarize the two "tribes" of Poles and Gypsies. As Michael Beckerman wrote in his keynote address for the Polish-Jewish Music Conference of 1998, ethnic hatred is coined in terms of physical rejection and disgust—as if we the human race were genetically and neuro-physically "wired" for ethnic purity, for the preservation of the familiar gene pool and rejection of the foreign blood.[60]

In the first Act, the villagers reject the foreign Gypsy and expel his wife Ulana from her community of origin, because she became tainted by associating with the "unclean." In the second Act, the focus shifts to the Gypsies and the marital dysfunction of the unhappy couple. Manru lives through the torment of the "call of his blood" urging him to return to the freedom of Gypsy life: "I curse the day I left the band And follow'd love's decoys. I envy them the wind-swept camp, The canvas homes unfurl'd, Their tents unfurl'd! I long to stroll thro' forests damp, And roam thro' all the world!" His conscience tells him of duty to reciprocate the love of his wife: "She is so gentle, patient, kind, So wondrous mild." Yet, his memory tells him of passionate Gypsies he used to love: "But there are women fill'd with fire, With passions wild!" Here is a dysfunctional marriage at its worst, replete with endless arguments between an unhappy husband longing for his former lovers, an unhappy wife trying to change her husband, a hapless child suffering for the faults of his elders, and a wicked mother-in-law.

After being expelled from her village and cast out by her own mother, Ulana focuses on her child and on regaining Manru's affection. She obtains love potion and makes him drink it; a love duet ensues. Apparently, only in self-delusion and abandonment could Manru be happy with his life as a blacksmith in a hut half-way between the pastoral village and the wild forest. He knows of the peasants' hatred and rejection, citing the villager's opinion of himself: "Falsehood, seduction, theft, conjurations, These are the Gypsy's true occupations." In this "racially-determined" internal conflict, Manru fights a losing battle between the sense of duty and obligation and the pull of his heart and instinct.

While expressing his longings for the freedom of roving the countryside, Manru sings: "With longings wild my soul is fill'd, Spring's voices shout within me. . . Thus rolls the molten lava stream, Dispersing havoc dire, supreme, Enfolding, whelming all in wreck! . . Is it a curse? There is no other life for me." Manru cites "the book of fate" condemning the Gypsies to "wander, rove eternally!" Again, the libretto's equation between the Gypsy and the Jew, the Eternal Wanderer, becomes transparent. Furthermore, the judgments of the "book of fate" are predetermined and cannot be changed.

While trying to follow his individual choice to love Ulana, Manru agrees to drink love potion and professes his undying love for the gentle wife: "A torrent through my veins is throbbing, like balsam sweet, yet like a fire's fierce glow! 'Tis joy in living! 'Tis joy in loving!" Ulana thinks that magic would restore their love and keep Manru "safe from roving..." In the delusional love duet, Ulana pressures Manru to admit his love for her and luxuriates in the illusion of its permanence: "Such heavenly rapture does past grief repay!" Manru, inspired by the drink, overflows with praise: "my sun, my treasure, thou my bliss divine, ever, ever I am thine!" The tense, dramatic love duet ends Act II.

Nonetheless, the force of fate, the "Gypsy blood" is stronger than the human will and love of Manru, as we see in Act III. In Manru's "moon madness" scene, the doomed hero again fights his true calling to the Gypsy way of life. His longings are stirred by eerie moonlight, portrayed in rich harmonies and impressionistic orchestral colors. His solitude is interrupted by distant, offstage voices of approaching Gypsies; a similar gesture of expanding the stage was effectively used in Strauss's *Salome* and Szymanowski's *Harnasie*. This scene fascinated Strauss and was echoed in a similar moon-madness scene of *Salome*. Paderewski's Manru sings: "The blood within my veins doth surge! A nameless impulse onward doth me urge!" He falls asleep and wakes up to the appearance of the Gypsies in one of the most powerful, dramatically, moment of the opera. They march in with a song that reveals their true nature: "Let us wander from place to place!... Onward, onward let us wander!" The males of the band initially reject Manru as "a traitor he to us, a renegade" and curse him for abandoning his tribe: "Who deserts his father's race, seeks the black blood to debase, which thro'his own veins doth chase, he be accurst!"

However, Gypsy women and elders are more generous. Manru's former Gypsy lover, the voluptuous Asa and the old fiddler Jagu tempt him with songs and dance as they want him to return. After hearing an enchanting Gypsy melody on the violin and cimbalom, Manru gives up his doomed struggle against fate and decides to rejoin the Gypsy band and return to his lover, Asa: "Ah, anew my blood is gushing, Manru's fiery, fuming blood! Thou 'tis to destruction rushing, I will float on passion's flood! Thine am I, thine!"

Nossig's text absolves Manru from personal responsibility for abandoning Ulana. The Gypsy man's actions are inevitable, motivated by ethnic predestination: "As heaven knows, I meant no wrong! My love was ardent, my patience long! My heart was thine in ev'ry mood, deceived was I by my own blood." Only when reunited with his tribe could Manru find true freedom: "Asa! Kinsmen! I to you belong! 'Tis freedom call! My fetters fall! With ye I'll rove! No more a slave!" The chorus's response is expressive of Nossig's revolutionary, socialist leanings and sounds almost like a Soviet anthem: "No more a slave! Away with bonds and slavery! Away with bonds and slavery! The world's our chattel, we alone are free!"

Rejected by her mother, her village compatriots, and, finally, by her husband for whom she left them, Ulana is entirely alone, abandoned in the empty space between the two eternally separate, preordained tribal-racial identities. No wonder, she can think of only one way out, to drown herself in the lake. "Overwhelmed with sorrow and anguish!... Cast aside, rejected and scorned! Deserted!" This is what Halka did in Moniuszko's opera—a peasant girl abandoned by her noble lover who married a woman from his own social class. This is all that Ulana can and has to do. Her fate was predestined and foretold in Act I and inevitably played out in Act III.

According to Nossig and Paderewski, Gypsies and Polish villagers could not live together. There was no middle ground, no compromise. Foreigners and outsiders would not be accepted in either culture; moreover, they were unable to accept such a transgression of ethnic norms themselves. Thus, the two inescapable deaths come quickly, for there is nothing to add: after Ulana's drowning, Manru is killed by his rival. Neither her departure, nor his return is possible in the world of narrowly defined ethnic borders, of strict, impermeable limits between cultures and "bloods," of the Gypsies and Polish peasants.

These groups could be called Jewish and Polish, with the same effect. For Nossig, an ardent Zionist and a "racist" of a peculiar sort, a Jew could not settle in a Polish village and become Polish. Not only would he be perennially rejected, also his own inborn tendencies ("blood") would continue urging him to return to his rightful place, within his community of origin. Similarly, a Polish girl, would be forever tormented after abandoning her religion, the village of her peers, and her sense of belonging and place in society. If, like Ulana, she'd peg all her hopes on her husband, she would become needy and unbearably annoying, but where else could she go for affection? She could not transform herself into a Gypsy woman without losing herself. Or, could she?

With a tragic ending of a double death of lovers rejected by both communities (comparable to the archetypical Romeo-Juliet story), the opera's true narrative was not romantic, but rather, "ethnic/racial," i.e., focusing on the inescapable strength and permanence of ethnic belonging exemplified by the "Gypsyness" of the title character, Manru, and the "Polishness" of his wife, Ulana. If it fails to appeal to the public, it is because of its crude racial determinism: the emphasis on the fixed character of ethnic identities and intransigent borders between co-existing, hostile communities.

Musically, though, the opera has much to offer. In some of its most radical and adventuresome pages, Paderewski brought together elements from Wagner (arioso, Leitmotif, Vorspiel) with traits of French (Bizet's *Carmen*) and Italian (Verdi's *Othello*) operas, linking them with stylized folklore of Polish highlanders and the Gypsies. The rich harmonic language (sequences of parallel augmented triads, etc.), colorful orchestration, and arioso dialogs bring to mind impressionist *Pelleas et Melisande* by Debussy and place Paderewski at the forefront of compositional avant-garde of the time, a location he abandoned for the sake of serving the political cause of independent Poland. Only the March of the Gypsies from Act III and the love duet from the finale of Act II may be taken out and performed independently, in concert.

The music flows in a continuous stream, sparkling with instrumental colors, melodies and rhythms. A wonderful dramatic scene at the beginning of Act II contrast the hard-working, angry Manru, hating his fate and his chains to sedentary life, with the lovely, delicate Ulana who sings a lullaby to their child. After the New York premiere, critics praised this song as the most memorable fragment of the opera, which, they said, should have ended with a happy end of a love duet and the ecstasy of reunited lovers in Act II.

Seeing *Manru* on the stage so impressed Richard Strauss that he ordered the score to study it while working on his masterpiece, *Salome* (1902-1905). The operas by Paderewski and Strauss share an emphasis on the orchestra in their portrayal of emotions and thoughts of the character, the use of arioso-recitativo instead of set pieces (Wagnerian traits), as well as the use of an eclectic range of musical means, from stylized folklore and modal melodies, to advanced and dissonant harmony saturated with chromaticism and sequences of tonally-ambiguous parallel chords. Both composers introduce brief conventional strophic passages amidst continuous arioso singing; both precede the action of the opera with an orchestral *Vorspiel* that leads into the following scene. A very important similarity is the expressive soliloquy of the tragically disturbed title characters, Manru and Salome, in both operas triggered by the moonlight.

The Oriental subject matter of Szymanowski's *Hagith* (1912-13) is an echo of *Salome;* yet its colorful, rich orchestration and vivid emotional outbursts in fragmented melodic lines evoke traits also singled out for praise in *Manru*. It is not well known that, *Hagith* has Paderewski's work hidden in its genealogy. In addition to the indirect influence through Strauss's opera, the theme of *Manru*, portraying ethnic conflict between Gypsies and Highlanders (the opera was called the first "opera tatrzanska" by some of its reviewers), may have inspired the setting of *Harnasie*, with the topical opposition of the sedentary villagers and wild, exotic Highland Robbers (Szymanowski) or Gypsies (Paderewski). The wildness of Szymanowski's Siuhaj seduced a village girl, a bride to be; similarly, the exotic, nomadic Gypsy, Manru, charmed and seduced the peasant Ulana.
In *Harnasie,* there is a reversal of values, though, accompanied by a positive transformation of the symbols of wild, untamed energy, associated with the wildness of mountain landscapes: the highland robbers are wild, but not evil, "black-blooded" as are *Manru's* Gypsies.

The Gypsy March, one of the most inspiring segments of the opera, foretells the March of the Highland Robbers in Szymanowski's *Harnasie* written 30 years later. The parallels are very strong, both in the dramatic setting and the music's impact: wild, powerful, with prominent base line, low melody, pounding rhythms, and syncopation. The role of the wildly disruptive highland brigands who are a symbol of threatening primordial power, in union with nature in Szymanowski's *Harnasie* was first played by Paderewski's Gypsies, who are neither cute and ornamental as in endless Hungarian Rhapsodies, but are genuinely dangerous and threatening, with their wonton disregard for rules of settled life, their anarchic way of choosing their leaders, their free-spirited, sensuous, passionate and wildly arrogant women who do as they please.

V. Paderewski's "Polonia"

It is clear from Paderewski's writings and from his decision to abandon music for the "greater" good of national cause that he considered ethnic identity of a Pole and serving the cause furthering the benefits to the Polish race to be a primary value in his life. The composer-politician was at one point unjustly accused of anti-Semitism because of his one-time support of Roman Dmowski's publications in 1910s.[61] He subscribed to a vision of a multiethnic Poland which he called a "United States of Poland" and where all ethnic minorities peacefully coexisted and collaborated, as in the golden age of the Jagiellonian kingdom (16th century). Yet, Paderewski's speeches contain countless appeals to the sense of an exclusive, racially-based Polish identity. A powerful expression of such sentiments may be found in his speech at the Chopin Centennial celebrations in 1910.[62] Paderewski said: "Why should the spirit of our country have expressed itself so clearly in Chopin, above all others? Why should the voice of our race have gushed forth suddenly from his heart, as a fountain from depths unknown, cleansing, vital, fertilising?"

The composer's most ambitious patriotic work is his Symphony in B minor, Op. 24, "Polonia" completed in 1909. This monumental three movement work (each movement lasts about 30 minutes), may have been inspired by the vast historic canvas of the same name, by Paderewski's friend, Jan Styka. The painting "Polonia" was completed in 1891, for the 100th anniversary of Poland's May Third Constitution and, in the words of historian Patrice Dobrowski, "reads like a 'Who's Who' of Polish fight for independence."[63] Led by Tadeusz Kościuszko, Styka's gathering of patriots includes poet Adam Mickiewicz, composers Chopin and Moniuszko, and painters Jan Matejko and Artur Grottger. Similarly rich is the array of allusions in Paderewski's Symphony, with numerous patriotic anthems and songs. According to a contemporary critic, Paul Cook, the work is a virtual compendium of early 20th century musical styles, inspired by the symphonies of Anton Bruckner. It contains "shards of Elgar, Delius, and Bax. Listen even closer, and you'll even hear Nielsen and Sibelius floating in the background."[64]

Interestingly, Paderewski's patriotic zeal inspired yet another work entitled *Polonia*—a symphonic prelude composed and premiered by Edward Elgar in 1915 (it is his Op. 76). Like Paderewski's Symphony, Elgar's piece includes numerous quotations from Polish songs and anthems, with a fragment of Paderewski's own *Fantasie Polonaise* serving as a tribute to the great Pole. After World War I, Paderewski's *Manru* and *Polonia* were largely forgotten, while he continued to tour and play the standard 18th- and 19th-century repertoire and his own piano pieces.

Fig. 7: Jan Styka's monumental painting, *Polonia*, which celebrated the 100th anniversary of the Third May Constitution in 1891; also at the Paris Salon. Postcard mailed from Lwów on 25 January 1914. Maja Trochimczyk Collection.

He abandoned the field of composition with a spectacular and telling gesture: by writing an anthem for the Polish Army in America, penning both words and music for this patriotic trifle of 1917. Paderewski was one of the organizers of this army, established in 1917-1918 in order to increase Poland's presence on the battlefields of World War and to give credence to the country's claim to a seat at the Peace. The composer penned the text for his anthem on a letterhead page from the Gotham Hotel in New York, his venue of choice during his American tours.

The song was immediately sent out to be performed in the recruitment camps in the U.S. and Canada.[65] The four-stanza poem is addressed to the emblem of Poland, a proud white eagle. The author reminds this symbol of free nationhood that it is time to fight for freedom of all the parts of the country and remember the heritage of ancient kings from Piast and Jagiellonian dynasties:

On, white eagle, once so severely wounded
Too long the funereal bells have resounded
With mad despair and mournful tunes.
Lead us to brave and fearless deeds.

On to fight! to fight! Where liberty is dawning!
On to fight for the Polish shore of sea!
For Poland free from tyrants' thrones!
For Poland—proud—of Piasts and Jagiellons.[66]

Fig 9: Postcard from World War I, the Polish Eagle surrounded by bloody bayonets: "Blood reddened the black soil, but there will be a hundred-fold harvest from such seed of God." Painting by A. Grzybowski for the widows and orphans of the Polish Legion. Krakow: Wydawnictwo Salonu Malarzy Polskich, n.d..

During World War I Paderewski was touring America advocating for the rebirth of the Polish state and his attention turned exclusively to the national cause. Nossig continued thinking and writing about his favorite subject, that is the necessity of Jewish return to Palestine. They were both fiercely dedicated to their respective national causes and shared a belief in ethnic predestination. The dissemination of such narrowly defined and limiting concepts of ethnicity and national identity extended to the views and music of Karol Szymanowski (1882-1937), whose relationship to these issues was somewhat ambivalent; one could say that he did not join the "national" camp without a fight.

VI. Paderewski and Szymanowski

Historical sources leave no doubt that Karol Szymanowski's slow rise to fame took place in Paderewski's shadow. In accordance with Harold Bloom's theory of the "anxiety of influence"[67] felt by a younger artistic generation towards that of their fathers, Szymanowski's ambivalence towards national style should be seen through the prism of his relationship to Paderewski. Bloom would have said that Szymanowski was compelled to reject and destroy Paderewski's heritage in order to emerge into his own. It is my thesis that Szymanowski's "individuation" as a composer led through a) youthful inspiration with Paderewski and the "national style" of Noskowski and the late romantic generation, to b) a rejection of this influence around 1906-1907 during the inception of "Young Poland" for the sake of a universalist style based predominantly on German models, to c) the creation of a fully individual, mature style based on universalist ideas, reaching its summit by 1921, and to d) a return to folklore, national style and ideology in Szymanowski's later period, foreshadowed by the first patriotic songs he composed in 1920. After returning to the heritage of national music that Paderewski represented and embodied prior to World War I, Szymanowski took over his predecessor's place, blending his new musical language with national traditions. Thus, it is only in the 1920s that he started composing mazurkas and stylizations of Polish folk dances, the staple of Polish music and Polish-inspired music in the late 19th century and the "visiting card" of every Polish composer seeking to affirm their ethnic identity as a Pole. These works, however, assume an entirely different harmonic and tonal guise than those of Paderewski.

As a composer, Paderewski was the paragon of Polish national style and expression in the 1890s and early 1900s: his compositions dealt with national subjects (e.g., Symphony "Polonia" and the opera *Manru*), included stylized Polish national dances (e.g., the krakowiak and mazurka), and the regional folklore from the Tatra Mountains (*Manru* and *Tatra Album*). In 1883, when Paderewski was transcribing *Górale* music played by Bartek Obrochta and other musicians from Podhale, Szymanowski was just a small child.⁶⁸ Szymanowski's first conscious encounter with the unadulterated folklore of the Tatras took place in the summer of 1921, forty years after Paderewski's. The younger composer had visited Zakopane before World War I in his childhood, but did not pay any attention to the area's music. Only in 1921, Szymanowski had a chance to listen to the famed *Górale* fiddler, Bartek Obrochta—the same musician whose performances Paderewski heard and transcribed forty years earlier.

Szymanowski belonged to a different generation than Paderewski, yet his early pieces, up to the *Variations on a Polish Folk Theme* in B major (1904), were heavily influenced by Paderewski and the romantic nationalism of his teacher Zygmunt Noskowski. If there is a clearly recognizable voice in the Variations it is that of Chopin (especially in the eight variation, *Marcia funèbre*), but it is Chopin heard via Paderewski.⁶⁹ The Variations, dedicated to Zygmunt Noskowski, composed in 1904, and premiered at a Young Poland concert of 1906, are based on a melody taken from Jan Kleczyński's collection of *Górale* folksong, *O muzyce podhalańskiej* (1888). Paderewski used this minor-mode contemplative melody in his *Tatra Album* in the 1880s.

Interestingly, this Podhalean theme of Szymanowski's *Variations* is in itself a "Paderewskian" element, since it most likely originated under the pianist's pen. As previously mentioned, Szymanowski's source, i.e., Kleczyński's transcription, was actually drawn from Paderewski's notebooks. In the form presented in Szymanowski's Variations, this theme does not sound particularly "Polish," as it is enveloped by lush late-romantic chromatic harmony and displays of virtuosity comparable with that of Liszt, Rachmaninoff, Scriabin, or Paderewski.⁷⁰ However, we can easily spot many stylistic parallels when juxtaposing Szymanowski's work with Paderewski's *Variations and Fugue* in A minor, Op. 11 (1884), *Thème varié* from *Miscellanea*, Op. 16, No. 3 (1885-1887), or what some scholars consider to be his best work for piano, *Variations and Fugue* in E-flat minor, Op. 23 (1885-1903).

Paderewski's influence may also be detected in the form of Szymanowski's Variations: a fantasy-introduction and ten variations, ending with a four-part fugue (the fugal closure is typical of the older composer, though it also expresses a tradition dating back to Beethoven). The coupling of the forms of variations with the fugue returns in two other major works by Szymanowski: Sonata No. 2, Op. 21 in A major (second movement), composed in 1910-1911 (published by Universal in 1912) and the finale of the Second Symphony (1909-1910). Both works reveal an impact of Paderewski's monumental *Variations and Fugue* in E-flat minor, often considered his best composition, filled with thick counterpoint, complex harmonic gestures, and a richness of textural and expressive means.

Paderewski-style textures are also evident in Szymanowski's *Fantasy* in C major, Op. 14 composed in 1905 and published in 1911.

The introduction's expressive marking in the introduction to Szymanowski's *Variations on a Polish Folk Theme*—i.e., *andante doloroso rubato*— brings associations with Paderewski's fascination with the spontaneous and flexible *tempo rubato* and the theme of "żal" or sorrow, understood as one of the main characteristic of musical Polishness at the turn of the century.[71] "Doloroso rubato" stands for two national characteristics ascribed to the "Polish spirit"—shaped by the sorrow caused by the country's loss of independence and the essentially nostalgic, though also noble and spontaneous nature of the Polish folk.[72]

The critical reception of this early work after its 1906 premiere led to what may be called Szymanowski's "Crisis of Emergence"—stung by accusations of being derivative and lacking talent, the composer left behind folksong, national themes, style and quotations, for the sake of more universal subjects. Thus, he expressed his opposition to the "parental" generation of Paderewski and Noskowski by abandoning the national interests of his predecessors in order to follow foreign, mostly German models. The Young Poland composers sought fame in Berlin and Vienna; they adopted Strauss and Wagner as their idols, thus enraging Polish music critics, such as composer Aleksander Poliński. His strongly voiced criticism of Szymanowski and Young Poland accused them of betraying the national cause by imitating German musicians and failing to "develop their own, Polish school:"

> What kind of 'Poland' it is which does not serve its homeland, as Chopin and Moniuszko served it, but who serves like slaves of the seasonally fashionable German musicians and promotes the ideas of musical 'Bund'?[73]

Participating in the Young Poland movement was just a step in Szymanowski's quest for an individual musical voice. After imitating Paderewski and Chopin, he continued to search abroad. Adolf Chybiński warned his colleague Zdzisław Jachimecki, one of Szymanowski's staunchest promoters, about the composer's chameleon-like adaptation of different styles: "Szymanowski should not be placed on a pedestal because if you knew all of his things well you would be able to recognize traces of influences by Chopin, Liszt, Reger, and particularly Scriabin."[74]

The turning point in Szymanowski's emergence from under Paderewski's shadow may be associated with the years 1910-1911: the 1910 Chopin Centennial in Lwów and the 1911 Vienna concerts featuring symphonies by both composers. Szymanowski did not attend the Chopin

Anniversary Celebrations and the First Congress of Polish Musicians in Lwów (22–28 October 1910) and his indirect role in the proceedings was minor. He won first prize in the composers' competition for his First Piano Sonata Op. 8, submitted by Zdzisław Jachimecki. In contrast, Paderewski was the most important guest: he gave the famous speech about Chopin as a national composer and seemed to have been "crowned as a king" of Polish music world, with his status confirmed by a performance of the second movement from the programmatic Symphony "Polonia" of 1907. A report in *Scena i Sztuka* pointed out that "the tone for the discussions was set by Paderewski—only he could with his authority enforce the attentive reason and with zeal strengthen the holy fires of love of Polishness."[75]

These holy fires failed to burn in Szymanowski who mocked Paderewski's ultra-patriotic style in the Chopin lecture that he dubbed his "'coronation,' i.e., inauguration" speech. In December 1910, Szymanowski thus criticized Paderewski's approach to Polish music: "Oh, these awful papercuts, these obereks, these dana-danas, this is the curse of our art."[76] The dislike that Szymanowski felt for Paderewski's patriotic rhetoric, both in words and music, soon developed into a strongly-voiced rejection. The younger composer attended the 1911 Vienna premiere of Paderewski's Symphony in B minor "Polonia" conducted by Grzegorz Fitelberg. The program also included Brahms's Violin Concerto, and Fitelberg's symphonic poem, *Pieśń o sokole* (Song about a hawk). After the premiere of Paderewski's patriotic Symphony, Szymanowski wrote to Jachimecki that this work was "an unbelievable abomination for which no words are insulting enough."[77] Other critics did not share his negative opinion and the concert was not an occasion of national embarrassment, as Szymanowski portrayed it. Obviously, the younger composer was anxious about the reception of his own Symphony No. 2 in B-flat major that he completed in 1910 and that was scheduled for performance ten days after Paderewski's monumental work. His comments expressed this nervousness and insecurity. Yet, they also summarized his approach to the topic of the national style and expression in music, as articulated by Paderewski's lofty goals of capturing Poland's history in sound: "patriotism in the realm of music is a complete absurdity."[78]

When viewing these two composers from a 21st century vantage point, we should remind ourselves that Szymanowski played a "junior" role in the Polish music world ruled by the world-famous Paderewski. The older master's presence and participation in festivals featuring Szymanowski's music among other young Polish composers was considered essential to their success. On 17 April 1914, the director of Universal Music in Vienna, Emil Hertzka, wrote to Szymanowski in London, asking him to contact Paderewski and request his participation in the planned festival to raise the event's public profile:

> I would like unconditionally to assure the participation of Paderewski, so that he would appear with an orchestra in his piano concert and during his evening of piano or chamber music would play piano works of you, himself and other Polish masters.[79]

Alas, World War I broke out and the festival was cancelled. The war and its aftermath, the rebirth of independent Poland, changed Szymanowski's attitude towards the national in music. After Paderewski abandoned composition and performance for the sake of extensive political campaigns for the country's independence, fundraising activities for the war victims, and a role in the Polish government, Szymanowski took over his place as Poland's greatest composer. This shift was symbolically captured in their turn to a functional genre, soldiers' songs.

Paderewski's 1917 hymn of the Polish Army in America *Hej, Orle Biały*! (Hey, White Eagle) was his last work, an earnest expression of patriotic zeal in words and music, and a trivial way to close an illustrious compositional career. Szymanowski's soldiers' songs, written in 1920 to cheer up the defenders of Warsaw against Soviet invaders, though equally insignificant musically, played an extremely important role in his oeuvre; they indicated a new direction, a return to musical patriotism. One of these songs, entitled *Wiedzie nas Haller* (Haller leads us), recently discovered by Elżbieta Jasińska Jędrosz and published in *The Songs of Szymanowski and His Contemporaries*,[80] praised the general of the victorious Polish Army that brought to Poland from the West under the leadership of Paderewski.[81] *Hej, Orle Biały!* was that Army's anthem.

In the year 1919, Paderewski served as Poland's Prime Minister and the Minister of Foreign Affairs, after representing the country at the Peace Conference in Versailles and signing the Peace Treaty on behalf of his country. The position of Poland's "national composer" was left empty when Paderewski' compositional career ended due to his focus on politics. Instead of claiming it back, Paderewski left for a self-imposed exile to Switzerland following a year of service in Polish government. During the same period, Szymanowski's musical identity as a Pole was confirmed in a series of political upheavals and musical events following the Soviet revolution. His family estate of Tymoszówka was in Ukraine; the rejection and expulsion of Poles by the briefly independent and fiercely nationalistic country resulted in the composer's exile and move to Warsaw. Here, again, Soviets were at the door: the invasion and the siege of Warsaw ended when

Poles defeated and pushed back the Red Army. These crises placed Szymanowski's Polish identity, earlier taken for granted, in the spotlight.

Szymanowski's first article published after the return to Poland in 1919, "Remarks Concerning the Contemporary Musical Opinion in Poland," return to the ground treaded earlier by Paderewski.[82] The article portrayed Chopin as a paradigmatic Polish composer who created "great, Polish, national music" permeated with expressions of the "soul of the nation (*lud*), in its fathomless racial depth."[83] The racially-charged language and patriotic rhetoric almost literally reflects Paderewski's remarks that so angered Szymanowski nine years earlier.[84] Both composers positioned Chopin's music as an expression of the spirit of the nation arising from its racial depths, though, Paderewski said it first, and expressed his racial ideals of ethnic identity in a more florid, rhetorical language.

Szymanowski's exposure to *Górale* music since 1920, including meetings with the famed fiddler Bartek Obrochta, who played for Szymanowski in 1922 and for Paderewski almost 40 years earlier (as discussed above)[85] resulted in the younger composer's use of the Podhalean folklore and its successful stylization and quotation in a full range of pieces, culminating with the ballet *Harnasie*. This choice of the Tatra Mountains as the site of Polish national identity was clearly articulated a generation earlier by Paderewski.

The shared "intransigent" views on immutable ethnic/racial identity, another common trait of Paderewski and Szymanowski, found an interesting expression in Szymanowski's controversial encounter with Paderewski's long-time friend and supporter, American music critic Henry Krehbiel. During his 1922 travel to the U.S., to the composer's dismay, the influential music critic mistook Szymanowski for a Polish Jew and while apologizing admitted to preferring Paderewski's works to those by Szymanowski.[86] In a review of a new music concert, published in *The New York Tribune*, Krehbiel listed Szymanowski among Polish Jews who—along with Russians—were transforming the image of contemporary music. Krehbiel complained about the invasion of composers from Russia and the Polish Jewry, naming Poldowski (i.e. Irena Wieniawska, from the Polish-Jewish family of Wieniawski), Szymanowski and Prokofiev as the main culprits.[87]

The composer was disturbed by this transformation of his national/ethnic identity and wrote two letters to the critic explaining his purely Polish heritage. On 15 February 1922, Krehbiel thanked Szymanowski for writing to him and thus expressed his view on the subject of racial identity in music:

I could not even remember whether during writing these observations about Russian and Polish invasion I remembered your name, however after consulting the article I realized that you were right that I placed you in the group of Polish Jews who gave guest performances and because this was obviously unpleasant for you, I sincerely ask you to forgive me this mistake. I never associate an offensive meaning with the description "Jew" and I have many friends among people of this race. But this designation awakens in my mind artistic problems and the possibility of their discussion – without awakening an accusation about acting under the influence of personal or racial prejudices, this should be my and your privilege.[88]

On 28 February 1922, Krehbiel responded to another missive from Szymanowski and explained that his criticism of the Polish composer's symphony and songs was not formed under the influence of personal racial or political emotions: "I have my ideas about music, its scope, possibilities and limitations as art, I also have my ideas about other arts. I can see that you also accept that you have aesthetic views. We have an equal right."[89] Krehbiel claimed that being a personal friend of a composer would not change his opinion about their music:

> my opinion about singing of Mme Sembrich and Brothers de Reszke and the playing of Paderewski as well as his Symphony, Fantasy and opera, (he also was a Polish composer whose works were performed here), was not influenced by the sincere friendship that I felt for them.[90]

Durng this *quid-pro-quo*, Krehbiel defended his dislike of Szymanowski's music as a matter of personal taste, while proclaiming an admiration for Paderewski's Piano Concerto, the opera *Manru* and the Polish Fantasy. In the eyes of this music critic, Paderewski's stature far transcended that of Szymanowski.

It is possible to see this debacle as an additional reason that Szymanowski's decision to further assert his Polishness in music. He started to think about the definitions of the "Polish race" and introduced this term into his studies of Chopin and Podhalean music.[91] Szymanowski's celebrated essay about Chopin of 1922 continued some national/racial themes from Paderewski's 1910 speech, but primarily emphasized international significance of Chopin's talent.[92] While preparing the Chopin study, he worked on versions of an unpublished article "The Question of Jewry" that contained disturbingly anti-Semitic ideas.[93] The character of his unfinished essay is evident in the first sentence in the notebook: "If the Jews did not so mercilessly hate us, Aryans, and if they did not fill their lives to the brim with this hatred —they would probably die of disgust with themselves."[94]

Szymanowski, offended to the core by being identified as a Jew, rejected Jewish influence in music and attempted to define its essence. Musically, Szymanowski proved that he was not a Polish-Jewish "modernist" by returning to the folklore of the Tatra Mountains, inspirations by Chopin, and stylized folklore following in the footsteps of Paderewski, and not—as it is generally acknowledged—solely foreigners, like Stravinsky and Bartók. He bought a villa in Zakopane and called it *Atma* (Breath), seeking rest and respite from his illness in the pristine clarity of mountain air. The fascination with Chopin and *Górale* music brought Szymanowski back into the sphere of Paderewski's influence, from whence he ventured and into his own musical world.

* * *

When Szymanowski and his "Young Poland" colleagues sought recognition for their music in Berlin in the early 1900s, only one living Polish composer was known in every country of the Western world: Ignacy Jan Paderewski. Now primarily remembered for its virtuosity, his music was once as well-regarded as his performing talents. In contrast to the maligned Paderewski, Szymanowski is often portrayed as a musical giant emerging from a field of nothingness.

Jim Samson stated in the entry on Szymanowski's works in the online edition of *The New Grove*, that "the poverty of indigenous traditions after Chopin forced Szymanowski to look outside his homeland, and . . . his development as a composer can be viewed as a series of responses . . . to German, French and eastern European styles respectively." In his appreciation of Szymanowski, Samson discredited the music of a generation of Polish composers directly preceding Szymanowski, including Żeleński, Noskowski, Paderewski, Stojowski, Statkowski, and others. True, their oeuvre does not equal the work of Wagner. Is this the only context, though? Perhaps the late-Romantic Polish national tradition should be compared not with the German avant-garde but with the music written in England by Ralph Vaughan Williams, Edward Elgar, Gustav Holst, Frank Bridge, and others associated with the "English renaissance" movement of the same period? The English composers, while failing to invent new musical languages, created a strong national school that continues to provide staple works for classical concerts and radio broadcasts in the English-speaking world. Nobody blames Elgar for not being Britten . . .

Why was it so important, then, to present Szymanowski as appearing "out of nowhere," from a cultural vacuum? Why was it so important for him to abandon the national path, for the sake of emulating the German and French avant-garde? Why was it crucial from 1920s onwards to return to the "national" in music, to return to the roots of Chopin and the folklore of Tatra Mountains, first discovered, collected, and stylized by Paderewski?

In a 1902 article about Paderewski's attitude to folk music, Helena Windakiewicz wrote:

> Paderewski found immediately path that Chopin followed… Without returning and getting lost he walks further and more confidently to the sources from which both drew. He knew that one does not have to imitate an external manner, that was done by so many imitators of mazurkas and polonaise with little talent, but he used the genial predecessor as an initiator in the research and comprehension of the spirit of national music.[95]

Paderewski's attempt at "elevating the folk to the universal" (to paraphrase Norwid's statement about Chopin from his epic poem, *Fortepian Chopina*), resulted in attractive, well-written solo miniatures, eminently playable concert pieces, one opera tainted by its pessimistic racial ideology, and one "monster symphony" overburdened with good intentions and an unduly detailed program. Szymanowski found and followed Paderewski's national path while avoiding its pitfalls. He did not start from a vast field of nothingness that was Polish music after Chopin. He developed his own highly original and significant musical voice by, in turn, imitating, rejecting and sublimating a national tradition that was rich, vibrant, and unjustly forgotten.

ENDNOTES

[1] Cited from Charles Phillips. *Paderewski: The Story of a Modern Immortal* (New York: Da Capo, 1978. Original edition, New York: The Macmillan Co., 1933). This chapter is based on my research papers presented at the following conferences: "Towards Poland's National Style: Paderewski or Szymanowski?" presented at a session on "Karol Szymanowski," Third International Conference on 20th Century Music, Nottingham, U.K., June 26-29, 2003; "Poland's National Composer: Szymanowski or Paderewski?" presented at a session on "Polish National Composers" at the 61 Annual Meeting of the Polish Institute of Arts and Sciences of America, McGill University, Montreal, Canada, June 6, 2003; "Paderewski and Nossig, Szymanowski and Fitelberg: Polish - Jewish Collaborations in Music." Session on "Jewish Presence in Polish Music" at the 62nd Meeting of the Polish Institute of Arts and Sciences of America, Pittsburgh, 3-4 June 2005. I published some ideas in editorials to Polish Music Journal vol. 4 nos. 1 and 2; a study of Manru appeared in Polish, "*Manru* Paderewskiego" (Paderewski's *Manru*). *Przegląd Polski (Nowy Dziennik)*, 26 June 2005, 1-2.

[2] Jim Samson, Entry on "Paderewski," *The New Grove Dictionary of Music and Musicians* (online, London: Mcmillan, 2002; accessed on 12 May 2002).
[3] See Małgorzata Perkowska and Maja Trochimczyk, "Selected bibliography: Ignacy Jan Paderewski," *Polish Music Journal*, vol. 4 no. 2 (2001).
[4] Henry T. Finck, Paderewski and His Art. (New York: Whittingham & Atherton, 1895); Edward Algernon Baughan, *Ignaz Jan Paderewski* (London, J. Lane; New York, J. Lane Company, 1908).
[5] Charles Phillips, *Paderewski: The Story of a Modern Immortal* (New York: Da Capo, 1978). Original edition, New York: The Macmillan Co., 1933. I discuss and cite Phillips's poem in "Paderewski in Poetry: Master of Harmonies or Poland's Savior?" *Polish Music Journal* vol. 4, no. 1 (2001), online.
[6] Paderewski & Mary Lawton, *The Paderewski Memoirs,* (New York : C. Scribner's Sons, 1938).
[7] Józef Orłowski, *Paderewski i Odbudowa Polski*, (Paderewski and the Rebuilding of Poland), vol. 2 (Chicago: The Stanek Press, 1940).
[8] Antoni Gronowicz, *Paderewski: Pianist and Patriot* (Edinburgh, New York, T. Nelson and Sons, 1943).
[9] Simone de Pourtales Giron published, among other titles, *Paderewski's Drama* (1947) and *The Mystery of Paderewski's Last Will*, issued in Poland as *Tajemnica testamentu Paderewskiego* (Paderewski's secret legacy), trans. by Hanna Olędzka, Renata Opechowska and Elżbieta Reis, (Kraków: PWM, 1996). Giron's claims of fraud lacked proper documentation, though were accepted by some scholars as factual. The book was withdrawn after a libel lawsuit won by the heirs of Strakacz.
[10] Aniela Strakacz, *Paderewski As I Knew Him: From the Diary of Aniela Strakacz* (New Brunswick, NJ: Rutgers University Press, 1949).
[11] Charlotte Kellogg, *Paderewski* (New York: Viking Press, 1956); Czesław R. Halski, *Ignace Jan Paderewski: Dzieje wielkiego Polaka i wielkiego Europejczyka* (The story of a great Pole and a great European) (London, Gryf, 1964).
[12] Adam Zamoyski, *Paderewski* (New York and London: Atheneum, 1982). A new book by Marek Żebrowski, *Paderewski in California*, is forthcoming from Figureoa Press, 2009.
[13] I edited these volumes of online *Polish Music Journal* (vol. 4, no. 1) dedicated to the music and life of the pianist-composer. Vol. 4 no. 1 from the spring of 2001 marks the beginning of my interest in Paderewski. The Journal's vol. 4, no. 2 was also dedicated to Paderewski; source documents appeared in *Polish Music Journal* vol. 5 no. 2. In 2002, my paper on Paderewski's image constructed with the help of Helena Modjeska and on his American female audiences was presented at the national meetings of American Musicological Society and Polish Institute of Arts and Sciences of America. A research paper, "Paderewski, His Art and His Audiences," is unpublished. Two articles are forthcoming in peer-reviewed or invitation-only publications, "An Archangel at the Piano: Paderewski and His American Audience," in *Polish-American Studies*, vol. 67 no. 1 (spring 2010), and "Celebrity in Decline: Paderewski's Political and Musical Reception in America 1919-1939" in Proceedings of the Third Conference *Topos Narodowy w Muzyce Polskiej*, F. Chopin University of Music, Warsaw, Poland, 2010.
[14] This subject has been examined in several dissertations written at American universities: David J. Morck, *Ignace Paderewski and the Re-Birth of the Polish State, 1914-1919*, (M.A. thesis, California State University, Fullerton, 1994); Joseph T. Hapak, *Recruiting a Polish Army in the United States, 1917-1919*, (Ph.D. diss., University of Kansas, 1985); Mieczyslaw B. Bienkowski-Biskupski, *The United States and the Rebirth of Poland, 1914-1918*, (Ph.D. diss., Yale University, 1981).

[15] Wieńczysław, Brzostowski, ed., "Ignacy Jan Paderewski," special issue of *Życie muzyczne i teatralne* vol. 2 no. 5/6 (May- June 1935), published in Poznań.

[16] Andrzej Piber, *Droga do Sławy: Ignacy Jan Paderewski w latach 1860-1902* (The Path to Fame: Ignacy Jan Paderewski in the years 1860-1902), (Warszawa: PIW, 1982).

[17] Małgorzata Perkowska, "Wczesne utwory Paderewskiego w świetle źródeł prasowych" (Paderewski's early works in the light of press sources), *Muzyka* 3-4 (1981): 117-20; "Nieznane kompozycje I.J. Paderewskiego w świetle badań żrodłowych" (Unknown works in the light of source research), *Muzyka* 33 no. 3 (1988): 21-32; Perkowska with Włodzimierz Pigła: "Katalog rękopisów I.J. Paderewskiego" (Catalogue of manuscripts by Paderewski), ibid., 53-70; *Wykonawstwo i koncepcje polityczne Ignacego Jana Paderewskiego* (Kraków: PWM, 1991); *Diariusz koncertowy Ignacego Jana Paderewskiego* (Paderewski's Concert Diary) (Kraków, 1990). Perkowska and Anne Strakacz-Appleton, eds.: *Za kulisami wielkiej kariery. Paderewski w dziennikach i listach Sylwina i Anieli Strakaczów. 1936-1937* (Behind the scenes of a great career: Paderewski in the diaries and letters of the Strakaczes) (Kraków, Musica Iagellonica, 1994).

[18] Mieczysław B. Biskupski, "Paderewski, Polish Politics, and the Battle of Warsaw, 1920," *Slavic Review* (1993): 503-513; and Mieczysław. B. Biskupski, "Paderewski as Leader of American Polonia, 1914-1918," *Polish American Studies* 43 no. 1 (1986). See also Anna Cienciała, *Poland and the Western Powers in 1938–1939. A Study in the Interdependence of Eastern and Western Europe* (Routledge & Kegan Paul, London; 1968); Anna M. Cienciala and Titus Komarnicki, *From Versailles to Locarno. Keys to Polish Foreign Policy 1919–1925*, (University Press of Kansas, 1984).

[19] Authors of Paderewski's political biographies in Poland: Marian Marek Drozdowski, *Ignacy Jan Paderewski. Zarys biografii politycznej* (Outline of a political biography) (Warsaw, 1979; Eng. trans., 1981, enlarged 1988); Henryk Przybylski, *Paderewski: Między muzyką a polityką* (Paderewski: Between music and politics) (Katowice: Unia, 1992).

[20] Małgorzata Woźna-Stankiewicz, "Poezja C. Mendesa w pieśniach Paderewskiego i kompozytorów francuskich" (C. Mendes's poetry in songs by Paderewski and French composers) in Wojciech Marchwica and Andrzej Sitarz, eds., *Warsztat kompozytorski, wykonawstwo i koncepcje polityczne Ignacego Jana Paderewskiego* (Composers workshop: Performance and political conceptions of Ignacy Jan Paderewski) (Kraków: Musica Iagellonica, 1991. English translation in *Polish Music Journal*, vol. 4 no. 2 (2001).

[21] Jerzy Jasieński, *Ignacy Jan Paderewski: Antologia* (Ignacy Jan Paderewski: Anthology), (Poznań: Ars Nova, 1996).

[22] See dissertations about Paderewski as musician: William Hunter Heiles, *Rhythmic nuance in Chopin performances recorded by Moriz Rosenthal, Ignaz Friedman, and Ignaz Jan Paderewski*, (D.M.A. thesis, University of Illinois, 1964); Paul A. Carlson, *Early Interpretation of Debussy's Piano Music*, (D.M.A. thesis, Boston University, 1998); and Albert W. Zak, *Paderewski's "Theme Varié" op. 16 no. 3: An Eclectic Analysis* (D.M.A. thesis, New York University, 1999). See also Maja Trochimczyk, "An Archangel at the Piano: Paderewski and His American Audience," forthcoming in *Polish-American Studies, op. cit.*

[23] "A Peaceful Solution: At the Next World's Fair Paderewski Will Play on All the Pianos at Once," caricature on the cover of *World Fair Puck*, published in Chicago, 15 May 1893. New York Public Library, Performing Arts Division, Research Collection, Paderewski scrapbooks. Used by permission. I first reproduced this caricature in my editorial, "Rediscovering Paderewski," in *Polish Music Journal* vol. 4 no. 2.

[24] I discuss this work in the first chapter, "From Mrs. Szymanowska to Mr. Poldowski: Careers of Polish Women Composers."

[25] The International Paderewski Piano Competition in Bydgoszcz, Poland is a site of repeated performances of his concerti, chamber, and solo piano music. Established in 1961,

it was banned by the government until its revival in 1986; the seventh competition was scheduled for 2009. Dux recording company has issued numerous CDs of Paderewski's music, including the first ever recording of *Manru*.

[26] The anthem is preserved in the Polish Museum in Chicago; its text and English translation have been published, in *Polish Music Journal*, vol. 4 no. 1. The distinction between free people of action and people dedicated to production (*homo faber*) is borrowed from Hannah Arendt's *The Human Condition* (Chicago: University of Chicago Press, 1958).

[27] See samples of these patriotic appeals in *Polish Music Journal* vol. 4 no. 2 (2001).

[28] Ignacy Jan Paderewski, "Poland" in Program of *A Recital for the Polish Victims' Relief Fund*. Boston, MA, Symphony Hall, 10 October 1915, cited in PMJ vol. 4/2.

[29] Ignacy Jan Paderewski, "Appeals for Polish Victims' Relief Fund, in *Polish Music Journal*, vol. 4 no. 2, Winter 2001.

[30] Zofia Helman,"The Dilemma of Twentieth-Century Polish Music: National Style or Universal Values," in Maja Trochimczyk, ed. *After Chopin: Essays in Polish Music* (Los Angeles: Polish Music Center at USC, 2000), 240. Translated by Joanna Nizynska and Peter J. Schertz from "Styl narodowy czy wartosci uniwersalne – dylemat muzyki polskiej dwudziestego wieku," in Anna Czekanowska, ed. *Dzidzictwo europejskie a polska kultura muzyczna w dobie przemian* (Krakow: Musica Iagellonica, 1995), 175-200.

[31] Wojciech Nowik, ed., *Topos narodowy w muzyce polskiej pierwszej połowy XIX wieku* (Warsaw: F. Chopin University of Music, 2006); *Topos narodowy w muzyce polskiej okresu postromantyzmu i Młodej Polski* (Warsaw: F. Chopin University of Music, 2008). The third conference was held in November 2009 and proceedings are forthcoming in 2010.

[32] I focus on this issue in my study of shifting identity of Jewish émigrés from Poland to America, in "The Question of Identity: Polish-Jewish Composers in California." *Polin: Studies in Polish Jewry* vol. 19 (2007), "Polish-Jewish Relations in North America," Anthony Polonsky and Mieczysław Biskupski, ed.

[33] See Magdalena Dziadek's two chapters in the present volume, "Polish Reception of Wagner's Music and Ideas," and "Portraits of Composers and Musicians in 19th Century Music Criticism."

[34] See Maja Trochimczyk, "Sacred/Secular Constructs of National Identity: A Convoluted History of Polish Anthems." In Maja Trochimczyk, ed., *After Chopin: Studies in Polish Music*. (Los Angeles: Polish Music Center, 2000), 246-268.

[35] Barbara Milewski, *The Mazurka and National Imaginings*, Ph.D. Dissertation, 2002. For a history of the mazurka see also my entries on Mazur(Mazurka), Oberek, and Kujawiak in Polish Dance site at USC Polish Music Center.

[36] Norman Davies, *God's Playground: A History of Poland* (New York: Columbia University Press, 1982).

[37] Anna Czekanowska, *Polish Folk Music: Slavonic Heritage, Polish Tradition, Contemporary Trends* (Cambridge: Cambridge University Press, 1990). I discuss this issue in *Polish Dance in California* (New York: Columbia University Press, 2007); see also my entry on *krakowiak* for the Polish Dance website of the Polish Music Center at USC: http://www.usc.edu/dept/polish_music/dance/krakowiak.html.

[38] Włodzimierz Poźniak, "Opera po Moniuszce," [Opera after Moniuszko], in *Z dziejów polskiej kultury muzycznej* [From the history of Polish musical culture], vol. 2 (Kraków: PWM, 1966), 307-310.

[39] Timothy Cooley explored this topic in his dissertation and several studies: "Authentic Troupes and Inauthentic Tropes: Performance Practice in Gorale Music," *Polish Music Journal* 1 no. 1 (Summer 1998), http://www.usc.edu/dept/

polish_music/PMJ/issue/contents.html; "Constructing an 'Authentic' Folk Music of the Polish Tatras," in Maja Trochimczyk, ed., *After Chopin: Essays in Polish Music* (Los Angeles: Polish Music Center at USC, 2000), 243-262.

[40] Timothy J. Cooley, *Making Music in Polish Tatras: Tourists, Ethnographers, and Mountain Musicians*, Bloomington, IN: Indiana University Press, 2005.

[41] Timothy J. Cooley, "Authentic Troupes and Inauthentic Tropes: Performance Practice in Gorale Music," *Polish Music Journal* vol. 1 no. 1 (1998).

[42] My account of interactions of Paderewski with the Chałubiński circle is based on Andrzej Piber's *Droga do sławy, op. cit.*, 95-6.

[43] I discuss Modrzejewska's relationship to Paderewski and her impact on the start of his international career in "An Archangel at the Piano: Paderewski's Image and His American Audience," forthcoming in Polish American Studies, vol. 67 no. 1 (Spring 2010); earlier versions, entitled, "How Paderewski Plays: *Chant d'amour* and the Aestheticism of America's Gilded Age," were presented at national meetings of American Musicological Society and Society for American Music in 2002.

[44] Piber, *op. cit.*, 113. Jan Kleczyński: "Zakopane i jego pieśni" (The Zakopane region and its songs), *Echo Muzyczne i Teatralne* 1 (1883-4): 419-21, 429-30, 447-8, 468-70; "Wycieczka po melodie" (Excursion for melodies), *Echo Muzyczne i Teatralne* 1 (1883-4): 567-9, 588-90, 610-11, 631-2, 653; "Melodie Zakopiańskie i Podhalskie" (The melodies of the Zakopane and Podhale regions), *Pamiętnik Towarzystwa Tatrzanskiego* 12 (1888): 39-102.

[45] The work's subtitle: "Tanze und Lieder des polischen Volkes aus Zakopane."

[46] *Tatra Album. Tänze und Lieder des polnischen Volkes aus Zakopane* [Polish folk dances and songs from Zakopane, arranged by the composer for 4 hands], (dedicated to Chałubiński) 1884, 6 mvts.; published in Berlin in 1884 by Ries und Erler: Part I: 1. *Allegro con brio* 2. *Andantino* 3. *Allegro con moto*; Part 2: 4. *Allegro maestoso* 5. *Allegretto* 6. *Allegro ma non troppo*.

[47] There is one, small-book-length study of Manru by pianist Lidia Kozubek, *Opera Manru Ignacego Jana Paderewskiego* (Katowice: 1993). Aleksandra Konieczna and Andrzej Piber published articles about this work in 1991, and I wrote a short reevaluation in 2005, but otherwise, *Manru* remains unknown.

[48] Nossig's publications include *Jüdische statistik,* (Vienna: C. Konegen, 1887); *Ueber die bestimmende Ursache des Philosophirens; Versuch einer praktischen Kritik der Lehre Spinozas* (Stuttgart: Deutsche Verlags-Anstalt, 1895); *Kolonizacya żydowska w Palestynie* (Lwów: "Kadimah," 1904); *Nowe drogi w syonizmie* (Lwów: "Moriah," 1905); *Die neue Turkei und ihre Führer* (Halle: O. Hendel, 1916); *Zionismus und Judenheit: Krisis und Lösung* (with Davis Ertracht; Berlin and New York: Interterritorialer Verlag "Renaissance," 1922); *Polen und Juden die polnisch-jüdische Verständigung zur Regelung der Judenfrage in Polen* (Wien: Interterritorialer Verlag "Renaissance," 1921). He also wrote plays: *Die Hochstapler: Schauspiel in 3 Aufzügen* (Leipzig: Hermann Seemann Nachfolger, 1902); *Abarbanel: das Drama eines Volkes* (Berlin: H. Steinitz, 1906); *Die Legionäre: Drama in drei Akten* (Berlin: Kühling & Güttner, 1900, 1937); *Don Juan als moralist; lustspiel in einem aufzug* (Berlin: Concordia, 1910s). He even penned a book on Paderewski (*I.J. Paderewski*; Leipzig: H. Seemann Nachfolger, 1901).

[49] According to the *Encyclopedia of the Holocaust,* Nossig became director of the department of culture and the arts in the Judenrat (Jewish Council) in the Warsaw ghetto. He collaborated in the Holocaust as he believed that the trains taking Jews to their death were taking them on the first stage of their journey to Palestine. Nossig was executed by the Żydowska Organizacja Bojowa (Jewish Fighting Organization; ZOB), at the end of January or in February 1943 (the precise date is unknown).

[50] His death was a subject of a recent surrealist play performed in New York in 2004. Written by Lazarre Seymour Simckes and performed at Theater for the New City in May *Nossig's Antics* received mixed reviews.

[51] I thank Steven Huebner for bringing this work to my attention. See also James Parakilas, "The Soldier and the Exotic: Operatic Variations on a Theme of Racial Encounter, Part II," *The Opera Quarterly* 10, no. 3 (spring 1994): 43-69.

[52] Aleksandra Konieczna, ""Manru Ignacego J. Paderewskiego - Kilka uwag o stylu i dramaturgii" in, *Warsztat kompozytorski, wykonawstwo i koncepcje polityczne Ignacego Jana Paderewskiego* (Composers workshop: Performance and political conceptions of Ignacy Jan Paderewski). Conference proceedings. Edited by Andrzej Sitarz and Wojciech Marchwica. Kraków: Musica Iagellonica, 1991:134-148. English translation as "Stylistic and Artistic Features of Paderewski's Manru," *Polish Music Journal*, vol. 4 no. 2 (2001).

[53] Cited from *Listy Stanisława Witkiewicza I jego korespondentów*, ed. Maria Olszańska and Anna Micińska, 1. *Listy o stylu zakopiańskim* (Kraków, 1979), 116; letter of 24 June 1901 written after the Lvov premiere of the opera, 444.

[54] Piber, Andrzej. "Recepcja Manru w USA" (The reception of Manru in the USA). In *Warsztat kompozytorski, wykonawstwo i koncepcje polityczne Ignacego Jana Paderewskiego* (Composers workshop: Performance and political conceptions of Ignacy Jan Paderewski). Conference proceedings. Edited by Andrzej Sitarz and Wojciech Marchwica. Kraków: Musica Iagellonica, 1991, 120-133. English translation in Polish Music Journal, vol. 4 no. 2 (2001).

[55] Cited from Piber, *op. cit.*

[56] Charles Godfrey Leland, *The Gypsies* (Boston, New York, Houghton, Mifflin and Co., 1898). Fragment reprinted in Paderewski's *Manru*, piano-vocal score, New York: Schirmer, 1901.

[57] Egbert Swayne, "Paderewski's 'Manru," *Music* vol. 21 (January 1902): 153-162.

[58] Emily Grant von Tetzel, "At the Opera," *The Theatre* vol. 11, no. 13 (March 1902: 24-26.

[59] Both cited studies were published in 1991 and reprinted in English translation in Polish Music Journal vol. 4 no. 2 (2001).

[60] Michael Berckerman, "Neuro-Nationalism, or Why Cant' We All Just Get Along?" *Polish Music Journal*, vol. 6 no. 1 (2003).

[61] Adam Zamoyski, *Paderewski* (New York: Atheneum, 1982), 143-44.

[62] Ignacy Jan Paderewski, "Fryderyk Chopin," (1910), *Polish Music Journal*, vol. 4 no. 2 (2001).

[63] Patrice M. Dabrowski, *Commemorations and the Shaping of Modern Poland*. (Bloomington and Indianapolis: Indiana University Press, 2004),105.

[64] Peter Cook, review for Amazon.com, http://www.amazon.com/Paderewski-Symphony-Maksymiuk-Ignace-Jan/dp/B00000G3ZC

[65] There are two sources for this song, entitled in both *Orzeł Biały* (White Eagle): a 1918 edition, New York: T. Wroński (arrangement for male choir and piano or brass band); and an undated arrangement for mixed choir and brass band, copied by Henryk Opieński. See, Małgorzata Perkowska and Włodzimerz Pigła, "Katalog rękopisów I.J. Paderewskiego" (Catalogue of manuscripts by Paderewski), *Muzyka* 33 no. 3 (1988): 53-70.

[66] "Hej, orle biały, ongi tak zraniony, / Zbyt długo brzmiały pogrzebowe dzwony, / Rozpaczy szały i żałosne tony. / Wiedź nas na śmiały czyn, nieustraszony. Hej na bój, na bój, gdzie wolności zorza, / Hej na bój, na bój, za polski brzeg morza. / Za Polskę wolną od tyrańskich tronów, / Za Polskę dumną—Piastów, Jagiellonów." Full text is reproduced in Appendix II to Maja Trochimczyk: "Paderewski in Poetry: Master of Harmonies or Poland's Savior," Polish Music Journal vol. 4 no. 1 (2001).

[67] Harold Bloom, *The Anxiety of Influence: A Theory of Poetry* (New York, Oxford University Press, 1973).

[68] See Magdalena Dziadek, *Polska krytyka muzyczna w latach 1890-1914. Koncepcje i zagadnienia* (Polish music criticism in 1890-1914: concepts and issues), vol. 1, Katowice: Wydawnictwo Uniwersytetu Śląskiego, 2002, see Chapter VII, "Programy muzyki narodowej."
[69] See a letter to August Iwański, on 20 Jan 1919 that "Paderewski could help a lot, especially in regards to myself and my family" 572, and 591, trying to leave Tymoszówka by seeking Paderewski's protection. *Korespondencja* vol. 2, 1.
[70] According to Tadeusz Zieliński.
[71] Ignacy Jan Paderewski, "Tempo Rubato" and "The Best Way to Study the Piano," in *The Paderewski Paradox / Le paradoxe Paderewski* (Lincoln: Klavar Music Foundation, 1992); the first article was originally published in Henry Finck, *Success in Music and How it is Won* (Charles Scribner's Sons, New York, 1909) and reprinted in *Słowo polskie* 15 no. 491 (1910); the second article first appeared in *The Strand* in 1895. For more information see Ronald Stevenson, "The Paderewski Paradox" and "Preface to Paderewski's Essay on Tempo Rubato," in *The Paderewski Paradox / Le paradoxe Paderewski*, ibidem.
[72] See the discussions of national spirit in texts by Zielinski (1901), Piduch, and Anderton, reprinted in the *Polish Music Journal* Vol. 5, No. 2, winter 2002, http://www.usc.edu/dept/polish_music/PMJ/issue/5.2.02/contents.html.
[73] Cited from *Kurier Warszawski's* second review of 22 April 1907, entitled "Młoda Polska w muzyce" and followed by a polemical response by Szymanowski and Fitelberg.
[74] Letter from Munich written by Chybiński to Jachimecki on 14 May 1907; published in vol. 1 of *Karol Szymanowski: Korespondencja*, ed. Teresa Chylińska (Kraków: PWM), 129.
[75] Report on 9 Nov 1910 in *Scena i Sztuka* no. 46: 7, "Zjazd chopinowski a przyszłość muzyki polskiej" reprinted in Chylińska, ed., *Karol Szymanowski: Korespondencja*, 247.
[76] Karol Szymanowski, letter to Zdzislaw Jachimecki, 4 December 1910, reprinted in Chylińska, ed, *Korespondencja* vol. 1, 245.
[77] Letter written on 13 November 1911 from Vienna to musicologist Zdzisław Jachimecki in Kraków. See Karol Szymanowski, *Korespondencja* (Correspondence), ed. T. Chylińska, vol. 1 (Kraków: PWM, 1994), 310.
[78] "Patriotyzm w dziedzinie muzyki jest niemożliwym zgoła absurdem," ibidem.
[79] Teresa Chylińska, ed. *Korespondencja, op. cit.*, vol. 1, 439, originally in German.
[80] Zofia Helman, Teresa Chylińska, and Alistair Wightman, eds., *The Songs of Karol Szymanowski and His Contemporaries* (Los Angeles: Polish Music Center, 2002), 210-228.
[81] It may be worthwhile to note as an aside that Józef Koffler, Poland's first twelve-tone composer and later a Holocaust victim, fought as a soldier defending Warsaw in the campaign that inspired Szymanowski's songs.
[82] Karol Szymanowski, "Uwagi w sprawie współczesnej opinii muzycznej w Polsce" (Remarks concerning the contemporary musical opinion in Poland), published in *Nowy Przegląd Literatury i Sztuki* no. 2 (July 1920). Reprinted in Szymanowski, *Pisma muzyczne, op. cit.*, 33-47
[83] Szymanowski, "Remarks," *op. cit.*, cited from p. 40. English trans. Alistair Wightman, in *Szymanowski on Music*, op. cit., 73-94. I discuss Szymanowski's racial views on Chopin in "Chopin and the 'Polish Race': On National Ideologies and the Chopin Reception," chapter in Halina Goldberg, ed., *The Age of Chopin: Interdisciplinary Inquiries*, Bloomington: Indiana University Press, 2004, 278-313.
[84] Szymanowski, "Remarks," *op. cit.*, cited from p. 40. English trans. Alistair Wightman.
[85] *Sabałowa nuta* in Chybiński's trascription is used in *Słopiewnie* and *Harnasie* in many variants. Szymanowski initially studied the music in transcription, not live: in March 1920 he first received Adolf Chybiński's transcription. He heard the piece played by Obrochta in 1921.
[86] Letters of 15 and 28 February 1922, from Henry Krehbiel to Szymanowski (translation not provided, retranslated from Polish by Jerzy Zawadzki).

[87] Henry E. Krehbiel, "New Composers Get Hearing as Slavic Invasion Continues. Songs by Lazare Saminsky. Cantata by Samuel Thewman. Presented at Town Hall by Society of Friends of Music." *The New York Tribune* (6 February 1922). Reprinted in Karol Szymanowski, *Pisma*, vol. 2, *Pisma literackie*, ed. Teresa Chylińska (Kraków: PWM, 1989), 230. The account is based on Teresa Chylińska's introduction to Szymanowski's "Kwestia żydostwa" (The Question of Jewry), in Karol Szymanowski, *Pisma*, vol. 2, *Pisma literackie* (Kraków: PWM, 1989), 226-23. Szymanowski's essay appears on pp. 238-240 and is preceded by fragments on Judaism and Christianity, "Pansemityzm- Panaryjskość," and Gustav Mahler (pp. 231-237).

[88] Krehbiel's letter to Szymanowski, in T. Chylinska, ed., Korespondencja, op. cit., vol. 2, part 1, 342-343.

[89] Krehbiel's letter to Szymanowski in Chylinska, ed. op. cit., letter No. 153, 350-1.

[90] Krehbiel's letter to Szymanowski, *op. cit.*.

[91] Statements based on Kornel Michałowski's introduction to Karol Szymanowski's essay "Fryderyk Chopin," in Szymanowski, *Pisma muzyczne*, op. cit., 89.

[92] According to Kornel Michałowski, first drafts of his earliest and most extensive text about Chopin were probably written during his stay in New York (two trips in 1921 and 1922).

[93] Karol Szymanowski, "Kwestia żydostwa" (The Question of Jewry) in Szymanowski, *Pisma literackie,* op. cit., 238-240. According to Chylińska's introduction to this essay, the earliest notes about readings on the "Jewish question" date back to 1918-19, a longer fragment was written after 1920 and the essay completed in 1922 (Chylińska in Szymanowski, *Pisma literackie*, op. cit, 227-228).

[94] Szymanowski, notes for "the Question of Jewry," n.d., in Szymanowski, *Pisma literackie*, op. cit., 231.

[95] Windakiewicz, Helena. "Stosunek dzieł Paderewskiego do muzyki ludowej. Studium analityczne." (Relation between Paderewski`s works and folk music.) *Echo Muzyczne, Teatralne i Artystyczne*, nos. 956, 958, 959, 961 (1902).

A Romantic Interlude VI

Fig. 14: *In Love*. A postcard of a Polish nobility couple in stylized national costumes. Published in Kraków, Poland, ca. 1890. Maja Trochimczyk Collection.

Fig. 15: *Engaged*. A postcard of a Polish nobility couple in stylized national costumes. Published in Kraków, Poland, ca. 1890. Maja Trochimczyk Collection.

Fig. 16: *Married*. A postcard of a Polish nobility couple in stylized national costumes. Published in Kraków, Poland, ca. 1890. Maja Trochimczyk Collection.

Chapter 8

Feliks Nowowiejski – A Polish Composer from the Warmia Region

Krzysztof D. Szatrawski

When browsing through periodicals published in the first twenty years of the twentieth century we are likely to encounter numerous references to one young, but already highly esteemed composer, Feliks Nowowiejski (1877-1946). At that time, he was one of the most famous Polish composers and his compositions were performed in all the great musical centers of Europe. Nowowiejski was born in Warmia ("Ermland" in German - M.T.), a part of East Prussia that was under German rule since the 13th century when it had been conquered by the Teutonic Knights.[1] In his youth, Nowowiejski, though a Pole, was a subject of the king of Prussia; he received his education in German lands, in Regensburg and Berlin. After the composer had consciously selected being "Polish" as his national identity in the 1920s, the German music press ignored his oeuvre. However, his works could still be heard in the concert halls on several continents. A recipient of numerous awards and honors in the 1930s, the composer produced a large number of pieces; sadly, his musical legacy was partly destroyed by the ravages of World War II. Nonetheless, a far more significant "destruction" of his accomplishments occurred on a more abstract level after the war. It stemmed from the lack of recognition and appreciation of the true value of Nowowiejski's music by people who imposed their judgments on results of artistic activity and who claimed ownership over a right to determine the value of works. I believe that their claims were false since the art that they condemned and rejected often transcended their level of expertise. Until the present time, despite the efforts of other, more positively-minded scholars and dedicated music lovers who were able to comprehend the significance and quality of Nowowiejski's oeuvre, the composer has remained under-appreciated, undeservedly neglected, and—at times—completely forgotten. This article, as the first English-language survey of Nowowiejski's accomplishments serves to redress the omissions and errors that marred his reception in Poland and abroad.

Feliks Nowowiejski was born on 7 February 1877 in the village of Barczewo (it was called "Wartembork" at that time); his family had lived in Warmia for many generations.[2] He was the fifth child of Franciszek and Katarzyna Nowowiejski; his musical interests were already apparent when he attended elementary school. As a child, young Feliks composed a piano suite called *Łatwe Tańce Klasyczne i Współczesne* (Easy Classical and Contemporary Dances).[3] After noting such a musical accomplishment, his parents decided to send him to a music school in the village of Święta Lipka (the school's original German name was "Musik-Anstalt in Heiligelinde"). Despite the fact that this school enjoyed a reputation of "the best music school in Warmia" during the time when Feliks Nowowiejski studied there, its years of glory were long past before his enrollment. Founded in 1722 by the Jesuits as Seminarium Musicum, after 1816 the School continued to be managed by Catholic priests working for the sanctuary in Święta Lipka. At first, this status of a private church school was beneficial for its development. Unfortunately, this situation did not last long. Since the final years of the nineteenth century, the school's building had been slowly disintegrating; simultaneously, the lack of funds and growing competition from state schools caused the number of students to decline. Inevitably, the decision was made to close the school in 1909.[4] Nowowiejski studied in Święta Lipka from 1887 to 1893. From his certificate of graduation we learn that, in addition to lessons in singing and harmony, he also studied violin, piano and organ performance.

Fig. 1: A postcard of Olsztyn (Allenstein) in 1915. Maja Trochimczyk Collection.

However, we should assume that these three instruments were not all that he was able to play. He was quite a multi-instrumentalist. It is known that after leaving the school, he joined the Second Division of Grenadiers and performed in the Military Orchestra in Olsztyn as a cellist and French horn player.

In this early period of study, Nowowiejski composed a series of popular pieces, including a march entitled *Unter der Friedensflagge*, which, in July 1898, received the first prize in a competition organized by a magazine, *The British Musician*. Subsequently, it was published and popularized in many European countries.[5] Other well-known military marches by Nowowiejski include: *Deutschlands Stolz, Under den Schwingen Des Deutschen Aars,* and the *Zeppelin-Marsch*. The popularity that the fledging composer achieved in Olsztyn thanks to his youthful compositions inspired his friends to offer him financial assistance so he could travel to Berlin to continue his advanced music studies. It also influenced Nowowiejski's decision to continue studying music performance during a summer program for organists at the Stern Conservatory in Berlin.[6] He enrolled in the Conservatory on 1 April 1898 and completed his studies in September of the same year. In an opinion expressed on his graduation certificate by the director and faculty members of the Conservatory we read:

> Despite a short time of study he has managed to become educated as a confident, professional organist. His great diligence and impressive musical gifts allowed Nowowiejski to learn to play great compositions by Bach and modern composers properly and with understanding. He revealed this ability several times during organ recitals organized by his professor... He also dedicated himself, with great enthusiasm and surprising success, to piano performance, working under the direction of Adolf Stemler, and ending up being able to acquire both pianistic agility and the ability to interpret classical works with stylistic faithfulness... In the area of composition, which he studied with Mr. Ernest Edward Taubert, he exhibited a fluent musical invention. He learned the ability to shape various musical forms with confidence and has been able to master, with assuredness and indications of unique talent, all the principles of constructing a great symphonic form.[7]

Both the diploma from the Stern Conservatory and a series of positive opinions by teachers with whom he studied confirmed the young musician's professional capabilities. Nowowiejski did not treat his studies as a mere academic exercise: he sent these opinions to Father Józef Teschner, the priest and dean at St. Jacob Church in Olsztyn, upon whom the choice of the church organist depended.⁸ After receiving his graduation certificate from the Stern Conservatory on 1 October 1898, Feliks Nowowiejski was accepted for the organist position in Olsztyn. Unfortunately, while he striving to fulfill all the varied duties of a church organist, he was not able to work on his own music to an extent commensurate with his ambitions. What, for a musician from a military orchestra, could have been the summit of a professional career, appeared far less enticing to a graduate of Berlin Conservatory. Therefore, instead of remaining at his post, Nowowiejski decided to continue advanced music studies. In 1899, he filed a petition with Warmia Bishop, Andrzej Thiel, for a Church scholarship. When he did not receive an answer, the composer announced his intention of departing from Olsztyn and abandoning his job, in order to join the students at the School of Church Music in Regensburg. He traveled there at the beginning of 1900. In Regensburg, Nowowiejski participated in a three-month advanced music course, held at the Kirchenmusikschule from 1 January to 16 April 1900. As it was the case at the Stern Conservatory, teachers noticed his diligence and abilities. They expressed these observations in positive evaluations that the composer received upon completing the courses. Thus provided for, yet without any sources of income or prospects of a suitable position abroad, the young musician unwillingly returned to Olsztyn to his work as an organist. Nonetheless, having tasted creative freedom, he felt that his duties as an organist were constricting his development as a composer to an increasingly large extent. Consequently, on 1 October 1900 the composer finally resigned from his church organist position.

    Armed with a handful of letters of recommendation, Nowowiejski chose Berlin as his future residence. This choice was probably influenced by personal contacts that he had made during his studies there. We may assume that the composer may have maintained these contacts through correspondence, though there is no information about any letters surviving from this period. Already in the summer semester of 1901, Nowowiejski was simultaneously enrolled in two music programs: the School of Masters at the Royal Academy (Königliche Musikakademie) and the Fryderyk Wilhelm Royal University. As a University student, he attended lectures given by Prof. Schmid (German folksong), Prof. Max Friedländer (general history of music), Prof. Oskar Fleischer (history of church music and history of 19th-century music), and Prof. Max Dessor (history of 19th-century music aesthetics). At the School of Masters, his professor of composition was none other but Max Bruch; Nowowiejski owed this composer the most at the threshold of his own compositional career. In 1902, three compositions by Nowowiejski received the annual Giacomo Meyerbeer's Prize for composition: *Uwertura Romantyczna* (Romantic Overture), a fugue for eight-part chorus with orchestra, and an oratorio on a biblical theme, *Powrót syna marnotrawnego* (Return of The Prodigal Son). This prize was paid out in cash installments, with the purpose of funding an eighteenth-month artistic travel throughout Europe, including visits to various cities in Italy, as well as short-term residencies in Paris, Brussels, Vienna, Munich, Dresden, Leipzig, and Berlin. In addition, during the Meyerbeer Prize travels the prizewinner was obliged to send in two new compositions back to the awards committee. Therefore, after almost three semesters spent at the University, Nowowiejski interrupted his studies and began his artistic tour through Europe. During his concert travels, he encountered music and culture of many European artistic centers and established personal contacts that proved to be incredibly fruitful for his further development as a composer. For instance, after many years, Nowowiejski wrote the following about his visits with Antonin Dvorak:

> In Prague, Antonin Dvorak welcomed me warmly and became interested in me, a fledging artist, to such an extent that he decided to give me numerous important guidelines for my compositions. He also conducted with me several analyses of the greatest masterpieces of music literature. I will never forget these lessons to which the genial composer dedicated himself with his whole soul. Therefore, I must say that I benefited greatly from them, and from Dvorak's belief in the necessity for original creativity, a need that I considered to be well-accorded with the character of the Slavic race. The master of Czech music placed the strongest emphasis on two ideological principles (i.e., artistic originality and faithfulness to one's national identity - M.T.) that remained the main guideline and a signpost for artistic activities during my whole life.[9]

The statement cited above becomes particularly significant in the context of Nowowiejski's crystallizing Polish national consciousness. During his travels through Europe, perhaps under the influence of encountering so many different national and ethnic cultures, the composer became aware of his belonging to Polish culture and of his Polishness. The first mention of this subject can be found in his letters and notes written still in German. It needs to be explained that particular national and cultural circumstances prevailing in Warmia of his youth often led Nowowiejski to doubts and anxieties about his national identity.

Although Polish language was spoken in the composer's family home, it was not used as a literary language. As was the case with many Warmian families, the Nowowiejskis used Polish in daily life, but wrote in German. The first gesture the young composer made towards self-definition as a Pole was in his concert overture, *Swaty Polskie* ("Polish Matchmaking"), for which he received a prize in 1903 at the Ludwig van Beethoven Competition in Bonn. Nowowiejski inscribed the title of the work in Polish, while giving the German translation, *Polnische Brautwerbung*, in brackets. Local music critic responded to this overture with enthusiasm in a multitude of positive reviews.[10] The overture was also welcomed with great interest by the Polish music world; it was Nowowiejski's first work included in the repertoire of Polish orchestras in Lwów, Warsaw, and Kraków.

After returning to Berlin, Nowowiejski established contacts with the Polish community; studied Polish literature; composed songs to Polish poetry; directed Polish amateur choirs; was in contact with Polish composers in Poznań, Warsaw and Kraków; and last but not least, searched for a suitable subject for a Polish opera. In 1903, the composer received the Paderewski Prize in Bonn. In 1904, he won the Meyerbeer Prize for the second time. On this occasion, it included a scholarship allowing him to continue his music studies at the School of Masters in Berlin; he commenced his studies immediately and completed the advanced course of studies in 1906. In an opinion given by Max Bruch at the conclusion of Nowowiejski's studies, we may read, among other statements, that

> His inborn capabilities and melodic talents directed Nowowiejski primarily towards composing for chorus and orchestra. Thanks to his diligence, intelligence, endurance and meticulous studies of outstanding works of art, he was able to acquire valuable knowledge in this domain. Furthermore, he was also capable of using this knowledge in his own compositions. The results of these studies were primarily two oratorios: *Quo Vadis?* and *Znalezienie św. Krzyża* (The Discovery of the Holy Cross).[11]

Both works mentioned by Bruch opened Nowowiejski's path to recognition as a composer. The *Discovery of the Holy Cross*, premiered on 11 April 1906 in Lwów, and *Quo Vadis?* premiered on 4 May 1907 in Usti at Łaba, were greeted with very warm welcome. Nonetheless, the composer was not yet entirely pleased with these compositions and continued to revise them. The premiere of a second, thoroughly revised version of *Quo*

Vadis? took place seven years after the original—on 7 March 1914, in Amsterdam. The work, based on a German libretto by Antonina Jüngst, loosely interpreted scenes from Henryk Sienkiewicz's Nobel-prize winning novel of the same title. During the Amsterdam premiere, the ensemble, consisting of soloists, chorus and Conzertsgebouw Orchestra was conducted by Johann Schoonderbeek. Like the premiere of the original version, the revised oratorio's premiere was received with enthusiasm by the public and music critics. Performances in other cities and countries followed, thus transforming *Quo Vadis?* into Nowowiejski's most acclaimed large-scale composition.

In 1909, Nowowiejski announced his candidacy for the position of the director of the Kraków Music Society, in ancient Polish capital in southern region of the country; then the capital of Galicia, a part of Austro-Hungarian Empire. On 13 March 1909, he conducted a concert with a program that included Beethoven's Eroica Symphony and his own compositions. This concert, warmly received by local music critics and the members of the Music Society, was decisive in Nowowiejski's appointment to the position of the Society's music director. He worked as the director and conductor of the Music Society Orchestra from September 1909 to April 1914. Unfortunately, these five seasons that Nowowiejski contributed to the musical life of Kraków were locally interpreted in a different, more critical light than the original, highly successful concert that brought the composer to the capital of Galicia. In press reviews and articles, the composer was accused of succumbing to "directionless chaos" in his programming. Worse still, suspicions were voiced about possible weaknesses in his own music. In opposition to these critical statements, Nowowiejski's supporters emphasized the consistency of his programming and praised his "rational direction and planned thought." Already after his first concert as the Music Society's director, Kraków music critics regarded Nowowiejski coldly, some even with open hostility. They accused him of a variety of absurd transgressions and mistakes; they did not refrain from highlighting Nowowiejski's supposed non-Polish background and suspiciously "anti-Polish" (German) education. The military marches that he composed while serving in the Prussian Army were used as a proof of Nowowiejski's purported "German identity." Unfortunately, it was not the first time that personal insults and jealousy influenced judgments about this composer; neither was this the only occasion when nationalistic cliques opposing an "outsider" appealed to xenophobic feelings.

Fig 2: A Postcard of Krakow, view of the Wawel Castle, 1901.
Maja Trochimczyk Collection.

The Music Society Orchestra consisted of professors and students of the Conservatory, as well as of amateurs. In terms of its size, it was a symphonic orchestra. In performances of larger pieces it was assisted by musicians from military bands and ensembles. Under Nowowiejski's directorship, the Orchestra, despite being quite mediocre before his time, performed several "single-composer" concerts dedicated to the works of Zygmunt Noskowski, Robert Schumann, Johannes Brahms, Ludwig van Beethoven, Franz Liszt, and Richard Wagner. Furthermore, Nowowiejski did not ignore works that required performing forces that actually transcended the capabilities of the Music Society Orchestra, such as Symphony No. 3 by Gustav Mahler, Symphony No. 9 by Ludwig van Beethoven (without the choral finale), and Symphony No. 9 by Anton Bruckner. It is easy to notice that all of the composers that Nowowiejski admired and wanted to promote in Kraków, came from the sphere of German culture, Austria and Prussia. Clearly, he did not have any interest in French, Italian, Russian, or English music. These were the early years of Debussy, Ravel, and Stravinsky—composers associated with a completely different aesthetic orientation than the one upheld by Nowowiejski through his programming choices.

During his residency in Kraków, Nowowiejski was also engaged in lively concert activities as an organist and teacher. As a result of all these duties and activities, he composed far less than before. However, one song he created during this period, *Zagasły już* (They Were Extinguished Already), was honored at a composition competition organized in Lwów to celebrate the 100th anniversary of the birth of Fryderyk Chopin. Karol Szymanowski won that competition with his Piano Sonata; Ignacy Jan Paderewski was the guest of honor at the celebrations and gave a well-known speech about Chopin.[12] Also during the Kraków period, for the occasion of the unveiling of the Grunwald Monument in 1911 (the monument's design and production was sponsored by Paderewski, here the paths of the two composers crossed for the second time),[13] Nowowiejski composed a song entitled *Grunwald* to a patriotic poem by Maria Konopnicka. In its original printed version, the song appeared with the title *Hasło* (Password). Later it became known under yet another title, that of *Rota* (The Oath), under which it is known today as one of Poland's most popular anthems.[14]

Fig. 3: Fragment of Rota (The Oath), with text by Maria Konopnicka, translated by Maja Trochimczyk.

We shall not abandon the land of our ancestors!
We shall not allow to bury our language!
We are the Polish nation, the Polish folk,
We are the royal descendants of Piast,
We shall not allow the enemy to oppress us,
So help us God! So help us God!

Germans will not spit in our faces,
they will not germanize our children,
our troops will stand with weapons,

the peasants will be our leaders,
We shall go when the golden horn will sound,
So help us God! So help us God!¹⁵

From the moment of its first performance, this song was considered to be one of Poland's national anthems, notable for its praise of the tenacity of Polish peasants, who were so attached to their land that they solemnly swore they would never "abandon the country of their forbearers." In addition, the song's strongly voiced anti-German sentiments were well aligned with the generally "anti-Teutonic" character of the entire Grunwald celebration, marking the 500th anniversary of the victory of allied Polish and Lithuanian troops over the Teutonic Knights who had attempted to take over their land. Nowowiejski's memorable "military-march-style" melody amplified the feelings of zealous patriotism, energy and devotion to Poland expressed in the song's text.

During the period of working for the Kraków Music Society, Nowowiejski frequently traveled abroad, participating in "one-composer" concerts of his music that were organized, among other places, in Warsaw, Amsterdam, and New York. He also often appeared in guest performances as a conductor. However, despite this strenuous work and continuous concert activities, Nowowiejski failed to win the good will of local music critics. This fact is hardly surprising, if we were to consider that the most important music critic active in Kraków at that time, Zdzisław Jachimecki, had also been seeking the position of director of the Music Society which was awarded to Nowowiejski. Furthermore, Jachimecki's continuous critical attacks on Nowowiejski stemmed from an additional, less-known source, not just from his disappointed personal ambitions. In the early 1900s, the music critic embarked on a personal mission to transform Karol Szymanowski into the leading "national" composer of Poland. This personal agenda skewed his reporting about other composers, including Nowowiejski, Noskowski, and Paderewski.[16]

Finally, besides the unfavorable critical reviews, there were several other negative factors influencing Nowowiejski's growing discomfort in Kraków. The absence of a permanent opera company, or, at least, a larger orchestral ensemble of greater professional quality were very discouraging. In 1914, tired by the lack of recognition and scant musical resources, the composer left Kraków and moved to Berlin. Unfortunately, he could not have made such a choice at a worse time, since his move took place close to the outbreak of World War I. As a subject of the Prussian King, Nowowiejski was drafted to serve in the Prussian Army. Luckily, he managed to spend World War I in Berlin, working for a garrison orchestra. However, his compositional activities came to a halt. Only on 15 December 1918 did he return to an active musical life as a composer, by giving a concert of his music in the aula of Hochschule der Musik in Berlin. The program of this concert included *Dumka* "Klaglied um die gefallene Soldaten" for organ; *Legende*, Op. 32, for violin and piano; and two world premieres—the *Częstochowa Litany* for violin and organ (dedicated to the Black Madonna from the shrine of the Bright Mount in Częstochowa) and a work entitled *Christmas* and scored for solo organ. Programs of subsequent concerts organized by Nowowiejski included an increasingly greater number of works by Polish composers. In after-war Berlin such public displays of Polishness were not welcome by predominantly German audiences, especially since the Eastern borders of Germany were not established yet. In the state of geographic flux after the Versailles Treaty ending World War I, such areas as Silesia, Nowowiejski's home province of Warmia, and other large districts could either become parts of the new Poland or remain in Germany. As a result of musical demonstrations of Nowowiejski's Polish patriotism in Berlin, demonstrations that were not welcome by the German music society, the Hohschule's administration banned the composer from entering the school's campus. Other music institutions soon initiated a boycott of his compositions. We saw that he was unwelcome in Kraków as too German; paradoxically, he was rejected in Berlin as a Pole.

In October 1919, after ten months of weathering these nationalistically motivated sanctions and attacks in Berlin, Nowowiejski returned to his home province of Warmia. Almost immediately, he became involved in political activities of the Polish Referendum Committee, giving concerts in numerous Warmia towns and advocating for the vote in favor of Warmia joining Poland. After the referendum was held on 11 July 1920 and the Polish side lost, he did not accept the results of the vote that kept Warmia in Germany. He left for Poland. At first he intended to live in Warsaw; at the end, he settled in Poznań, where he maintained continuous contact with Poles living in Warmia. He also provided support for their activities by teaching classes for organists and choral conductors; his students later enriched the ranks of Polish activists in Eastern Prussia.[17]

In Poznań, Nowowiejski started working as a theory professor at the new State Music Academy and School, which was founded on 16 October 1920. Initially, he taught counterpoint, harmony, choral harmonic settings, and orchestration. After 1923, he limited his teaching activities to organ performance and improvisation. Finally, after 1927, he gave up working at the Conservatory entirely and dedicated all his time to composing full-time. During the interwar years, 1919-1939, Feliks Nowowiejski was a household name in Poznań. He directed choirs; assisted choirmasters; advised other musicians; taught hundreds of students; and created a new repertoire for the amateur choral movement. Already in the mid-1920s, he enjoyed a respect and admiration so widespread that tram and trolley conductors refused to accept his money for tram tickets. Writer Leonard Turkowski, whose father was a Poznań conductor at that time, remembered that "if a tram conductor would demand from him (Nowowiejski - K.D.S.) a fee for travel he would be once and for all completely compromised in his professional environment of tram conductors.[18]

During the interwar period, Nowowiejski composed a series of interesting stage works. The young composer had written his first opera, entitled *Busola* (Compass), while still enrolled as a student at the Berlin School of Masters; unfortunately, this work was never performed. A second attempt at an opera was not made until the composer's years in Poznań. The new opera, *Legenda Bałtyku* (The Legend of the Baltic Sea), premiered on 28 November 1924 at the Poznań Opera House, was enthusiastically received by music critics and the audience. The accumulation of folk motives, monumental choral parts, and the content—based on a legend about a sunken city, Wineta— were the features that caused *The Legend of the Baltic Sea* to be so welcome in Polish music theaters. The composer used here some material from his unperformed early opera, *Busola*. At the end of the 1930s, he composed another opera, *Ondraszek* (the title, in Silesian dialect, means "Little Andrew"), but its score did not survive the war.

In the same period, Nowowiejski composed two ballets, *Malowanki ludowe* (Folk Paintings), and *Król wichrów* (The King of Winds). Both ballets were based on melodic ideas borrowed from Polish folklore and earlier used in Nowowiejski's other compositions. In *Malowanki ludowe* we may find motives from an earlier composition, *Swaty Polskie*. Additionally, the finale of the ballet features a Polish folk dance, *kujawiak,* also composed earlier. As it was his custom with large-scale compositions, after the Poznań premiere of *Malowanki ludowe*, the composer withdrew this piece and made numerous revisions to the score. Sadly, the new, revised and improved version was not performed during the composer's lifetime. The second ballet, *Król wichrów* is based on the folklore of southern Poland, the Podhale (Foothills) area of the Tatra Mountains. In its first, original version, this ballet was entitled *Tatry*; the second version featured a new title, *Leluja* as well as other changes; but only the third, final version was presented to the public.

In the 1920s, besides stage works, Nowowiejski composed a series of monumental oratorios. From the time he had studied in Święta Lipka, religious music occupied a privileged place in his oeuvre. The composer was a deeply religious person. Since 1926, he served as the president of the Association of Church Choruses. His most esteemed compositions include oratorios on religious themes: *Quo Vadis?*, mentioned above, *The Return of the Prodigal Son*, and *The Discovery of the Holy Cross*. Sadly, he did not manage to complete another oratorio entitled *Misterium Crucis* (The Mystery of the Cross), a work which included his oft-performed setting of Psalm 136, also known under the title *Ojczyzna* (Homeland). Beside the oratorios, Nowowiejski's list of large-scale vocal instrumental works includes a series of Mass settings. The best known masses are: *Missa de Lisieux, Missa Mariae Claramontanae, Missa pro Pace, Missa Stella Maris, and Missa de Lourdes*. Due to their monumental proportions these works were not performed frequently: the approximate duration of the youthful oratorio, *Quo Vadis?* is two hours; other works in this genre had similar proportions. It is, perhaps, for this reason that numerous fragments of these oratorios continue to be performed independently and have a separate concert life of their own.

The cultural significance of Nowowiejski's oratorios on religious themes was recognized when the composer received the title of the Papal Chamberlain from Pope Pius XI in 1935. Almost at the same time, in February 1935, he was awarded a State Music Prize from the Polish government. During the following year he received an Honorary Medal from the Union of Polish Vocal and Instrumental Ensembles. On 11 November 1936 he was honored for his "achievements in the development of the arts" with the Commander Cross of the Order Polonia Restituta, the highest state honor in Poland.

Nowowiejski was active as an organist for most of his life; therefore, music for organ constitutes an important part of his oeuvre. His organ symphonies may be located at the border between religious and concert music. In the 1930s, Nowowiejski wrote nine Organ Symphonies, Op. 43, and four Organ Concertos. These Symphonies and Concertos are for the same instrumental setting, i.e., a solo organ; they are also connected by numerous formal similarities, so they differ mainly in name. It is probable that the number of organ symphonies is limited to nine because the composer greatly respected Beethoven's symphonic works and followed the example of other composers (such as Bruckner), who did not want to transcend the number of Beethoven's Nine. Perhaps for that reason, Nowowiejski called the last four works for organ solo "concerti." These organ compositions are considered Nowowiejski's artistic testament as well as the apex of organ symphonic writing in Poland.[19]

In the 1930s, the composer returned to symphonic forms and to writing for the orchestra. He had withdrawn two of his earlier symphonies after their premieres in Frankfurt-am-Mein in 1905 and in Usti at Łaba in 1907.[20] In 1930 he revisited the score of his Second Symphony, revising the work and re-designating it as his official Number 1. During the decade 1930-1940, Nowowiejski completed the final version of Symphony No. 1, in B minor, subtitled *Siedem barw Iris* (The Seven Colors of Iris); wrote his Symphony No. 2, *Praca i Rytm* (Work and Rhythm), which was premiered during the Week of Polish Music held in Poznań in October 1938; and composed his Symphony No. 3, subtitled *Białowieska* ("of Białowieża") and named after the most revered old-growth forest in Poland, associated with legends about the founding of the country and with the Polish royalty who used to hunt there. It may be seen as a paradox that Nowowiejski completed his Symphony No. 4, *Symphony of Peace*, only after the outbreak of the war, in German-occupied Poznań in 1941. During the Poznań period of his life, he also composed a Cello Concerto (1938) and the Piano Concerto in D minor, the latter was completed on 18 September 1941. Nowowiejski's vocal-instrumental compositions from the Poznań period include a symphonic poem for soprano and orchestra, entitled *Róże dla Safo* (Roses for Sappho), based on love poetry by Maria Pawlikowska-Jasnorzewska, and composed in 1935-1939.

Following the outbreak of the war, almost immediately after the German army entered Poznań, the composer was denounced by collaborators as a famous Polish patriot harboring anti-German beliefs. Luckily, after being questioned by Gestapo, Nowowiejski was not arrested nor imprisoned. Nonetheless, after this incident he did not feel secure at home and went into hiding; he found refuge in a hospital run by the Sisters of St. Elizabeth (Elżbietanki). Soon, however, he decided to move from Poznań to Kraków and to seek escape from the dangers and horrors of war in the peaceful world of music. He continued to compose, writing almost incessantly during the whole war period. It is interesting to note that Nowowiejski wrote his final compositions in haste, as if he were urged to write by an internal compulsion, as if he could foretell that he was running out of time and that he would soon suffer debilitating problems with his health. In December 1941, not long after moving to Kraków, the composer suffered a stroke. A slow convalescence and repeated attacks of illness made it impossible for him to continue his creative work on a scale to which he was accustomed. Consequently, his musical activities during the war years were limited to home concerts. Though seriously ill, he survived the war and returned to Poznań, where he died on 18 January 1946.

Nowowiejski's music enjoyed a widespread popularity during his lifetime, with concerts organized in the greatest music centers and the participation of the most distinguished orchestras. However, the respect that surrounded him passed very quickly. Right after his death in 1946 plans were made to rename the village of Wartembork where he was born to honor his name, so that it would have been called "Nowowiejsko." This, however, did not happen and the village received the name of "Barczewo" instead.

One reason for this changed attitude towards Nowowiejski was rooted in the conflict of public and private attitudes to religion in the new socialist Poland. The composer's monumental works of straightforwardly religious nature were not appreciated by the official music critics, historians, and, most importantly, governmental decision-makers, active during the Stalinist period of the 1940s and the early 1950s. As a result, the interest in Nowowiejski's oeuvre that peaked in late 1930s waned soon after his death. In the late 1950s and 1960s, the years of triumphs of the avant-garde, he was mainly remembered as the composer of *Rota* and a huge number of choral songs, including arrangements from Warmia folklore. A few enthusiasts of his music tried to preserve works that often remained only in manuscripts. For instance, the manuscript of the score for *Quo Vadis?*, Nowowiejski greatest oratorio, provided the basis for a full reconstruction of this piece. Numerous other works, though, were lost without a trace. A full catalog of Nowowiejski's compositions has not been compiled until today.

Most efforts to preserve and promote the music of Nowowiejski took place in north-eastern Poland, the region of his birth. The Olsztyn Music Society made the largest contribution to the promotion of Nowowiejski's oeuvre. Scholarly research about the life and activities of the composer commenced in the 1950s with articles commemorating his accomplishments and emphasizing the significance of his music. On the occasion of the 15th anniversary of the Olsztyn Symphony Orchestra, celebrated on 1 February 1962, two mono-thematic concerts dedicated to Nowowiejski's music were held. Simultaneously, the Olsztyn Symphony

Orchestra was re-named after the composer. On 25 February 1963, the world premiere of Piano Concerto in D minor, Op. 60, took place in Olsztyn. Nowowiejski's compositional achievements were often presented in Olsztyn throughout the 1960s. Opportunities for an increased interest in Nowowiejski's music was provided by the celebrations of the 20th anniversary of his death in 1966 and the 90th anniversary of his birth in 1967.[21] In his home village of Barczewo, a Nowowiejski Museum was opened.

Jan Boehm published a biography of the composer in 1968; it was reprinted in 1977 in a book series issued in Olsztyn by the local publishing house, "Pojezierze." In 1977, on the occasion of the 100th anniversary of the composer's birth, a scholarly conference was organized in the region of his birth; its results were later published by the State Higher School of Music (PWSM) in Gdańsk in collaboration with the conference's main sponsor, the Higher School of Education (WSP) in Olsztyn. On the same occasion of Nowowiejski's centenary, in May 1977, his monumental *Missa Pro Pace* was performed in Poznań at the Church of All Saints, with the participation of two choruses, conducted by Father Zdzisław Bernat and Stefan Stuligrosz respectively. Polish music recording company, Veriton, issued a double-LP album from this performance.

The next milestone in publicizing the oeuvre of Feliks Nowowiejski may be traced back to mid-1980s, when "Feliks Nowowiejski Music Days" were first organized in Olsztyn. Gradually, concerts of Nowowiejski's music and of various works by contemporary composers became an important and memorable element in Olsztyn's musical life, so much so that the six editions of the festival constitute an impressive chapter in the history of the city. A part of these events was always a scholarly conference, most of the time dedicated to Nowowiejski's music. Materials from two of these sessions were issued in two volumes of studies, published in 1986 and 1989. Earlier, in 1985, the composer's biographer, Jan Boehm, published another book about him, entitled *Feliks Nowowiejski, Artysta i Wychowawca* (Feliks Nowowiejski: An Artst and a Teacher). While such scholarly publications provided opportunities for more comprehensive appraisal of the composer's activities and for making his figure more visible in the local artistic milieu, music editions and recordings of his works still remained rare.

Only in the 1990s, did the Chopin Academy of Music in Warsaw issue a 16-volume edition of Nowowiejski's organ works, edited by the distinguished organist, Prof. Jerzy Erdman. We did not have to wait long for the evidence of the impact of this edition. In 1998, a German recording company, MDG, issued three CDs with a complete set of nine Organ Symphonies, Op. 45. The editor of Nowowiejski's organ works, Prof. Erdman, also recorded a two-CD album for the company CPO, with a program that included Organ Symphonies nos. 4, 5, 7, as well as the Fourth Organ Concerto. Both publications are of great artistic and historical significance, since they fill a huge void and bring Nowowiejski closer to the awareness of the general public. We should hope that future releases complete the range of recordings of Nowowiejski's organ music and of all the remaining works. The publication of Nowowiejski's organ compositions resulted in a renaissance of interest in this composer among organists. The efforts of the Chopin Academy of Music and the Feliks Nowowiejski Society have led to the organization of international competitions dedicated to monumental organ compositions by Nowowiejski. So far, the jury of the competition has included such famous organists as Julian Gębalski, Daniel Roth and Wolfgang Zerer.

Furthermore, selected works from Nowowiejski's oeuvre finally entered the repertoire of Polish orchestras. This group of compositions, besides the oratorio *Quo Vadis?* Op. 30, also includes: the Symphony No. 3, Op. 53; the Symphonic Poem, *Pożegnanie Ellenai* (Farewell to Ellenai), Op. 17, No. 3; the Concert Overture *Legenda Bałtyku* (The Legend of the Baltic Sea); and the Piano Concerto in D minor, "Slavic," Op. 60. In 1991, on the occasion of the visit of the Pope John Paul II to Olsztyn, during the solemn welcoming ceremony, the Olsztyn Symphony Orchestra played the "March of the Pretorians" from Nowowiejski's oratorio *Quo Vadis?*. On 14 May 1993, in Święta Lipka where Nowowiejski began his formal musical education, the world premiere of his oratorio *The Return of the Prodigal Son* took place, with the participation of soloists Maria Olkisz, Błażej Grek, and Ryszard Smeda, as well as the choirs of the Higher School of Education and the Cathedral of St. Jacob in Olsztyn, and the orchestra of the Olsztyn Philharmonic directed by Piotr Borkowski.[22] The same work was featured during celebrations of 125th anniversary of the composer's birth, held at the Academy of Music in Poznań, in October 2002. In 2000, Nowowiejski's *Quo Vadis?* was stylishly produced by Silesian Opera in Bytom, in Zbigniew Bogdański's staging inspired by paintings by Henryk Siemiradzki, Joseph Turner and Salvadore Dali. In 2008, his villa in Poznań, a historical monument, was transformed into a site of chamber music concerts and festivals, organized by the Feliks Nowowiejski Society.

Despite these signs of renewed interest, we should conclude that the oeuvre of Feliks Nowowiejski, recognized and appreciated during his lifetime, has been largely and thoroughly forgotten after the war. Efforts on his behalf, made by a small group of scholars and music critics, did not yet bring expected results.

Perhaps one reason for the rejection of Nowowiejski's music by wider contemporary audiences stems from its wide stylistic range, encompassing popular patriotic works and neo-romantic concert compositions. Another reason for a distrustful attitude towards Nowowiejski's music could be a general lack of interest in traditional, romantic aesthetics during the 1960s, the years when the Polish school of "sonorism" came into being and caught the attention of music critics, musicians, and audiences in Poland and abroad. In contrast to the avant-garde, Nowowiejski's music was traditional and romantic. It was filled with emotion and pathos, sometimes seemingly grandiose, but never ironic, doubting, or self-reflective in ways that would appeal to the avant-garde. There was no room for his fascination with religion and romantic poetry in a culture so ostensibly celebrating an image of optimism, secularism, and progress, with such profoundly ingrained and widespread traits of doubt, anxiety and depression. Times have changed since then and romanticism is no longer a "dirty word." We should now revisit the repeatedly postulated issue of publishing all of Nowowiejski's music in print and sound recordings. Such a publication effort seems to be, at present, the most important condition for the restoration of the composer's proper place in Polish culture. Nowowiejski's music remains controversial, with critical judgments ranging from accusations of epigonism, to praise for the aesthetic integrity of his vision and the remarkable unity of his musical language during the fifty years of music-making. Regardless of evaluations and opinions of artistic quality of the music, recovering its original place in Polish music history is a moral and intellectual duty that reaches beyond what can be accomplished in Warmia and transcends the efforts of the local enthusiasts of Nowowiejski's oeuvre.[23]

Translated by Maja Trochimczyk

ENDNOTES

[1] Warmia (Polish: Warmia, Latin: Warmia or Varmia, German: Ermland or Ermeland) is a region between Pomerania and Masuria in northern Poland. It is located in a border area which has been under the rule of many different rulers from several countries over its long

history; the most notable of these rulers were those of the Teutonic Knights (approved by Emperor Frederick II in 1228 and by a Papal Bull in 1234), Poland (prior to the Teutonic conquest; after the battle of Grunwald in 1511 until the partitions in 1772; and since 1945) and the Kingdom of Prussia (since the partitions until its integration into united Germany and the end of the Third Reich in 1945). Data cited from an online dictionary, http://www.wordiq.com/definition/Ermland, accessed on August 12, 2004.

[2] The Nowowiejski genealogy is recorded in a family tree, comprising of five generations of the composer's forebearers. This family tree was made in the 1940s, upon request of Bernard Nowowiejski, a brother of the composer. See J. Boehm, *Feliks Nowowiejski. Zarys biograficzny,* (Felisk Nowowiejski: A Biographical Outline), (Olsztyn: Pojezierze, 1977), p. 12. The fact that the family's home language, Polish, was not the official language (German) used at schools and offices of the government reveals the complexity of linguistic issues associated with the lives and travails of ethnic minorities. Polish, used in every-day conversations, was more colloquial than the formalized, official version of German.

[3] This suite was later published as Nowowiejski's Opus 2, No. 3.

[4] J. Oblak, "Szkoła muzyczna w Świętej Lipce" (Music School in Holy Linden), in (*Komunikaty Mazursko-Warminskie* no. 3, 1960): 351-371.

[5] J. Boehm, op. cit., 20.

[6] These studies were probably financed by Salo Staub from Olsztyn, an owner of a furniture factory located at Dworcowa 12 Street. See J. Boehm, op. cit., 20 and 121. However, from the fact that the parish priest in the church of St. Jacob in Olsztyn, Father Józef Teschner, received a steady stream of letters from Nowowiejski, containing opinions of teachers from Stern Conservatory about the progress of his studies, one can surmise that a chance of gaining employment in the largest Olsztyn church provided a motivation for commencing these studies.

[7] Originals of these certificates may be found in the collection of the Nowowiejski family in Poznań. Cited from J. Boehm, 21.

[8] This position remained vacant since the retirement of I. Herrmmann on 1 April 1895. Another candidate who applied concurrently with Nowowiejski, W. J. Gross, was a graduate of the Berlin Royal Academy of Music and a teacher at the Veit Conservatory in Berlin.

[9] Nowowiejski prepared this text for the Poznań press. Cited from Boehm, 36.

[10] Jan Boehm, "Prezentacja twórczości Feliksa Nowowiejskiego we Frankfurcie nad Menem i w Usti nad Łabą" (Presenting the works of Feliks Nowowiejski in Frankfurn-am-Mein and in Usti at Łaba), in *Kultura muzyczna Warmii i Mazur. Przeszłość i terazniejszość* (Music Culture of Warmia and Mazury: The past and the present") (Olsztyn: Wydawnictwo WSP w Olsztynie, 1989), 57-65.

[11] See Boehm, op. cit., 32ff.

[12] See Ignacy Jan Paderewski, "Fryderyk Chopin" (1910), reprinted in Maja Trochimczyk, ed., "Selected Writings and Speeches by Paderewski" *Polish Music Journal* 4, no. 2 (Winter 2001). http://www.polish-music.orgarchives.html, accessed on 14 August 2004.

[13] See Ignacy Jan Paderewski, "Address at the Unveiling of the Grunwald Monument" (1911), reprinted in Maja Trochimczyk, ed., "Selected Writings and Speeches by Paderewski" *Polish Music Journal* 4, no. 2, op. cit.

[14] For an overview of Polish national anthems see Maja Trochimczyk, "Sacred/Secular Constructs of National Identity: A Convoluted History of Polish Anthems," in Maja

Trochimczyk, ed. *After Chopin: Essays in Polish Music* (Los Angeles: Polish Music Center, 2000), 246-268.

[15] Nie rzucim ziemi skąd nasz ród!
Nie damy pogrześć mowy!
Polski my naród, polski lud,
Królewski szczep Piastowy,
nie damy by nas gnębił wróg
Tak nam dopomóż Bóg!, Tak nam dopomóż Bóg!

Nie będzie Niemiec pluł nam w twarz,
Ni dzieci nam germanił,
Orężny stanie hufiec nasz,
Lud będzie nam hetmanił,
Pójdziem, gdy zagrzmi złoty róg -
Tak nam dopomóż Bóg! Tak nam dopomóż Bóg!

[16] Its alumni included, among others: Antoni Barczewski, Antoni Broz, Hubert Brzeszczyński, Jan Lubomirski, and Franciszek Popin. They were active as teachers of Polish schools and social workers after the Referendum in Warmia. See Krzysztof D. Szatrawski, *Jan Lubomirski. Szkic biograficzny* (Jan Lubomirski, A Biographical Outline). No. 17 in "Biblioteka Olszyńska" series (Olsztyn: Wydawnictwo Wspólne Wojewódzkiej Biblioteki Publicznej i Ośrodka Badań Naukowych im. Wojciecha Kętrzyńskiego, 1991), 23.
[17] L. Turkowski, "Feliks Nowowiejski w środowisku artystycznym międzywojennego Poznania" (F.N. in the music millieu of inter-war Poznań), in *Feliks Nowowiejski: W setną rocznicę urodzin* (Feliks Nowowiejski: On the 100th anniversary of birth) (Gdańsk: Wydawnictwo PWSM, 1978), 64.
[18] Jan Erdman, "Symfonia organowa w twórczości Feliksa Nowowiejskiego," in *Kultura muzyczna Warmii i Mazur*, op. cit., 73-79.
[19] Boehm, "Prezentacja," op. cit., 59.
[20] Composer later removed the subtitle of "Białowieska."
[21] The concert of Nowowiejski's music held on 14 February 1966 included works that soon became the basis of the repertoire of the Olsztyn Philharmonic. These works included: Cello Concerto, Op. 55; Poem for Soprano and Orchestra, *Róże dla Safo*, Op. 51, Overture, *The Legend of the Baltic Sea*, the Overture *Polish Match-makers*, and a symphonic poem for clarinet, reciting voice, and orchestra, *Pożegnanie Ellenai* (Farewell to Ellenai). See Krzysztof D. Szatrawski, "Orkiestra Symfoniczna Filharmonii Olsztyńskiej w latach 1945-1995," in *50 lat Orkiestry Symfonicznej Państwowej Filharmonii im. Feliksa Nowowiejskiego w Olsztynie* (Olsztyn, 1996), 19-22.
[22] The fact that this oratorio had not been performed earlier was confirmed by the composer's sons. See F. M. and K. Nowowiejski, "Charakterystyka spuścizny rękopiśmiennej Feliksa Nowowiejskiego" (A characterization of the manuscript legacy of Feliks Nowowiejski). *Rocznik Olsztyński* vol. 2, (Olsztyn, 1959), 227ff.
[23] Krzysztof D. Szatrawski, op. cit., 49.

INDEX

absolute music (Absolute Musik), 3, 100
Amati, Andrea, 77-97
Amsterdam, 229, 232
Anti-Semitic, 101, 210
Austro-Hungarian Empire, 49, 91, 191, 229
Bacewicz, Grażyna, married name Biernacka, 6, 21, 22, 23, 37, 40, 41; *Desire*, 37
Bach, Johann Christian, 32
Bach, Johann Sebastian, 32, 64, 68, 100, 106, 111, 115, 225
Bach, Karl Phillip Emmanuel, 68
Barczewo, 224, 237, 238
Bartók, Bèla, 189, 211
Bayreuth, 131, 135, 136, 142,
Bądarzewska-Baranowska, Tekla, 4, 5, 11, 19, 33; *The Maiden's Prayer (La prière d'une vierge)*, 4, 5, 15
Baugan, Edward Algernon, 179
Beethoven, Ludwig, van, 8, 51, 60, 64, 67, 77, 81, 100, 102, 103, 112, 116, 138, 157, 205, 228, 229, 230, 235, 236
Bellincioni, Gemma, 157
Berlin, 9, 15, 16, 55, 107, 108, 109, 111, 112, 113, 191, 206, 211, 223, 225-228, 232-234
Berlin Conservatory, 226
Beydale, Cecilia, 3, 11, 26
Białkiewicz, Irena, married Andrault de Langeron, 11, 21, 22, 31
Biskupski, Mieczysław, 180
Bizet, George, 192, 199
Błaszczyk, Leon, 11
Boehm, Jan, 228
Bogdański, Zbigniew, 239
Bogusławski, Władysław, 129, 154-5
Bogusławski, Wojciech, 187, *Cud mniemany, czyli Krakowiacy i Górale*
Borkowski, Piotr, 239
Borkowicz, Maria, 12
Boston, 183, 192
Boujukli, Vsievolod, 157
Brahms, Johannes, 14, 101, 102, 103, 105, 115, 116, 207, 230
Bridge, Frank, 211
Britten, Benjamin, 211
Bruch, Max, 115, 226, 228

Bruckner, Anton, 201, 230, 235
Brzezińska, Filipina, née Szymanowska, 12
Brzowska, Jadwiga, married name Mejean, ps. Jadwiga Jagiełło 12, 18, 20, 25
Brzostowski, Wieńczysław, 180
Brzozowska, Julia, married name Niewiarowska, 12
Brzozowski, Stanisław, 142
Burzyńska, Jadwiga, b. Eminowicz, 12
Catholic, 17, 137, 224
Ciechomski, Stanisław, 128, 133, 154,
Chaminade, Cecilia, 33, 44
Chałubiński, Tytus, 187-188
Chicago, 6, 14, 21, 37, 181, 182
Chlebowski, Bronisław, 155, 162
Chopin, Fryderyk Franciszek, 6, 7, 8, 14, 15, 16, 17, 28, 31, 150-152, 155, 156, 161-167, 168, 169, 170, 171, 183, 185, 186, 201, 205-207, 209, 210, 211, 212, 238, 239. Works: Piano Sonata in B-lat minor, Op. 35, 161, 183; Polonaise in A-flat major Op. 53, 183; K*rakowiak - Grand rondeau de concert*, Op. 14, 186; Preludes Op. 28, 150-152; nocturnes, 167
Christian, 127, 165, 166
Chrzanowski, 155
Chybiński, Adolf, 184, 206
Citron, Marcia, 1, 2
Classical, 6, 19, 38, 49, 102, 113, 114, 128, 129, 132, 133, 166, 211
concerto, 8, 11, 16, 21, 22, 34, 51, 54, 60, 61, 65, 68, 101-104, 106, 108, 111, 112, 113, 115, 116, 181, 207, 210, 235, 236, 239,
Crawford-Seeger, Ruth, 37, 38. Works: *Suite for Five Wind Instruments and Piano*, 37; *Piano Study in Mixed Accents*, 37
Cooley, Timothy, J., 188
Czertwertyńska-Jełowicka, Janina, Countess 12, 26
Dali, Salvadore, 239
Debussy, Claude, 34, 143, 199, 230
Dessor, Max, 226
Dean Paul, Lady, see Wieniawska

Dean Paul, Aubry, 24, 25, 32
Dean Paul, Aubrey Donald Fitzwarren, 39
decadent, 136, 144, 159, 165, 172
Dorabialska, Julia Helena, 13, 21
Drozdowski, Marek, 180
Dvorak, Antonin, 116, 190, 227. Work: *Slavonian Dances*, 190
Dziadek, Magdalena, 11, 24, 124-149, 153-178
Eksteins, Modris, 145
Elgar, Edward, 180, 201, 211
Erdman, Jerzy, 238, 239
Erwest, Ida, 13
Finck, Henry, 179
Fitelberg, Grzegorz, 207, 212
Fleischer, Oscar, 226
Folklore, 49, 185-190, 199, 200, 204, 205, 211, 212
Forster, E. M., 1
Friedländer, Max, 226
Fromme, Richard, 144, 172
Galicia, Galician, 5, 48, 49, 50, 71, 91, 92, 127, 190, 193, 229
Gdańsk, 81, 90, 238, 239
German, Germany, 5, 7, 9, 10, 54, 88, 89, 90, 91, 99-119, 124-127, 129, 131, 133, 135, 139, 142, 145, 181, 189, 190, 192, 194, 206, 211, 212, 223, 224, 226, 22-230, 231, 232, 233, 236, 239
Glinka, Mikhail, 10, 77
Goethe, Johann Wolfgang von, 7, 9, 141, 144
Gostomski, Walery, 136-138, 140,
Górale, 187-189, 192, 204, 205, 209, 211
Górski, Artur, 134, 140, 141-142
Grabowska, Klementyna, 13
Grainger, Percy, 190
Grek, Błażej, 239
Grewe Sobolewska, 13
Grieg, Edward, 5
Gronowicz, Antoni, 179
Grottger, Krystyna, 13, 22, 23
Grodzicka-Rzewuska, Julia, 13, 22
Gruszecka, Maria, 13
Grünberg, Max, 82, 102, 108-113
Gwozdecka, Gabriela, 13, 19
Great Composer, 2, 4, 7, 19, 20,
Guarneri, Bartolomeo Giuseppe Antonio, del Gesù, 77-97
Guyau, Jean Maria, 136, 137, 138, 144

Gypsy, 190, 191-194, 196, 197-200
HAKATA, 125
Halicz, Czesław, 139
Haller, Józef, General, 208
Helman, Zofia, 184
Hensel, Fanny, b. Mendelssohn, 5, 26-7
Hertzka, Emil, 207, 208
Holmes, Augusta, 33, 34, 45
Holst, Gustav, 211
Horowitz, Joseph, 145
Ivanovski (Ivanowski), Sigismond, 150-152
Iwanowska-Płoszko, Zofia, see Ossendowska, 14, 22, 24
Jabłonowski, Władysław, 134, 135-138
Jachimecki, Zdzisław, 16, 143, 144, 167, 172, 184, 206, 207, 232
Jagiellon, 186, 202, 203,
Janotha, Natalia Maria Cecylia, 14, 18, 20, 28
Jarecki, Zygmunt, 126
Jasińska Jędrosz, Elzbieta, 208
Jellenta, Cezary, 134, 145
Jeske-Choińska, Ludmiła, 4, 6, 14, 21, 181. Works: *Rusałka*, 21, 181
Jesuits, 224
Jewish, Jew, 183, 190-193, 196, 199, 204, 209, 211
Joachim, Joseph, 99-119,
Karłowicz family, 126
Kasprowicz, Jan, 30
Kitsch, 4, 5, 11
Klechniowska, Anna Maria, married name Klechniowska-Sas 14
Kleczyński, Jan, 15, 128, 129, 131, 132, 156, 159, 161, 162, 163, 188, 205
Kleinemeister, 19, 20
Kochanowska, Franciszka, 3, 14
Kowalewska, Wiktoria, 14, 19
Kraków, 11, 13, 15, 16, 21, 28, 47, 52, 56, 59, 106, 120-122, 137, 144, 175-178, 180, 186, 229, 229-232, 233, 239
krakowiak (cracovienne), 4, 47, 48, 120-122, 175-178,186, 195, 204
Krasiński, Zygmunt, 140, 166
Krehbiel, Henry, 192, 209-210
Krechowiecka, Anna, 20
Krokiewicz, Apolonia, 14
Kruszelnicka, Salomea, 126
Krzyżanowska, Halina, 15, 20, 22, 27
Kujawiak, 186, 234

244

Lachowska, Stefania, 15
Landowska, Wanda, 15, 18, 19-23
Landau, Ron, 179
Lawton, Mary, 179
Lemaître, Jules, 154, 155
Leonardo da Vinci, 141, 144
Leśniewicz, Iza 15
Lessel, Helena, 15, 19, 26, 27
Lessel, Franciszek, 11, 27
Lessel, Wincenty, 27
Lew, Henry, 23
Lipińska, Natalia, married name Parczewska, 15, 26, 27
Lipiński, Karol, 15, 49-76, 77-97, 105, 111, 175
Liszt, Franz, 8, 51, 67, 71, 77, 79, 103-105, 143, 158, 161, 205, 206, 230
Łopuska, Helena, married name Wyleżyńska, 15, 22, 25
Maciejewski, Roman, 186
Mahler, Gustav, 230
Marchwica, Wojciech, 181
Markiewicz, Henryk, 138, 140
Markiewicz, Władysława, 16
Markowska-Garłowska, Eliza, 16
Maszyński, Piotr, 154
Matejko, Jan, 201
Matuszewski, Ignacy, 140, 144, 172
Mazurka, 4, 8, 12, 15, 17, 18, 164, 183, 185, 186, 204, 212
Mazurrana, Dr., 81, 82,
masterpiece, 1, 2, 6, 37, 90, 140, 145, 200, 207,
Melcer, Henryk, 17
Meliński, Stanislaw, 157
Mendès, Catulle, 181
Mendelssohn, Felix, 5, 27, 81, 101, 105, 106, 109, 111, 114, 116
Messianic, 141, 166, 170
Mickiewicz, Adam, 6, 7, 10, 13, 16, 139, 140, 141, 142, 172, 201
Miller, Antoni, 129, 134
modern, modernism, 6, 19, 22, 35, 37, 38, 40, 106, 123, 136, 142, 143, 179, 211, 235
Modrzejewska, Helena, 188
Moniuszko, Stanisław, 6, 19, 107, 160, 167, 187, 198, 201, 206. Works: *Halka*, 187, 198
Münchheimer, Adam, 133, 154

New Grove Dictionary of Music and Musicians, The, 4, 10, 179, 212
Niemcewicz, Julian Ursyn, 3, 9
national, nationality, 3, 4, 5, 8, 182, 184-186, 191, 194, 201, 203-212
national-democratic (Narodowa Demokracja, Endecja), 125, 168, 169
Nazi, 191
neo-romantic, 38, 140, 141, 160, 165, 166, 172, 186, 240
New York, 35, 37, 179, 182, 192, 193, 195, 199, 202, 209, 232
New Grove Dictionary of Music and Musicians, The, 179, 211
Nietzsche, Friedrich, 134, 135, 137, 142, 145, 172
Niewiadomski, Stanislaw, 129, 157
nocturne, 8, 18, 32, 36, 163, 164, 183
Norwid, Cyprian Kamil, 212
Noskowski, Zygmunt, 19, 128, 131, 162, 187, 204, 205, 206, 211, 230
Nossig, Alfred, 190-191, 194, 198-199, 203
Nowowiejski, Feliks, 223-240; *Legenda Bałtyku* ; *The Discovery of the Holy Cross, 228, 235; Quo Vadis?* 228, 229, 235, 239; *Rota,* 231, 237; *The Return of the Prodigal Son,* 235; *Łatwe Tańce Klasyczne i Współczesne, 224*; military marches, *225;* masses, 235; organ symphonies, 235, 236, 239; organ concertos, 235, 239; Piano Concerto in D minor,"Slavic" 236, 238, 239; Symphony No. 1, in B minor, 236; Symphony No. 2, *Praca i Rytm*, 236; Symphony No. 3, Op. 53, 236; Symphony No. 4, *Symphony of Peace,* 236; Symphonic Poem, *Pożegnanie Ellenai*, Op. 17, No. 3, 236; symphonic poem *Róże dla Safo*, 236
Nowowiejski, Franciszek, 224
Nowowiejski (Nowowiejska), Katarzyna, 224
oberek, 4, 13, 186, 207
Obrochta, Bartek, 188-189, 204, 205, 209
Obtułowicz, Zofia, 16
Ogińska, Amelia, 16, 26, 27
Olkisz, Maria, 239
Olsztyn, 224-256, 237-239

245

opera, 13, 14, 15, 18, 19, 20, 21, 22, 34, 41, 192-196, 199, 200, 204, 210, 212, 228, 232, 239
Opieński, Henryk, 167, 169-171, 180
Orłowski, Józef, 179, 183, 184
Ossendowska, Zofia, née Iwanowska-Płoszko, 14, 22, 24
Ottawowa (Ottawa?), Helena, née Rogalska, 16
Paderewski, Ignacy, Jan, 19, 23, 35, 155, 159, 163, 166, 168-171, 179-212, 228, 231, 232; Works: *Dances polonaises*, Op. 5, 186; *Danses polonaises*, Op. 9, 186; *Cracovienne fantastique* in B major, No. 6 in *Humoresques de concert*, Op. 14, 186; *Fantaisie polonaise sur des themes originaux* in G-sharp minor, Op. 19, 186; *Hej, Orle Biały*, 182, 208; *Manru*, 181-212; *Tatra Album /Album Tatrzanskie,* Op. 12, 188, 189, 190; *Piano Concerto in A minor,* op. 17, 181, 210; Symphony in B minor, Op. 24, "Polonia" 201, 204, 207, 210, 212; *Variations and Fugue* in A minor, Op. 11 (1884), 205; *Thème varie* from *Miscellanea,* Op. 16, No. 3 (1885-1887), 205; *Variations and Fugue* Op. 23, 205
Paganini, Nicolo, 50, 51, 68, 71, 77, 79, 86, 91, 92, 103, 108, 109, 111,
Palestine, 191, 204
Papara, Teodozja 16
Paris (Parys?), Salomea, 3, 16
Parakilas, James, 2
Pawlikowski, Mieczysław, 171
Pekacz, Jolanta T., 5, 6. *Music in the Culture of Polish Galicia, 1772-1914,* 5
St. Petersburg, 7, 10, 17, 104, 105, 111, 114, 115
Piast, the dynasty,186, 202, 203, 231,
Piber, Andrzej, 180, 186
Picasso, Pablo, 37
Pigła, Włodzimierz, 180
Piłsudski, Jozef, Marshall, 181
Piniński, Leon, 15, 127, 131
Plater, Maria, nee Zyberk-Groel, 18, 22
Podhale, Podhalean, 185, 186, 187, 188, 189, 204, 205, 209, 210
Polanowska, Teofila, 16

Poldowski, Mr. (See also Irena Wieniawska), 1, 17, 18, 22, 23, 24, 26, 32-40, 209
Poliński, Aleksander, 129, 157, 207
polonaise, 4, 13, 16, 18, 51, 52, 164, 165, 183, 285, 286, 202, 212
Polonia, 179, 181, 186, 201-204, 207
Pope John Paul II, 239
Pope Pius IX, 235
Prokofiev, Sergei, 209
Promethean, 134, 140, 141, 142, 144
Przybylski, Henryk, 180
Puget, Loisa, 33
Pushkin, Alexander, 10, 191
Przybyszewski, Stanisław, 131, 164
Rachmaninoff, Sergei, 180, 191, 205
Regensburg, 223, 226
Reger, Max, 180, 206
Ravel, Maurice, 34
Romantic, 7, 21, 28, 30, 31, 38, 184, 186, 187, 193, 194, 199, 204, 205, 211, 227, 240
Russian, Russia, 3, 10, 11, 195, 196, 209, 210
Samson, Jim, 211
Sarnecka, Jadwiga, 16, 28-31
Schopenhauer, Arthur, 3, 131
Schumann, Clara, b. Wieck, 2, 7, 10, 14
Schumann, Robert, 71, 77, 93, 101, 102, 116, 230
Schuré, Eduard, 138, 139, 144, 172
Scriabin, Aleksander, 205, 206
Sembrich, Marcella (Sembrich-Kochanska, Marcelina), 193, 195, 210
Shakespeare, William, 144
Siemiradzki, Henryk, 239
Sitarz, Andrzej, 181
Słowacki, Juliusz, 139-141, 166, 172
Smeda, Ryszard 239
Spohr, Louis, 50, 51, 53, 80, 91, 108, 115
Staff, Leopold, 12, 13, 30
Stalewska, Jadwiga, 17
Stalinist, 237
Statkowski, Roman, 11, 13, 17, 211
Stattler, Juliusz, 155
Sternicka, Ilza, b. Niekrasz-Sternicka, 17, 22
Stefani, Jan, 187
Steinway, 179, 181
Stern Conservatory, 225, 226
Stojowski, Zygmunt, 211

246

Stradivari, Antonio, 77-97
Strakacz, Sylwin, 180
Strakacz, Aniela, 180
Strauss, Richard, 30, 143, 180, 194, 198, 200, 206. *Salome,* 194, 198, 200
Stravinsky, Igor, 211, 230
Styka, Jan, 201, 202
Sygietyński, Antoni, 129, 163
symphony, 15, 22, 138, 181, 204, 205, 207, 210, 229, 230, 236,
sonata, 8, 11, 12, 13, 15, 16, 17, 18, 161, 165, 183, 205, 207, 231
Szalit Paulina (Paula), 17, 22, 28, 29
Szymanowska, Celina, 10
Szymanowska, Maria Agata, née Wołowska , 1, 3, 6-10, 11, 12, 17, 18, 19, 20-22, 32, 40, 186
Works: etudes, preludes, mazurkas and songs, 8; chamber works, 17; *Śpiewy Historyczne, Jan Albrycht,* 9; *Vingt Exercices et Preludes,* 8
Szymanowski, Karol, 6, 15, 17, 21, 25, 26, 35, 37, 179-212, 231, 232; *Harnasie,* 189, 198, 200, 209; *Hagith,* 200; Sonata No. 2, Op. 21 in A major, 205; Symphony No. 2, 205, 207, *Słopiewnie,* 190; military songs, 208; Symphony No. 2, 181, 183, 201, 204, 207, 210, 212
Szymanowski, Józef, 8
Święta Lipka, 224, 235, 239
Taine, Hippolyte, 154, 155
Tansman, Aleksander, 186
Tarnowski, Stanisław, 165, 166, 167
Tartini, Giuseppe, 51, 80, 81, 84
Tatra Mountains, 179-212
Tchaikovsky, Piotr, 5, 16, 195
Teschner, Józef, 225
Teutonic, 126, 223, 232
Teutonic Knights, 223, 232
Thiel, Andrzej, Bishop, 226
Trivialmusik, 3, 33
Varèse, Edgard, 38
Variations, 13, 15, 16, 51, 53, 55, 60, 61, 65, 183, 205, 206
Verdi, Giuseppe, 51, 192, 196, 199. Works: *Othello,* 199
Wagner, Richard, 71, 77, 123-149, 166, 167, 172, 192, 196, 199, 200, 206, 211, 230
Walter, Edmund, 171

Waltz, 14, 17, 36, 164
Warmia, 223-226, 227, 233, 237, 240
Warsaw (Warszawa), 3, 11, 12, 13, 14, 15, 16, 17, 18, 57, 86, 104, 114, 125, 126, 128, 130, 135, 139, 143, 154, 159, 160, 161, 168, 180, 181, 185, 208, 232
Wasilewski, Wilhelm Josef, von, 83
Waydel-Dmochowska, Jadwiga, 146
Weltschmerz, 160, 161, 164, 166
Węsławska, Emilia, 138
Wieniawska, Iréne/Irena (also Régine Wieniawski, Mr. Poldowski and Lady Dean Paul), 1, 17, 18, 22, 23, 24, 26, 32-40; Works: 35-39
Wieniawski, Henryk, 17, 23, 24, 32, 99-119, 209
Williams, Ralph Vaughan, 190, 211
Wilson, Woodrow, President, 180
Wojciechowska, Leokadia, née Myszyńska, 17
Wołowska, Kazimiera, 10, 25
women composers, 1-46
Woźna-Stankiewicz, Małgorzata, 181
Wróblewska, Zofia, 18
Upton, George, 2
Turner, Joseph, 239
Young Poland, 14, 21, 30, 31, 133, 134, 135, 139, 167, 172, 204, 205, 206, 211
Zaleski, (Z Oleska), Wacław, 50, 175
Zamoyska, Zofia, married name Czartoryska, Countess, 3, 18, 26
Zdziechowski, Marian, 141
Zionist, 190, 191, 199
żal, 12, 31, 161, 169, 186, 206
Żeleński, Władysław, 17, 19, 154, 165, 186, 211

www.ingramcontent.com/pod-product-compliance
Lightning Source LLC
Chambersburg PA
CBHW022110150426
43195CB00008B/340